THE NEW
PYRAMID
AGE

Philip Coppens

THE NEW PYRAMID AGE

Philip Coppens

BOOKS

Winchester, UK
Washington, USA

Winchester, UK
Washington, USA)

First published by O Books, 2007
O Books is an imprint of John Hunt Publishing Ltd.,
The Bothy, Deershot Lodge, Park Lane, Ropley, Hants, SO24 0BE, UK
office1@o-books.net
www.o-books.net

Distribution in:

UK and Europe
Orca Book Services
orders@orcabookservices.co.uk
Tel: 01202 665432 Fax: 01202 666219 Int. code (44)

USA and Canada
NBN
custserv@nbnbooks.com
Tel: 1 800 462 6420 Fax: 1 800 338 4550

Australia and New Zealand
Brumby Books
sales@brumbybooks.com.au
Tel: 61 3 9761 5535 Fax: 61 3 9761 7095

Far East (offices in Singapore, Thailand, Hong Kong, Taiwan)
Pansing Distribution Pte Ltd
kemal@pansing.com
Tel: 65 6319 9939 Fax: 65 6462 5761

South Africa
Alternative Books
altbook@peterhyde.co.za
Tel: 021 447 5300 Fax: 021 447 1430

Text copyright Philip Coppens 2007

Design: Stuart Davies

ISBN-13: 978 1 84694 046 0
ISBN-10: 1 84694 046 X

A CIP catalogue record for this book is available from the British Library.

Printed and bound by CPI Group (UK) Ltd, Croydon, CR0 4YY

ACKNOWLEDGEMENTS

Just like pyramid building is not just one man's effort, neither is writing a book. On my trips to Peru, Mexico, Egypt "and beyond" (which should include England, France, Greece, Crete, Italy, etc.), I've met and been accompanied by many wonderful people, either local to those areas or fellow visitors. Thanks for making these journeys quite often more than enjoyable.

Closer to home and a more constant presence, thanks to: David Hatcher Childress for travelling the mysteries of the world and continuing to do so. Duncan Roads for publishing the articles about the Chinese and Bosnian pyramids, and continuing to provide a forum for alternative thought that remains – if not becomes more – desperately needed. André Douzet for providing me with his research on the Falicon pyramid and for being a real friend: through the good and the bad times. Herman Hegge, for building dreams now for over a decade.

Special thanks go to Wim Zitman, a close and true friend during the last 13 years. We have always tried to perform our research independently of one another, though were always aware of the other person's trail. I think that here, we finally become complementary.

Personal thanks also go to Hartwig Hausdorf and Sam Osmanagich, two people who I've had the pleasure of speaking to and who have done a tremendous amount of work, each in their own way, time and space, to transform the pyramid debate.

A personal thanks too to Pierre Demoustiez for underlining the importance of the Davidovits material.

I would also like to thank Fernando and Edgar Salazar. I have repeatedly tried to make contact with these two authors, to express my appreciation of their work, as well as provide pro forma authorisation to quote from their work as relevant to this book. Unfortunately, none of the contact details I have seem to be current; I hope that in the near future, we will be able to correspond, if not meet.

Thanks also go to: John Major Jenkins; Andy & Sue Collins; Cris Maier; Simon Cox; Gary Osborn; Steve Marshall; James Stokes and Lucinda Arnett; Mark Oxbrow & Ian Robertson; John Ritchie; Geoff Potts; Mark Foster; Andy Gough; Greg Taylor; Gay Roberts; Stéphane Chalandon; Katarina Miletic; Odile Martinez; Bill Ingle; my parents; and anyone whom I may have failed to mention.

Finally, to John Hunt, for inviting me to write this book. Collating the various pieces of ten years of writing and research on the pyramids in one book provided me with my own initiation: a true understanding of the pyramids, one which I hope that can be shared by many and which will contribute to the pyramid debate.

NORTH BERWICK
AUGUST 29, 2006

CONTENTS

INTRODUCTION

"MAN FEARS TIME, YET TIME FEARS THE PYRAMIDS."

ARAB PROVERB

Until ca. 1500 AD, Egypt was believed to be the only country where pyramids could be found. With the discovery of America, we learnt that the Mayan civilisation had its own pyramids. And that, it seemed, were the only two civilisations that were into pyramid building as a national pass-time, if not obsession. But in the last decade, pyramids are being found almost anywhere: in 1994, the existence of pyramids was confirmed in China; then, archaeologists announced the discovery of a pyramid complex in Caral, Peru, which was older than the pyramids of Gizeh; more recently, there have been controversial announcements of their existence in Northern Italy and in 2005, the latest in this series, a global media phenomenon with the announcement that there were pyramids in Bosnia.

The old status quo that it were but the ancient Egyptians and the Mayans that built pyramids has been upset and over the past decades, hardly a month seems to have gone by without a pyramid being found; and almost each year, a gigantic pyramid or pyramid complex is found somewhere. Today, it is clear that massive pyramids are a feature of many civilisations, whereas the pyramids of Italy and Bosnia are not easily associated with any culture that is known to have either built such large remains or built pyramids.

In 1995, I was the first outside of the German language to report on Hartwig Hausdorf's discovery in China: confirmation that rumours of pyramids in that vast country were in fact true. It was a pivotal moment in the pyramid debate, for the old status quo had been upset – and rumours that the scientific community had always been unable to address, had been confirmed.

Pyramids have not only intrigued, they have also continued to question science. Though most Egyptologists continue to argue that the Egyptian pyramids are tombs, no original burials have ever been recovered in them. In the Mayan world, archaeologists argue that pyramids are temples, yet some are tombs too. Underneath such apparent diversity, upon which the scientific and specifically archaeological world focuses, there are other aspects, which hint at a common "pyramid theme". I wil therefore address the important question whether each culture developed this rather unique shape on its own, or whether it means that there was a truly global movement – apparently starting somewhere around 3000 BC? That in itself should already feel like a welcome change, for in all popular books on the subject, the authors seem to have concluded that any such movement "had" to be approximately 10,000 BC and "had" to involve Atlantis. Though I do not see any evidence for such a conclusion – though remain open to the possibility, but nothing more – I hope the reader will discover that the "truth" is more complex and more intriguing than the commonly accepted opinions about pyramids.

Over the past decade, the landscape of the pyramid debate has changed and offers science a challenge. The last decade has seen a series of discoveries that has changed the archaeological world in such a manner, that it will take years before key questions are being properly addressed – hopefully. In this pioneering volume, the challenge will be set out, and some of the answers will be given. I hope that it will stimulate debate and can become a "foundation stone" of what I have termed "The New Pyramid Age".

The title has nothing to do with the "New Age" movement (which in the United Kingdom is more commonly referred to as "Mind, Body & Spirit" interest), but with a new "Pyramid Age". But unlike the first "Pyramid Age", in which ancient civilisations built them, the New Pyramid Age is hopefully going to be the era when those pyramids will be understood: why they were built; what they expressed, etc. In between "The Pyramid Age" and "The New Pyramid Age", as a species, we somehow have been able to "forget" what that odd five-sided structure placed on the landscape meant to our ancestors. I hope that remembering can begin...

CHAPTER 1

THE LAND OF THE NILE

A uthor Michael Rice noted that "amongst the most conforming and comforting of all archetypal shapes is the pyramid. [...] Its significance to the Egyptians can be gauged by the fact that, even in the Predynastic age, centuries before the pyramids themselves were built, paintings depicted lines of triangular hills on Naqada II pottery, suggesting the shape already lay somewhere deep in the Egyptian psyche."[1] Rice interprets the Egyptian Pyramid Age as the fulfilment of a profound archetypal experience, "the culmination of the first period of Egypt's existence as a nation". In his opinion, these ancient Egyptians had an almost "genetic" urge to build pyramids and finally accomplished their desire in what Egyptologists have named "The Pyramid Age".

But despite their gigantic presence over the horizon west of Cairo, despite the millions of visitors that have come to stare at them for centuries, despite its role in the imagination in movies such as *Stargate*, despite all of that and more, little is known for certain about these structures. British author Colin Wilson summed up the problem, stating that "the truth is that, where the pyramids are concerned, there are no absolute certainties: only certain established ideas that the 'experts' have agreed to accept because it is convenient to do so"[2]. Indeed: though tourists continue to flock to see the pyramids, Egyptologists wouldn't mind if these structures disappeared; few Egyptologists study pyramids, opting instead to dig in more tranquil (read: less controversial) structures elsewhere along the Nile. Some have gone so far as to argue that the pyramids are "incidental" to ancient Egypt. Are they?

NOT JUST ANOTHER PYRAMID

All pyramids are equal, but all are more equal than one. The Great Pyramid of Egypt is the sole surviving wonder of the ancient world. There is a simple reason for this: of all the ancient wonders, it is the oldest and the most massive, the only one that withstood the test of time. Hence the Arab proverb that time fears the pyramids. But contrary to common belief, only the Great Pyramid of Khufu (Cheops) and not all three pyramids that sit on the Gizeh plateau, just outside of Cairo, is on number one in the "wonders chart". That is somewhat bizarre, for the Pyramid of Khafre (Chefren) is only minimally smaller.

They – or the Great Pyramid specifically –bedazzle. In Antiquity, they were referred to as "The Granaries of Joseph" and "The Mountains of Pharaoh"; today, authors such as Christopher Dunn have interpreted them as an ancient "power plant" and Zecharia Sitchin as a "beacon" for spaceships on approach to a landing site in the Middle East. Amongst the famous visitors is Napoleon Bonaparte, who shouted during his invasion of Egypt in 1798: "Soldiers! From the top of these Pyramids, 40 centuries are looking at us." He was wrong: it was actually 50 centuries…

The Great Pyramid was built by the Egyptian Pharaoh Khufu, a ruler of the Fourth Dynasty (around 2560 BC), sometimes better known under his Greek name Cheops. The official Egyptological stance argues that the Great Pyramid was to serve as a tomb for the deceased Pharaoh. But no mummy has been found in any of these three structures, which Egyptologists explain as clear evidence of grave robbing, for which there has been ample occasion over a period of roughly 4000 years.

Khufu's remains have therefore never been found; and little is known of this man, whose rule stands out solely because of this accomplishment – and some people are not even willing to give him that honour; for many, the pyramid is the work of extra-terrestrials and/or descendants of the lost civilisation of Atlantis. To followers of this possibility, the pyramid is also more likely to date to ca. 10,000 BC and hence not a legacy of ancient Egypt.

Some go further, inspired as they were by the work of Erich von Däniken and his popularisation of the so-called "ancient astronaut hypothesis". As just mentioned, for Zecharia Sitchin, the Great Pyramid is a beacon for any approaching spacecraft, intent on landing further east in any of his theoretical spacecraft, reconstructed – i.e. interpreted – from wall drawings in Egypt and Iraq. In my humble opinion, those ancient spacemen could have put up a simpler homing beacon, in line with beacons for modern aviation; building the Great Pyramid merely to find your way to a

The Great Pyramid at Gizeh

spaceport seems extravagant – at best.

Sitchin was not the first who abandoned all reason when faced by the pyramids. In the 19th century, Robert Menzies had used certain incisions and lines inside the Great Pyramid to argue that the Pyramid contained prophecies of the world's history, including the Earth's creation in 4004 BC and a Great Flood in 2400 BC. Those who followed in his footsteps, including the Scottish Astronomer Royal Charles Piazzi Smyth, who was a Christian zealot, have since been labelled pyramidiots. What else can we think of someone who believed that the start of the Grand Gallery corresponded with the time of Christ's birth? For your information: he deduced Jesus' Second Coming as occurring in 1911 AD. Still, our descendants will probably look towards our era and notice that our preoccupation with industrial technology resulted in arguments that the Great Pyramid was actually a "water fuel cell", as well as a power plant, in which the unique acoustic properties of the edifice indicate it was designed as a form of 'Tesla-style' energy-generation device, which used harmonics to harness the Earth's natural vibrational energies and convert them into microwave radiation.[3]

Though in retrospect ancient Egypt's grandest accomplishment, there is in essence no contemporary evidence from Khufu's reign that speaks of it. In fact, some of the earliest history of the pyramid comes from the Greek traveller Herodotus of Halicanassus, who visited Egypt around 450 BC. His Egyptian guides told him that it took twenty years for a force of 100,000 oppressed slaves to build the pyramid. The purpose of the structure was as a tomb for the Pharaoh Khufu. Today, Egyptologists believe that most of what Herodotus was told was probably false – except that it was a tomb.

First, it is no longer believed that slave labour was used. Second, Egyptologists have calculated that fewer men and less years were needed than Herodotus states. The only thing it shows is that we are as far removed in time from Herodotus than he was from the actual building of the pyramid.

PYRAMID ORIGINS

If the "Wonders Commission" had decided to include the nearby and practically equally high Pyramid of Khafre (Chefren) and the smaller Pyramid of Menkaure (Mycerinos), those unwilling to adhere to the Egyptological party line would have had to frame their theories differently. Bizarrely, many "pyramidiots" argue that the Great Pyramid of Khufu was an impossible achievement for the ancient Egyptians... but seem to imply that they were able to build the Pyramid of Khafre, which in essence is equally difficult to construct than the Great one, both of which being to all intents and purposes equally high and built in identical fashion and fabric.

Too many people have taken – and continue to take – the Great Pyramid in isolation, as if it is the only pyramid in Egypt. As Rice mentioned, the idea is as old as Egypt itself. Egyptologists have clearly shown how the tradition of pyramid building started as a sophistication of the idea of a mastaba. The mastaba is in essence a rectangular tomb-chapel that was constructed from the earliest dynastic era, traditionally dated to ca. 3500 BC. Mastabas are structures with flat roofs, and normally built from mudbrick or stone. The mastabas had burial chambers that were often dug out in the ground, with shafts connecting to the entrance. All over Egypt, there are thousands of mastabas, with a great variety of wall paintings, many of high artistic value. These depict everyday life

The Zoser Pyramid complex at Saqqara

in Ancient Egypt, and the mastabas represent an important source of information of the rather idyllic living conditions that ancient Egyptians experienced. On the other hand, the wall paintings in the pyramids – a trend developed after the great pyramid achievements of Khufu and the other 4th Dynasty rulers – depicted life in the court and amongst the royals, as well as renditions of the "Book of the Dead", a manual that was to assist the deceased in reaching the Egyptian equivalent of Heaven.

The first pyramid worthy of that name is accepted to be that of Zoser, a ruler of the Third Dynasty. The theory is that his pyramid in Saqqara was at first constructed as a normal mastaba, even though it already differed from them in its usage of stones, rather than the traditional mud bricks. It is believed that the mastaba was extended by building five new, and gradually smaller, squares on top of it. By adding these new levels, the "step pyramid" was born.

The creation of the first pyramid did not only involve a change in material (stone instead of mud brick), it also involved a change of setting. The most sacred location to be buried was Abydos, about 300 miles south of Saqqara. Abydos is one of the most ancient cities of Upper Egypt, flourishing from the predynastic period down through Christian times (about 641 AD). Its fame was derived from the legend that the site preserved the sacred head of Osiris. Osiris was the Lord of the Underworld, the first being who had been able to resurrect from the dead – also known as "ascension" – which was the ambition of every ancient Egyptian, a feat which he hoped to accomplish upon his death – and hence why he wanted to be buried in Abydos.

Many tombs of predynastic rulers of ancient Egypt were located here, as well as the kings of the First Dynasty. In fact, during the Middle Kingdom, the tomb of a First Dynasty king, Djer, was identified as the "burial site of Osiris" (the structure is now known as the so-called Osireion). Festivals and the passion plays of Osiris' life and death were performed here from about the 12th Dynasty (1985-1795 BCE) until the Christian era... when the "Passion of Christ" shared many characteristics with passion plays of Osiris and Isis – his wife, who aided her deceased husband in his ascension.

Why was Abydos abandoned for Saqqara? The change of location is normally explained by the rise of the cult of the sun, whose cult centre was located in Heliopolis, now buried underneath the streets of Cairo. It is quite clear that as the power of the Heliopolitan priests rose – Zoser's architect Imhotep, who built the Step Pyramid, was their High Priest – the Pyramid Age commenced. Egyptologists have therefore concluded that the Pyramid Age coincided with the Age of Heliopolis, and its chief deity, Atum-Ra, the creator-sun god.

The Red Pyramid at Dahshur

The next Pharaoh to build a pyramid was Sekhemkhet, again in Saqqara, though he did not complete this project. Judging from an inscription on his pyramid at Saqqara, and from its very design, it is believed that Imhotep survived Zoser, Sekhemkhet's predecessor, and was again the mind behind the funerary complex. Next, Khaba built an unfinished pyramid in Zawiyet el-Aryan, four kilometres southeast of the pyramids of Gizeh. If it was indeed built for Khaba, that makes the structure only ten to thirty years younger than Zoser's pyramid. Khaba's short reign may explain why it never was completed, as the succeeding king would be more inclined to pay for his own burial complex than that of his predecessor.

But if pyramids are tombs, Sneferu must have suffered from multiple body disorder, for he built no less than three pyramids: one at Meidum and two at Dahshur: the Bent and Red Pyramid. Sneferu was the first to introduce the "true pyramid shape", though the pyramid at Meidum, five miles south of Saqqara, now looks more like a tower than a pyramid. What remains is actually the tower-like core that rises from the pulverized pieces of the original structure of the pyramid. But no doubt remains about the Dashur pyramids being "true pyramids" – and these pyramids are amongst my personal favourites, specifically the Red Pyramid. First, they are impressive in height (the Red Pyramid rises to 105 metres, versus 146 metres for the Great Pyramid), but more importantly, you can on occasion be the only person in or around the pyramids – which indeed implies that the guardians have wandered off somewhere themselves! Furthermore, the Red Pyramid is also seen as the immediate forerunner of the Great Pyramid and it thus provides evidence that the Great Pyramid was no anomaly, but that there is a clear line of evolution in pyramid building that culminated in the Great Pyramid.

Chronologically indeed, the next pyramid builder was Khufu, followed by Djedefre, who built at Abu Roash, followed by Khafre and Mycerinos, who returned to the Gizeh complex. With the Gizeh pyramid complex now constructed, many often assume that the Pyramid Age was finished, but successive Pharaohs of the 4th and 5th Dynasty continued constructing pyramids, with the Fifth dynasty efforts mostly centred on the sites Abu Sir, just south of Cairo, and Saqqara. Finally, there was a "Pyramid Revival" in the late 11th and 12th Dynasty (ca. 2100 to 1750 BC), but the building techniques were far inferior to those of previous Dynasties, and the Fourth specifically. As such, all these monuments were eclipsed by the brilliance of the Great Pyramid of Gizeh.

BUILDING THE PYRAMID

The Great Pyramid originally measured 145.75 metres (481 ft) high. Over the years, it has lost ten metres (30 ft) off its top. It ranked as the tallest structure on Earth for more than 43 centuries, only to be surpassed in height when the Eiffel tower was built in Paris in 1889 AD. It was originally covered with a casing of stones to smooth its surface, but these were later removed (like they have been at the nearby pyramids) to be worked into several buildings in Cairo, after an earthquake hit the city in 1222 AD. Most of the stones were used to rebuild the city's public buildings; the Grand Mosque is almost entirely built from the casing stones of the Great Pyramid. Only near the top of Khafre's pyramid can we see a glimpse of how the structure would have originally looked like. Reconstructions and ancient accounts speak of how they "shone" and to this day, tourists can try to imagine how they would shine in the sun, no doubt changing in colour and intensity as the sun moved across the sky, both during the day and the year.

The sloping angle of its sides is 51 degrees and 51 minutes; when you stand at the foot of the pyramid, you appreciate the steep angle the most. Realise that until recently, several people climbed these structures. The sides are carefully oriented to the cardinal points of the compass, with each side measuring 229 m (751 ft) in length. The maximum error between the lengths of the four sides is astonishingly less than 0.1 percent, underlining the engineering accomplishments of the architect in charge of this project. My parents' toilet, built in 1969, has one wall that deviates 1.5 cm over a distance of two metres; this 20th century builder managed almost the same error over a distance of two metres than his ancient colleagues allowed to occur over a distance of more than 200 metres.

Finally, the structure consists of approximately two million blocks of stone, each weighing more than two tons. The total volume is estimated to be between five and six million tons. It has been suggested that there are enough blocks in the three pyramids to build a three metres (10 ft) high, 0.3 metre (1 ft) thick wall around France. The area covered by the Great Pyramid can accommodate St Peter's in Rome, the cathedrals of Florence and Milan, and Westminster and St Paul's in London – combined.

WIND POWER?

Still, how the pyramid was built, remains an enigma. Author Clive Prince once observed that if we were to follow the writings of Egyptologists, then the Great Pyramid was not built. Their proposed theories of how the structure was built, some of which have been put into practice, have not worked and some theories can't even be put to the test, collapsing onto themselves – as the building would do.

One theory as to how the more than two million stones were moved into place involves the construction of a straight or spiral ramp that was raised higher and higher as the construction proceeded. This ramp, coated with mud and water, would have allowed for the transport of the blocks. But even though some Egyptologist claim they have found "evidence" of such a ramp, some of their colleagues point out that a straight ramp is highly unlikely: it would have contained more material than the pyramid itself, it would furthermore be immensely long and no single trace exists of a structure that is impossible to obliterate totally. Furthermore, the work that would have to go into the construction of the ramp would be more than the work that needed to go into the construction of the pyramid itself! A spiral ramp is often depicted on artist's drawings of how the pyramid was supposedly constructed, but how the laws of gravity would make them stick to the sides is a problem not tackled by the Egyptologists, who seem to merely like to draw them on sheets of paper, rather than underwrite their theory with engineering precision. A second theory suggests that the blocks were placed using long levers with a short angled foot, which originates from a story sold to Herodotus as to how the pyramids were built. Unfortunately, many Egyptologists are not versed in how levers and pulleys work, so little progress has been made here too.

But comparative analyses may help us out. Just like a massive amount of pyramids were erected in the Old Kingdom – and none afterwards – approximately 90 obelisks were raised in the New Kingdom period (1600-1100 BC) – and apparently none before. This in itself is an intriguing fact, as it shows "era specific types" of construction in Egypt. But though the eras were different in what they constructed, they may share identical construction techniques.

Dr Maureen Clemmons' interest in Egyptian building techniques started when she read an article in the January 1997 *Smithsonian*, about the attempt to raise a forty ton obelisk resting in an ancient quarry in Aswan, Egypt. The granite of Aswan was the favoured stone from which obelisks were carved. These were then transported – mostly via the river Nile – to the north, mostly to Thebes/Luxor, which at that time was the capital of the Egyptian Empire and the site of most building projects. Even though the obelisk was relatively small in monument terms (40 tons compared to other obelisks weighing 100–300 tons), the crew was unable to produce the lift required to raise the obelisk. Dr. Maureen

Clemmons pondered the problem and offered a new possibility as to how the ancient Egyptians may have erected their obelisks: wind power, using kites. For seven years leading up to January 2004, Clemmons was the main motivator of a team of amateurs whom received little to no funding, all of them trying to show practically that obelisks could be erected by harbouring the power of the wind.

Kites may seem a bizarre suggestion, but we know that the ancient Egyptians had been successful in controlling and harvesting the power of the wind: they sailed along the Nile, which formed the artery of ancient Egypt. Clemmons wondered whether the ancient Egyptians applied their acquired knowledge of the wind on the Nile also on land. The inspiration came when Clemmons saw a building frieze in a Cairo museum, showing a wing pattern in a bas relief that did not resemble any living bird, directly below of which were several men standing near vertical objects that could be ropes. Was this carving showing how the ancient Egyptians had built their monuments?

Kites are known to provide pull and lift, two great forces that, if harboured, could be great allies in their construction efforts. In the 20th century, Egyptologists have also uncovered that the ancient Egyptians were also familiar with pulleys, which is a required ingredient in harvesting wind power. In short, in theory, it was a possibility; but was it practical, and, above all, was it the method used by the ancient Egyptians?

After years of initially small tests, the first "real" test involved the erection of a 3.5 ton obelisk. The test site was at Quartz Hill in the Californian desert, as the team hoped to mimic some of the Egyptian desert conditions. During this endeavour, modern materials, such as nylon and steel, were used. In later tests, they would become replaced with traditional tools that were at the disposal of the ancient Egyptians; the steel frame into which the obelisk would be lifted would be replaced with a wooden frame, made from cedar and pine, which the Egyptians were known to import from the Lebanon; nylon kites would be replaced with linen kites; a metal sled on which the obelisk slid into place was replaced with a wooden sled; finally, nylon and steel ropes were replaced with hemp rope, whereby tests showed that twisted hemp rope when wet could stand the comparison with modern nylon ropes.

The first successful test occurred on April 14, 2001. In wind speeds of approximately 25 kilometres (15 mph), the obelisk was raised in approximately one hour. On June 23, 2001, the team raised the three metres tall obelisk into vertical position in winds of 35.5 km (22 mph) in under 25 seconds. Towards the end, the obelisk was seen to be swinging from the top of its lifting frame, like a giant pendulum. Erecting obelisks seemed to be that easy…

After this initial success, the more traditional components were introduced, as well as making the obelisk larger in size. An eleven ton obelisk, made out of cement and steel, to mimic the granite used by the ancient Egyptians, was the centre of these renewed attempts. The team now knew that the best operating conditions were steady winds, between 30-40 kph (20-25 mph). In 2003, the first attempt resulted in a partial lift of approx. forty degrees, or approx. three metres (10 ft). However, part of the set-up broke, which meant that this test had to be abandoned. Finally, in January 2004, working in optimal wind conditions, the obelisk raised itself to three metres after 27 minutes, at which (yet again) cracks were heard – even though this time nothing broke. An angle of 80 to 85 degrees was reached after 57 minutes, upon which it became clear that the lifting frame was too small to completely erect the obelisk – thus pointing out a basic flaw in the team's engineering drawings. Nevertheless, the test proved a success as it showed that a single kite was able to provide sufficient lift to raise an obelisk.

The team has only used a single kite. And if one kite can lift ten tones, then a constellation of many more kites could lift larger weights; to lift 400 tons, a constellation of forty kites could do the job; or larger kites could be employed, just like larger boats have larger sails. This also means that the "wind method" is quite "modular": depending on the weight, smaller or larger kites can be used, meaning that certain "kite operators" would need to be more knowledgeable than others, working with smaller kites.

Eleven tons is hundreds of tones away from the true weight of the Egyptian obelisks – but it is five times more than the average block of stone used in the Great Pyramid. Though the team focused on the erection of obelisks, the pyramid building technique was not neglected. In 2003, the team showed that two ton stones (the correct weight for the Great Pyramid) easily moved on rollers, propelled by the powers of the wind via a kite. The system also allowed stones to be lifted up a ramp. The average weight of the pyramid stones is 2.5 tons means that relatively small kites could be employed to move and lift these stones – or large kites could lift more than one stone at a time.

Intriguingly, if wind power was indeed used in the Old Kingdom, it shows that "wind technology" was thus subject to a learning curve as well: from the Old Kingdom onwards, the ancient Egyptians perfected their "wind method", whereby in the New Kingdom, they were able to lift obelisks that weighed several hundreds of tons.

With the initial success in showing that wind power can be harnessed and used in the building industry, Egyptologists have nevertheless pointed out that Clemmons has only shown a possible technique – but that this does not mean that the ancient Egyptians followed this technique. This in itself is true, but what Egyptologists fail to add is that their own preferred explanations equally fall short of that criterion. What makes Clemmons' approach specifically appealing is the speed at which these complex tasks are performed. Mass labour and massive ramps could indeed – possibly – build the Great Pyramid; but if this pyramid was built in less than twenty years, as Egyptologists argue, then it means that one stone was lifted into place approximately every two seconds (under normal working conditions). Speed is therefore of the essence, and mass labour and massive ramps are known to have been the slowest techniques so far imagined.

Clemmons' method has one final advantage: the bodies of the slave labour force have not been found; the remains of the giant ramps around the pyramids have equally not been found. There are, in short, no archaeological traces of a method that should have left traces. But the "wind method" would not leave such traces – and would also be a quick to clean up method once the work is completed. But is it fast enough?

CEMENT?

What if the stones were not quarried, but "made" on site? Professor Joseph Davidovits is an internationally renowned French scientist, born in 1935, who was honoured by French President Jacques Chirac with one of France's two highest honours, the "Chevalier de l'Ordre National du Mérite", in November 1998. Davidovits comes with a French Degree in Chemical Engineering and is a German Doctor Degree in Chemistry (PhD), as well as being professor and founder of the Institute for Applied Archaeological Sciences, IAPAS, Barry University, Miami, Florida, from 1983 till 1989, being visiting Professor, Penn State University, Pennsylvania (1989-1991) and Professor and Director of the Geopolymer Institute, Saint-Quentin, France (1979). He is a world expert in modern and ancient cements, as well as geosynthesis and man-made rocks, and the inventor of geopolymers and the chemistry of geopolymerisation.

These are just the highlights; his CV is longer than most books. But the reason why I include his career's distinctions is that all of his scientific credibility has made virtually no indent in Egyptological circles, who have largely disregarded his findings about how the pyramids were "really" constructed. The few Egyptologists that have criticised him, do not seem to have read his work, for they largely misquote or at best quote out of context, apparently unaware what Davidovits actually says. So why is there such an attitude towards this distinguished scientist? Because Davidovits has a radical theory: he argues that the limestone that constitutes the major pyramids of the Old Kingdom of Egypt is man-made stone.

Egyptologists dogmatise that the stones of the pyramids are hewn from nearby limestone quarries, which were then moved to the pyramid sites, where they were positioned in place. Davidovits argues that the stones were indeed hewn in the Turah and Mokattam quarries, but were more chopped rather than perfectly hewn out, and then transported. These rough blocks of limestone

Section of Khafre Pyramid where casing stones are left

were part of a construction method that resembles modern construction techniques: moulds had been placed, into which the stones and other compounds were placed, before a chemical process turned the mixture into the blocks we can now admire. In short, the stones of the Great Pyramid are "cement-like", rather than "hewn limestone blocks".

From an engineering perspective, this technique would make the construction much easier: there were no immense limestone blocks to be moved; there is no real need for a ramp and the transport of the stone material could be done faster, as less care was required in moving the limestone – the limestone was merely an ingredient and if it broke, no-one cared. Furthermore, the technique could also explain how the tremendous accuracy in the construction of the pyramid was achieved: the famous "no cigarette paper is able to be fitted between two stones". Rather than figuring out how two hewn stones were perfectly fitted into each other on site, instead, we would have wooden moulds that were placed next to a completed "block", upon which "cement" was poured into the mould, then left to dry, before the next stone was made. This guaranteed that each one fitted perfectly to the next.

For it to work, the only ingredient that is required, is to identify whether or not the ancient Egyptians were familiar with such "rock making", i.e. geopolymerisation. Davidovits is the – *the* – world expert in this technology and it is fair to say not a single Egyptologist was aware of the possibility until the mid 1980s, when Davidovits first proposed his hypothesis. Over the past two decades, Davidovits has been trying to educate this group of scientists, but they remain largely unwilling students, even though he sold more than 45,000 copies of his book: the general public wanted to understand, but as Egyptologists were largely unable to criticise – or had any credentials to – they chose to ignore.

Davidovits has used chemical analysis to show that the stones of the pyramids are different from the native stone in the quarries, showing that the traditional stance of the Egyptologists can, from a scientific point, no longer be maintained. The analysis shows that the stones did not "just" come from these quarries... and are indeed cement. To quote Davidovits: "The results [of the quarry samples] were compared with pyramid casing stones of Cheops, Teti and Sneferu. The quarry samples are pure limestone consisting of 96-99% Calcite, 0.5-2.5% Quartz, and very small amount of dolomite, gypsum and iron-alumino-silicate. On the other hand the Cheops and Teti casing stones are limestone consisting of: calcite 85-90% and a high amount of special minerals such as Opal CT, hydroxy-apatite, a silico-aluminate, which are not found in the quarries. The pyramid casing stones are light in density and contain numerous trapped air bubbles, unlike the quarry samples which are uniformly dense. If the casing stones were natural limestone, quarries different from those traditionally associated with the pyramid sites must be found, but where? X-Ray diffraction of a red casing stone coating is the first proof to demonstrate the fact that a complicated man-made geopolymeric system was produced in Egypt 4,700 years ago."[4]

Egypt was seen as the birthplace of alchemy, but for Davidovits, it is also the cradle of chemistry. He argues that certain names, such as *mafkat*, which Egyptologists have been unable to translate or explain, are very much "invented words", as they described compounds that ancient chemists had constructed – just like *cement* is an "invented word" – a technical term. He argues that when Imhotep is credited as "the inventor of the art of constructing with cut stones", it is actually a mistranslation of the Greek "xeston lithon", which does not translate as "cut stone", but rather means "the action to polish stone". For Davidovits, Imhotep is actually the inventor of working with agglomerates, or geopolymers.

Davidovits believes that Imhotep created two different chemical formulas: a very simple one for the casting of the limestone core blocks, and another one to produce the high quality stones of the exterior layer. The first and major ingredient in these techniques is soft limestone. Soft limestone can be easily disaggregated either under pressure or by diluting it in water. "Shallow canals were dug in the soft limestone along the Nile, forming ideal basins for producing large quantities of muddy limestone. Imhotep's men began disaggregating the clayish soft rock with its water, until the lime and the clay separated, forming a mud with the fossil shells at the bottom." Next, a substance called natron salt (sodium carbonate) was poured in. Salt is a very reactive substance that has a petrifying effect, which is why it is used to avoid the putrefaction of organic tissue (mummification). Natron is found in great quantities in the desert and in the Wadi-El-Natron (100 km to the north west of Cairo and named after the substance) and Davidovits has shown that the ancient Egyptians of the Pyramid Age used it in massive quantities.

Next, more lime, the mineral which binds, was added. Lime is a powdery residue obtained by burning and reducing to ashes sedimentary rocks such as limestone and dolomite. The fire oxidizes and converts the rocks into a powdery residue, and that is lime. Davidovits argues that as the ashes of plants are also rich in lime, the ancient Egyptians established the custom of receiving ashes from cooking fires from all over Egypt, to add them to the mixture. In short: recycling not to save the environment, but to build the pyramids.

Lime mixed with natron and water produced a third substance, a much more corrosive one, which sparks off a strong chemical reaction and transforms other materials. The water dissolved the natron salt and put the lime in suspension, forming caustic soda.

Caustic soda is the catalyst Imhotep needed to trigger off a powerful chemical reaction, one which would produce the fast integration of silica and alumina. According to Davidovits, they then mixed the ingredients in the canals until a homogenous binder paste was obtained. Imhotep had invented a water-based cement, which he had to convert into concrete. For this, he added more fossil shells, limestone rubble and silt from the river Nile, producing a concrete paste, which they carried to where hundreds of small wooden moulds had been prepared. These moulds had been smeared with rancid oil to facilitate the release of the concrete once hardened. The mixture was rammed into the moulds, becoming a dense re-agglomerated limestone, which was let to dry in the shade, to avoid its cracking under the glare of the hot sun.

The above is a proven chemical procedure, but was it known to Imhotep? For an untrained eye, the process seems terribly complex and outside of the scope of ancient Egyptians – after all, Davidovits himself discovered geopolymers only recently – how could it have been known millennia ago, and then forgotten?

Davidovits thinks that ancient records have left us clues... as wel as the total cost of the mineral mixing ingredients required in the above process. He believes that this information was actually left behind on the pyramid covering stones and pointed out to Herodotus when he visited Gizeh. Herodotus reported that a sum of 1600 talents, or roughly the equivalent 100 million Euros (dollars), was spent on garlic, onions and radishes, which he and everyone else considered a phenomenal amount of money for what seems to be secondary dietary requirements for the work-force. As such, the story is taken with... a pinch of salt, arguing that Herodotus was lied to by his locally hired tourist guide. But Davidovits believes that those names ("garlic, onions and radishes" were misinterpretations of what was actually written on the pyramid. Originally, we referred to substances based on their colours: rubber comes from the Latin word for red, yet when we today ask for a rubber... And so Davidovits argues that these words are not "garlic", "onion" or "radish", but technical terms whose true meaning had become lost and hence were misinterpretations, causing bafflement with anyone who came across them, like Herodotus. Davidovits has used other inscriptions, including several steles from the period, to show that specific mining venues were exploited during the Pyramid Age, but that the quaried materials have no clear purpose within the traditional methodology of how the pyramids were constructed – but they do make sense within his approach.

Was Imhotep an inventor? The answer is yes. Zoser's step pyramid was not only the first, but also the only one made entirely of small modular blocks weighing approximately sixty kilos apiece, easily carried by two men. It was a variation in which the traditional mud bricks had been replaced with the new limestone paste. This innovation was then improved by Imhotep's successors, to construct pyramids for the succeeding Pharaohs. The three Sneferu's pyramids that followed improved, step by step, the technology by increasing the size of the blocks and the height of the monuments. Whereas the small bricks for the Step Pyramid of Saqqara were still moved from the construction site to the building site, from Sneferu's Red Pyramid at Dashur onwards, much heavier blocks were moulded and cast directly on the spot, the technique also used for the Great Pyramids at Gizeh – which arose sixty years after the beginning of this new technology. In this hypothesis, the discovery of "ancient cement" meant that the ancient Egyptians were able to commence massive building projects, which would have otherwise remained impossible to accomplish. It made the "Pyramid Dream" a reality.

Is there hard evidence to credit Imhotep and his colleagues of the Third and Fourth Dynasty with the invention of geopolymers? Davidovits argues that the Famine Stele, found on the island of

Elephantine in southern Egypt, indeed describes the invention of building with stone through processing different minerals and ores, which could be chemicals involved in the fabrication of man-made stone, or a type of concrete. On the Gizeh plateau, he has shown that several stones have weathered unnaturally: one single block was sometimes left unfinished for the day, and thus hardened over night, before being brought to the desired height the following morning. This meant that one block was made in two phases, with slightly different materials and created under different circumstances. Six millennia later, it means that sometimes the lower section of a stone has weathered badly, but the higher section has not, even though the stones next to it, did not reveal such lower weathering. Such weathering is not conform the traditionalist point of view of quarried blocks.

Thes are just some examples in a long list of evidence that argues that the most likely method of construction was the use of geopolymers, and not hewn limestone slabs that were perfectly moved into position. But it is clear that it will take some time before it may ever be accepted as the most likely explanation... Let us note that as recently as 1951, Otto Neugebauer argued that "ancient science was the product of very few men; and those few happened not to be Egyptian."[5] In short: ancient Egyptians had, in his opinion, made no contribution to science whatsoever... though in the successive five millennia, not a single scientist has been able to explain or let alone reconstruct the Great Pyramid. Still, Neugebauer's statement was in sharp contrast with men like Aristotle, who saw Egypt as "the cradle of mathematics", crediting them with inventing geometry, astronomy and arithmetic. Eudoxus, like Pythagoras, studied in ancient Egypt, before being admitted in Plato's Academy in Athens, showing that the ancient Greeks throughout their history realised that Egypt held certain knowledge which was of vital importance for an educated Greek – and which was apparently a type of knowledge that they were unable to get in Greece itself. Intriguingly, Plato, a man who has been seen as standing at the cradle of Western civilisation, himself studied with the priests of Heliopolis, the body who had, two millennia before Plato, initiated the birth of the Pyramid Age.

A TOMB?

In the Middle Kingdom, the tombs of the Pharaohs were located in the Valley of the Kings near Thebes/Luxor; they were carefully sealed and their entrances as much as possible hidden. Despite these efforts, so far, only one intact tomb has been found: that of Tuthankhamun. All other tombs have so far proven to have been robbed, either in the distant past and – "it is assumed" – some in more recent centuries. Of all the things that can be said about the Great Pyramid, "hidden from view" does not apply. The Australian journalist Clive James once noted that the only thing missing from the top of the pyramid was a neon sign, announcing things like "tomb inside" or "treasure inside".

But despite its obvious spell-binding attraction on Mankind's imagination to explore that which could be inside, it was only in 820 AD that one Arab Caliph Abdullah Al Manum decided to penetrate into the pyramid and search for the treasure of Khufu. He gathered a gang of workmen, but was unable to find the location of the entrance door – no doubt the main reason why the pyramid had survived the previous centuries intact. So he started to burrow into the side of the monument in the hope of hitting at some point upon the internal structure – in the hope that indeed there was an internal structure. After about thirty metres (a hundred feet), they were about to give up, when they heard a heavy thud echo. Digging in the direction of the sound, they came upon a passageway that descended into the heart of the structure. On the floor they found a large block that had fallen from the ceiling, which they believed was the noise that they had heard. Going back to the beginning of this corridor, they found the door to the outside whose location they had missed from the outside.

Manum's men found themselves in the "Descending Passage", which ended into the natural rock of the plateau on which the pyramid was built, leading into a chamber that contained an empty that extended downward for about ten metres (30ft); beyond the pit, the chamber continued, but ended in a blank wall.

But the block that had become dislodged during their tunnel seemed to be an act of God – Allah – or the Pharaoh's Curse. When the workmen examined it, they noticed a large granite plug above it. Cutting through the softer stone around it (granite is one of the hardest materials), they found another passageway, this time ascending – and now known as "the Ascending Passage". They found several more granite blocks closing off the tunnel, but each time, they cut around them by burrowing through the softer limestone of the walls. Finally, they found themselves in a low, horizontal passage that lead to a small, square, empty room, now known as the "Queen's Chamber". But even though the room contained niches and thus implied the presence of statues, there was nothing of the kind to be found.

Now aware that this interior structure had hidden passageways, the workmen went back to the junction of the ascending and descending passageways, where the workers noticed an open space in the ceiling. Climbing up, they found themselves in a high-roofed, ascending passageway: the "Grand Gallery". At the top of the gallery was a low horizontal passage that led to a large room, some 11 metres (34 feet) long, 6 metres (17 feet) wide, and 6.5 metres (19 feet) high: the "King's Chamber". The room was empty, except for a huge granite sarcophagus, without a lid, in the centre. We can imagine how one or more men approached the structure with their torches at shoulder's height, bending forwards, lowering their torches over the sarcophagus, illuminating the structure and its interior... to find it empty.

If this is a tomb – Khufu's tomb – where was the body? What happened to the grave gifts, so numerous for a boy king like Tutankhamun (though these Arab explorers were more than a millennium away from that discovery), yet absent for this Pharaoh? "Grave robbers" is the standard reply given by the Egyptologists. But if we believe the accounts of Manum's men, the granite plugs that blocked the passageways were still in place when they entered the tomb, suggesting that the interior structure had not been penetrated before; they were the first "grave robbers" to enter the structure, and they found it empty; no tomb, no body.

Still, for those who were convinced that the pyramid was a tomb, salvation came in 1638, when the English mathematician John Greaves discovered a narrow shaft, hidden in the wall, which connected the Grand Gallery to the Descending Passage. Both ends were tightly sealed and the bottom was blocked with debris. This was, archaeologists afterwards suggested, the route used by the last of the Pharaoh's men to exit the tomb, after the granite plugs had been put in place. It was also, they claimed, how the thieves got inside. If this were so, these seemed be extremely tidy thieves, sealing the passage after them!

There are two problems with this theory. First, given the small size of the passageway and the amount of debris, it seems unlikely that the massive amount of assumed treasure to be located inside, including the huge missing sarcophagus lid, could have been removed this way. The lid would have been broken up and whereas this is a possible scenario, the question is whether it is likely; yes, the lid may have been seen as valuable, but if broken in several pieces, would it retain its value and be worth the effort? And if so, why not break up the entire sarcophagus and take it out in pieces too? Second, though it may explain how the Pharaoh's men could get out after putting the granite plugs in place, it does not explain how the tomb robbers got in. The funeral cortege could have ascended up the Descending Passage, leaving through the official door, which was then sealed – so well, that Manum could not discover it. We know that that door remained intact for millennia. So, with the original entrance not broken into, it means that any tomb robber would have had to dig a tunnel like Manum, and such a tunnel would be visible today. But there is no such tunnel. It thus seems that, in spite of what Egyptologists claim, the pyramid was not penetrated before Manum. And as he found no mummy, it means that when the pyramid was sealed, there was no body inside. Or, at least, if there is a mummy in the pyramid, it was not inside the King's Chamber, and if there is a mummy, it is located in a part of the pyramid that we have not been able to locate yet.

As the reader will appreciate, I am not the first to make the above argument, which is precise and clear in its reasoning. When others have argued similarly, some Egyptologists have argued that Manum's records are not detailed enough or that he "may" have just enlarged an already existing tunnel, dug by previous grave robbers. It is possible; but is it likely? I agree that there is vast evidence that many of the pyramids have been penetrated in the past – but where is the evidence for the Great Pyramid? And even though there is evidence of burglary, it is another question whether or not the burglars found anything inside. As such, the "pyramids are tombs" camp are too quick to identify evidence of penetration as evidence that the burglars found something inside... or, more importantly, that what they found inside was a mummy. The fact remains that no royal mummy has been found inside any pyramid – though a mummy of a young man was found in the coffer of the pyramid of the Sixth Dynasty king Merenre at Saqqara in 1971. This discovery could have vindicated the Egyptologists' stance, for "finally", there was evidence for their theory. But, amazingly, no scientific testing has been performed to determine its age, i.e. to determine whether it was the "original mummy", or an "intrusive burial", i.e. someone buried after the pyramid had been opened – by treasure seekers.

As such, the most convincing evidence for the "non-tomb" theory comes from Zakaria Goneim, who was excavating the pyramid of Sekhemkhet at Saqqara in the early 1950s. Making his way to the underground chamber, he removed the sealing blocks at the entrance, as well as those at the doorway to the burial chamber. In the opinion of this qualified Egyptologist, everything appeared to be intact. He also found some bones and multiple papyri written in demotic Egyptian, as well as a hoard of gold jewellery – which is convincing evidence that the structure was intact and had not been subjected to grave robbers, who would have been more than "intrigued" by the gold jewellery and would definitely have taken it away, rather than any mummified remains. Inside the burial chamber, he came upon an alabaster sarcophagus and found that the grooves for the sliding panel of the structure were still sealed with a layer of plaster. This was definitive proof that the sarcophagus had remained intact. So, what did Goneim find inside? Nothing. No mummy, nothing. The coffer was completely empty.

The reader may, of course, not have heard about Zakaria Goneim, and it is clear why. Goneim's discovery caused serious problems for the "pyramids are tombs" camp and hence some mention it without further comment, others speculate, arguing that this was a "false burial", to fool any burglar, and that the Pharaoh was buried elsewhere, etc., etc. It is all possible, just like the possibility that a time traveller from 35,643 AD travelled back in time, projecting himself into the inside of the sarcophagus, snatching the mummy with him back to his own time. It's possible, but it's hardly likely!

If the pyramid showed no signs of penetration, and the sarcophagus neither, if the sarcophagus was empty… the most logical conclusion is that sarcophagi were not installed inside pyramids to hold the royal mummy. Scientists like to poke Occam's razor into non-scientifically trained minds; the argument goes that the most logical conclusion should be taken as the most likely and hence upheld as "the" hypothesis. This rule, it seems, does not apply to Egyptology. The physicist Dr Kurt Mendelssohn levelled the same criticism against his Egyptology colleagues: "while the funerary function of the pyramids cannot be doubted, it is rather more difficult to prove that the pharaohs were ever buried inside them. There are too many empty sarcophagi and, what is worse, rather too many empty tomb chambers, to make the idea of actual burials unchallengeable."[6] Enigmatically, Mendelssohn then proposed that "as these were burials without a corpse, we are almost driven to the conclusion that something other than a human body may have been ritually entombed".

THE SEARCH FOR SECRET CHAMBERS

The pyramids are gigantic structures with a very limited amount of rooms inside them. In some cases, like Khafre's pyramid at Gizeh, the actual pyramid contains no rooms at all; the chambers and tunnels are confined to the lower levels, tunnelling into the bedrock. In this case, the pyramid sits on top of a subterranean cave-like network, rather than a "house with rooms" – and even in the case of the Great Pyramid, the lowest levels penetrate into the bedrock; in fact, there is evidence to suggest it was built on top of a natural cave, which was held to be sacred – hence why the pyramid was built on top.

But back on subject: with the advent of modern electronic detection equipment in the 1960s, non-destructive exploration of the pyramid became possible. In 1965, a proposal was submitted by an American team led by Dr. Luis Alvarez to scan Khafre's Pyramid. Their results did not find any hidden chambers in the area that they had analysed. In 1977, a team of SRI scientists[7] discovered two anomalies beneath Belzoni's chamber, the inner of its two so-far discovered chambers. They could lie in the extension of the two descending passages of this pyramid, but no further research has since occurred.

Though you would assume someone has tried to explore this potential discovery further, it is equally clear that the focus of most attention is on the Great Pyramid next door. Are there hidden chambers in this pyramid? The answer is a remarkable "yes, definitely". Even Colonel Howard Vyse (1784-1853) spoke of "sand filled cavities" that he encountered in the area of the Queen's Chamber. Another "anomaly" was detected by the SRI team, in an area between the King's and Queen's Chamber. In March 1985, French design technician Gilles Dormion and architect Jean-Patrice Goidin observed certain anomalies in the walls of the passage leading to the Queen's Chamber. Their instrument's readings indicated a cavity behind its west wall. Next to these, a Japanese team detected another cavity, along the same wall. The Frenchmen were given permission to drill three small holes. The third drill hole penetrated 2.65 metres and revealed a cavity containing sand of a very fine quality. The Japanese team discovered – or confirmed Vyse's observation – that a cavity existed beneath the floor of the horizontal passage, which contained once again sand. Rumours spread that this sand was radioactive, which was incorrect, but it was not just "any" sand either: the sand had been transported from El Tur, in southern Sinai, suggesting that someone wanted this type of sand and not the one that was locally available.

But sand is just sand (even though we have no idea why they wanted El Tur sand) and it is not as interesting as the saga that developed shortly afterwards. In 1993, German engineer Rudolf Gantenbrink co-operated with a German team led by Egyptologist Rainer Stadelmann to install a new air-conditioning system in the Great Pyramid, to accommodate the tourists. The project was given a scientific addendum when the robot was sent into the "air shafts" that lead up from two sides of both the Queen's and King's Chambers. Traditionally identified as "air shafts", their purpose was thought to be to let in air into the interior structure, a theory "confirmed" when J.R. Hill, the owner of the Cairo Hotel and friend of Colonel Howard Vyse, clambered up the pyramid and found their outlets. The shafts are only 20 by 20 cm (8 inches) wide and thus far, had only been probed by elongated brooms and other pliable material, which had indicated a possible length, as far as broomsticks and like could probe, before they seemed to be closed off. Gantenbrink's robot was equipped with a camera, which meant human eyes would see a structure that had been left intact since the building of the pyramids.

First, on its slow upward travel into the Southern shaft of the Queen's Chamber, the robot's journey proved that the shaft was much longer than previously assumed. But eventually, it came to a halt before a slab of white, Tura limestone with what appeared to be a small copper handle on it. On the floor of the shaft was another of these handles (if handles they are), which had broken off from the slab. Where it should have been attached, there was now only a tarnished, copper stump remaining. There was a small opening at the bottom, through which the robot's laser light disappeared.

This was an exciting find – and the cause of much speculation. What was behind the door? A secret chamber? If so, what would it contain? Speculation came from various corners, including the Director of the Gizeh Plateau, Dr. Zahi Hawass, who spoke of a potential statue of Osiris, or perhaps even the veritable tomb of Khufu… or perhaps something else. He "promised" that the project would soon be followed up, with attempts to penetrate through the door.

"Soon" turned out to be 2002 (nine years later), when a team sponsored by National Geographic continued the research, drilling a hole through the door, and sliding a camera through it. Result? Another door. Again, Hawass promised that research would continue, and "soon", but four years later, no new work has been planned.

Both Gantenbrink and the team of National Geographic have worked on the other shafts and have indicated that each has such doors – even though only one door has received most of the attention so far. Stories of secret chambers have since become rife, with certain people claiming they "know" there are secret chambers inside (some arguing Egyptologists like Hawass know their location and have actually entered them!) and others "convinced" that their work has pinpointed the location of a further cavity.

It is clear that the Great Pyramid has not yet revealed all of its secrets: whether the air shafts will indeed lead to chambers, or something else; whether the cavities filled with sand are indeed chambers or merely cavities... and why they were filled with such specific sand. But it is clear that progress is slow. Despite all work being carried out by people with the proper credentials and using due care and attention, projects are slow, noting that "soon" translated as "nine years". There is no specific reason why it should be this slow. Whereas Hawass is publicly infuriated with the speculation and conspiracy theories surrounding "his" plateau, he is also the primary cause of it: if you promise swift action, but for undetermined reasons it takes a decade, even though every robot engineer was virtually sitting outside your office, willing to send his robot up the passage, you have to wonder why it took so long. The answer is a mixture of "politics" and "money", as well as "esteem", but these should not be the main ingredients in a scientific endeavour – though of course they always are.

WRITTEN IN THE STARS?

Two British authors, Robert Bauval and Graham Hancock, are the main "culprits" in Hawass' eyes of all this speculation. But Bauval was originally only interested in the new discoveries Gantenbrink's robot had made – so interested that he single-handedly caused great distress to Gantenbrink and in a two-edged sword may have been a contributing factor as to why "soon" took nine years... which Bauval consequently identified as a possible sign of a cover-up.

But rather than their role in the controversy, let us look at Bauval's genuine contribution to the pyramid debate: the popularisation of the astronomical approach to the pyramids. In his 1994 publication *The Orion Mystery*, co-authored with Adrian Gilbert, he used the Gantenbrink discovery to underline his theory that these shafts were not air shafts, but actually "star shafts", with individual shafts aligned to Sirius, Orion's Belt, Alpha Draconis and Beta Ursa Minor. Each of these stars played an important role in ancient Egypt's mythology, Sirius identified with Isis (Osiris' content) and identified as the herald of the Egyptian New Year, which itself had astronomical origins, namely the rising of Sirius at dawn at the same time the sun rose above the horizon.

Though often attributed to Bauval, the suggestion that the shafts were astronomically aligned was actually the work of Virginia

Trimble, working with Professor Alexander Badawy, whom Bauval and Gilbert clearly credit for their work. Furthermore, even the Roman author Proclus stated that before the pyramid was completed, it served an astronomical function. Astronomer Richard Proctor observed that the Descending Passage could have been used to observe the transits of certain stars and also suggested that the Grand Gallery, when open at the top, during construction, could have been used for mapping the sky. It is, however, difficult to see how theories such as Proctor's may have any great contributions to the debate, for, of course, the Grand Gallery would not remain open at the top for very long – a matter of days or weeks, while construction progressed.

Bauval's contribution is that he transformed this astronomical debate, showing that the three pyramids of the Gizeh plateau represented Orion's Belt. To use one of his own favourite quotes: "As above, so below." Though Egyptologists do not like it, as a whole, they are equally unlikely to attack this hypothesis, if only because it is so strikingly visually similar. But unfortunately perhaps for himself, Bauval did not stop there: he then tried to use other nearby pyramids, in an effort to show that the builders depicted the entire constellation of Orion onto the surface. With this extrapolation, he ran into difficulties, for not only could he only find two of the four required stars to depict Orion, the bigger question that he failed to address was what to do with the dozens of other pyramids in the area... and why the "Orion project" did not seem to be a clear plan by Khufu and his sons, but haphazardly taken up and dropped by some Pharaohs – showing that even if they did wanted to depict Orion, they were not very devoted to this cause.

Bauval's "Orion Correlation Theory" followed the accepted dogma that the pyramid was a funerary complex. But rather than seeing the Subterranean and Queen's Chambers "just" as evidence that the Pharaoh had changed his mind twice before deciding to be buried in the King's Chamber (i.e. the standard Egyptological interpretation), Bauval speculated whether the chambers of the Great Pyramid were used in the Pharaonic funerary rites and thus were not the result of the Pharaoh's whims, but necessary ingredients in the Pharaoh's burial. Though controversial (why, for example, do other pyramids thus not have similar structures?), many were willing to go along with this, for, indeed, it made more sense than most theories. But where most jumped off his train of logic was when Bauval brought in the known fact that the position of the stars change through the Precession of the Equinoxes. An analysis of his depiction of Orion on the ground (which, in my opinion, is far-fetched) and the known movements of that constellation in the sky made him conclude that the Gizeh Pyramid Complex (and other pyramids part of the "Orion Correlation Theory") depicted a celestial configuration of the skies not in 2450

Gizeh Plateau

BC, when he believed the pyramids were built, but in 10,400 BC. Though he focused on arguing that the pyramids thus depicted the "Zep Tepi", or the "First Time of Osiris", a type of Golden Age – or Paradise – within Egyptian mythology, he also drew direct parallels with the myth of Atlantis, as well as making references to the American psychic Edgar Cayce's prophecies that argued that Atlanteans had left a Hall of Records in or near the nearby Sphinx. "Atlantis" and "Hall of Records" act on Egyptologists like the colour red on the emotional balance of a bull. It resulted in a veritable stampede in which Egyptologists tried to trample Bauval... and anyone who joined ranks with him, including his future co-author Graham Hancock, with whom he would later explore the same theories in more depth, but also in other directions.

Scientists tend to take one book as a whole, rather than take from it the nuggets of veritable ingenuity and innovation. It meant that Bauval's contribution in beginning to depict an astronomical framework into which the pyramids had been constructed, was largely ignored. Instead, it resulted in a five year long controversy, in which Atlantis and Edgar Cayce formed the nucleus of the controversy, with authors such as John Anthony West and Colin Wilson (in *From Atlantis to the Sphinx*) choosing Bauval's camp, with criticism, apart from the scientific community, also coming from "independent researchers" (a term Bauval favours) Chris Ogilvie-Herald and Ian Lawton's *Giza: The Truth* and Lynn Picknett & Clive Prince's *The Stargate Conspiracy*. The latter book, to which I was the principal contributor, tried to depict the "Cayce-10,400 BC"-frenzy within a larger framework, showing that there seemed to be a concerted effort by various individuals in abusing historical realities to rework them to suit their own theories, a theory which argued that we were on the brink of a major revelation, which would reveal the presence of a superior, perhaps alien civilisation that had left proof of its existence behind in the mystical "Hall of Records". Though I met Bauval in August 1995 at a conference where we were both speakers, by 1999 and with the publication of *The Stargate Conspiracy*, his demeanour to towards his fellow Belgian ex-patriate had changed dramatically from four years before...

DATING THE GREAT PYRAMID

For Egyptologists, there is no doubt whatsoever that the pyramids date from Egypt's Dynastic period. But for many popular authors, this is not the case. At least: they agree with Egyptologists on almost everything, except the Great Pyramid. For some authors, it is a remnant of an alien civilisation, being several tens of thousands of years old. As mentioned, Zecharia Sitchin is one of these defenders, arguing that the Great Pyramid was a space beacon for incoming spaceships (as well as serving as a temporary prison for an alien being). For others, the Great Pyramid was a memorial built by survivors of the destruction of Atlantis. Others see it is a pre-diluvian remnant of this lost civilisation. John Anthony West uses the nearby Sphinx to argue that it "clearly" reveals evidence of water-erosion and argues that insufficient rainfall has fallen since ca. 2500 BC to accomplish the level of erosion that we "clearly" see. Hence, he proposes the same 10,400 BC date, that mythical time which allows so many people to bring in the prophecies of Edgar Cayce – for some reason, a prophecy is deemed to outweigh a logical observation, or support it – and it is only logical why scientists and Egyptologists have had a go at people who bring in prophets into a scientific debate that really does not require the input of a visionary.

So what do scientific instruments date the pyramids as? In 1984, the Pyramids Carbon Dating Project was conducted, in which 64 samples of organic material was extracted from the pyramids. The conclusion was that Egyptologists had been off by almost 400 years; the pyramids were 400 years older. Still, some samples suggested that Egyptologists could be off by 1200 years. Mark Lehner summed up these findings: "Now this is really radical... I mean it'll make a big stink. The Gizeh pyramid is 400 years older than Egyptologists believe." Even though Lehner himself is an Egyptologist, it has to be said that he is more scientific than most – if only because he is willing to tackle the pyramids. Still, he is lacking in psychology, as he "clearly" did not understand most of his colleagues, as there was no "big stink": his colleagues opted to disregard the evidence, rather than confront it.

The revised average date for the Gizeh Pyramid, based on 15 samples, thus had it built in 2985 BC – roughly 500 years older than previously accepted, though by no means old enough to argue that it was built by an Atlantean civilisation in 10,400 BC. This is where most commentators stop, but I would like to go one step further, for the carbon dating also brought up several questions whether the assigned Pharaohs were truly responsible for the other monuments on the plateau.

The average date for Khafre's Pyramid is 2960 BC, 25 years after the Great Pyramid. This underlines the likelihood that the two major pyramids were part of the same building project, executed by consecutive (or the same?) pharaohs. But Menkaure's pyramid should logically sit within the next twenty to fifty years. Carbon dating, however, gave a date of 2572 BC, almost four centuries after the completion of Khafre's pyramid! To add to the problem, samples of the Sphinx Temple suggested a date of 2416 BC, which is half a millennium after Khafre's pyramid, though almost everyone assumes that the Sphinx and the Khafre pyramid were part of the same project...

The new date of ca. 3000 BC for the construction of the Great Pyramid does not please either camp – whether Egyptologist or "Atlanteologist". It shows that scientific tests can be unpopular... As such, both sides of the debate have tended to disregard this solid evidence, as it doesn't fit their preconceived ideas. Thus, we find articles that contain the following paragraphs: "Even if the radiocarbon dates for the 15 samples from the Great Pyramid that were tested are assumed to be reasonably accurate, there is still no certainty that they tell us its age. All of them came from the exterior of the Pyramid, from between the core masonry blocks or between the core masonry and the former casing stones, and they may therefore date from later repair work. The radiocarbon dates of 2085 BC and 2746 BC for the Sphinx Temple certainly do not indicate the date of its construction, for the huge limestone blocks from which it is built were obtained during the carving of the Sphinx, and the weathering patterns of the Sphinx prove beyond doubt – to most geologists, if not to conventional Egyptologists – that it must be at least 7-9000 years old."[8] Actually, there is just one such geologist who posits this seniority to the Sphinx, and that is Robert Schoch. But this ardent stance is all the more spiteful when we note that a second dating in 1995 with new but similar material obtained dates that confirmed the 1984 dates!

Sphinx with Great Pyramid behind

In the final analysis, it is clear that the Great Pyramid's status is just a mess. How disdainful we treat the only surviving Wonder of the World! But the same applies to the Pyramid Age as a whole. Egyptologists have too long and too childishly clung to outdated models, at the same time adding little to true understanding of these structures. Contributions such as those of Davidovits should have been welcomed and subjected to agreeable criticism, rather than vitriolic attacks or idiotic disregard. Radio-carbon dates should become integrated and form the centre of reinterpretation about the dating of the various pyramids. The absence of mummies in the pyramids should be seen as the possibility they were not tombs after all, even though it is clear that the walls of several pyramids do depict scenes of the Pharaoh's journey to Heaven. Though many of the alternative explanations have come up with equally ridiculous proposals, often foolhardishly going for the most popular, but equally preposterous theory ("Atlantis descendants built this in 10,400 BC"), both sides of the fence are clearly not going to contribute to a true understanding of what the pyramids truly represented... let alone who built them, when, why... But there is a new hope.

THE SUM OF THE WHOLE

In 2000, the Dutch engineer Willem Zitman proposed that there was a Master Plan at the foundation of the Pyramid Age. Rather than look at single pyramids in isolation, he looked at the entire collection – just like a project manager, a job role he performed within the building industry, would do.

In *Egypt: "Image of Heaven"*, he argued that all pyramids were positioned in predefined locations, so that the overall image revealed one particular part of the sky. To quote Zitman: "the ancient Egyptians were the first geographical planners to develop a system in order to establish an 'image of heaven' on Earth." He placed this project firmly within an astronomical framework, arguing that certain portions were built at certain times, to coincide with – i.e. mark – celestial events that the ancient Egyptians considered to be of great importance. In Zitman's approach, the ancient Egyptians coupled the observation of the heliacal rising of the star Sirius as the basis for their solar calendar. The places where these observatories were carried out would later become the prehistoric capitals of Egypt. But Zitman went further: he noticed that 365 arch-minutes exist between the two locations, one for each day of the year. From this basis, he was able to conclude that both the ancient Egyptians and Sumerians used the constellations in the sky to map the Earth as an "image of Heaven". His hypothesis stretches many's power of visualisation, if not imagination, as it implies that the ancient Egyptians possessed an advanced knowledge of geography and mapping. But the Greek grammarian Agatharchides of Cnidus, who lived in the 2nd century BC and tutored the pharaoh's children, was told that the base of the Great Pyramid was precisely one eight of a minute of a degree of the Earth's circumference, suggesting that such knowledge was indeed available at the time of the building of the Pyramid.

For Zitman, the "Pyramid Field" along the western side of the River Nile brought to life a specific portion of this "Heaven mapping on Earth-project". He argues that the design was based on two images. The first image dates back to the Old Kingdom and is the rendering of the ritual pose of "smiting the enemy". The second image dates from the Middle Kingdom and represents the "Hennu boat". Due to the many boat pits that were found (e.g. near the tomb of Pharaoh Khasekhemwy and near the pyramids of Gizeh), we may even consider the alternative possibility that work was undertaken during the Old Kingdom to create this image of the boat, a design that was completed during the Middle Kingdom and adapted to the style of this subsequent period. Still, the two images complement each other and jointly make up the completed "Hennu boat". To let Zitman speak for himself: "The outline of this Hennu boat, harbouring Osiris, is formed by the pyramids in Abu Rawash, Giza, Zawyet el Aryan, Saqqara, Dahshur, Mazghuna, El Lisht, Meidum and Seila respectively. The raised stern is marked out separately by the pyramids of Lahun and Hawara. The pyramids of Mazghuna and El Lisht form the belly of the ship. The location of the southern pyramid of El Lisht catches the eye because of its rather south-westerly position. It is striking how these two images complement each other to form a unity, in which the first image (from the Old Kingdom) serves as the prow while the second one (from the Middle Kingdom) contributes the belly and the stern. The stern had, to a large extent, already acquired its shape during the Old Kingdom by the pyramids of Meidum and Seila. This boat was imagined to sail on the Nile, the river Hapi, which is synonymous with Osiris."

Zitman thus argues that the Pyramids mapped on Earth a depiction of the souls' voyage to the Afterlife, which it made on the Hennu Bark: "Various Pyramid Texts [...] endorse the striking image of this region that was ruled from Sokar (i.e. Saqqara): 'But you shall bathe in the starry firmament, you shall descend upon the iron bands on the arms of Horus in his name of Him [Osiris] who is in the Hnw [Hennu]-barque.' And: 'O, Osiris the King, you are a mighty god, and there is no god like you. Horus has given you his children that they may bear you up; he has given you all the gods that they may serve you, and that you may have power over them; Horus has lifted you up in his name of Hnw-barque; he bears you up in your name of Sokar.' 'O Osiris the King, Horus has lifted you into the Hnw-barque, he raises you into the Barque of Sokar, for he is a son who raises up his father.' These Pyramid Texts show that, in the region of Sokar, Horus carried his father Osiris into the Sokar boat or Hennu boat."

As simple as the approach may be, connecting the dots of the various pyramids does indeed reveal an outline of a bark, sailing on the river Nile. It is simple, convincing, and Zitman has argued his case in such depth that Egyptologists will once again be confronted with two possibilities: leave it aside, or adopt it. His theory may become the straw that breaks the camels' back, but seeing how strong-headed Egyptologists are, it is highly unlikely to happen in his lifetime. Though I would dearly love to be wrong!

So where does it leave us? Chris Ogilvie-Herald and Ian Lawton concluded their investigation of the Gizeh complex as follows: "To sum up, despite reservations about initiations and ongoing rituals, we feel that as well as having a burial function the pyramids clearly did have a far deeper symbolic function specifically connected with the king's journey to the afterlife. In this context it is worth mentioning that the original Egyptian word for the Greek name 'pyramid' is *mer*, which *may* be derived from components that translate as 'the Place of Ascension'."[9] It is the perfect foundation from which to continue our quest for pyramids elsewhere... and the only hope we can take with us into a later chapter, in our search for the meaning of the Egyptian pyramids.

CHAPTER 2
A NEW WORLD

The discovery of the New World brought with it the discovery of new pyramids. In fact, most ancient Mesoamerican turned out to be people that built pyramid-shaped structures, suggesting that the pyramid was a central feature of their religious life – more so than in the Old War. But these pyramids were usually step pyramids, which like the original mastabas of ancient Egypt, ended in a platform, on which a temple was built. As such, many describe the Mayan pyramids as "more akin to the ziggurats of Mesopotamia than to the pyramids of Ancient Egypt". A correct statement would be: "the pyramids of Mesoamerica are raised platforms, with steps leading to the top, and thus similar to the ziggurats of Mesopotamia and the original mastabas of ancient Egypt, before they changed into the pointed pyramids that now typify ancient pyramid building."

One of the unsung heroes of the pyramid discoveries in the new world – the first New World Pyramid Tourist – is the Italian traveller Giovanni Careri, who visited Mexico in 1697, almost two centuries after Cortez's arrival. In Mexico City, he spoke to Don Carlos de Siguenza, a scientist, historian and priest, who spoke the language of the Indians and who was able to read their hieroglyphic script. Siguenza had been able to identify when the Aztecs had built their capital Tenochtitlan (1325 AD), and that the region was previously ruled by the Toltecs and before them, the Olmecs. Siguenza nevertheless could not stop himself from speculating that these Olmecs themselves had come from Atlantis.

Apart from reconstructing and interpreting the natives' history, Siguenza confirmed that the native civilisations had their own pyramids; and therefore he invited Careri to visit San Juan Teotihuacan, to see its pyramids. Our tourist was impressed, even though the pyramids at the time were partially buried in earth. He queried the local Indians how the giant blocks of stone had been moved from the quarries to the construction site, but none of them knew.

Careri published his round-the-world voyage in 1719, in nine volumes; it was greeted with hostility and incredulity; some even commented that "he never even left Naples", implying he had all invented it from the comfort of his living room. This incredulity originated from his descriptions of what he saw in Mexico: the structures that the Aztecs and the Mayans had built seemed to rival those of ancient Egypt. It was, of course, preposterous that a nation of "devil worshippers" had been able to rival – in fact, they should have said "outperform" – the West. The world-renowned Scottish historian William Robertson thus declared that "the Indian temples were merely mounds of earth covered with shrubs, without steps or facings of cut stone. There is not, in all that vast expanse, a single monument or vestige of any building more ancient than the conquest."[10] There is not a statement that could have been more wrong than Robertson's…

THE GREATEST PYRAMID

With the discovery of the new world, the "Great Pyramid" of Egypt remained great, but no longer the greatest: the Great Pyramid of Cholula, in the Mexican state of Puebla, is the largest in the world by volume – though therefore not the best known; in fact, it is largely off the beaten tourist track. It has a base of 450 by 450 metres (1476 by 1476 ft) and a height of 66 metres (217 ft) – making it much smaller than the Great Pyramid in height and thus largely preserving its status as "the heighest". But it is its total volume, estimated at 4.45 million m³, which makes it almost one third larger than that of the Great Pyramid of Giza.

Many have not heard of the pyramid of Cholula and few tourists visiting Mexico will find it on its path. There is a reason for this: the pyramid remains largely unexcavated; it appears to be a natural hill surmounted by a church. The Iglesia de Nuestra Señora de los Remedios (Church of Our Lady of the Remedies), also known as the Santuario de la Virgen de los Remedios (Sanctuary of the Virgin of the Remedies) was built by the Spanish on the site of a pre-Hispanic temple in 1594. It is this church's presence that is preventing the pyramid as a whole to be excavated and restored to its original glory. Still, archaeological excavations have occurred and some five miles (8 km) of tunnels have so far been uncovered inside. It has been established that the pyramid was begun in Pre-Classic times (2000 BC – 200 AD) and enlarged four times.

You might think that the Spanish weren't aware of the pyramid's existence when they built the church on top, but you would be wrong. The Franciscan Diego de Duran visited Cholula in 1585 and interviewed the town's elder, who was said to be more than one hundred years old. He told de Duran how "in the beginning, before the light of the sun had been created, this place, Cholula, was in obscurity and darkness; all was a plain, without hill or elevation, encircled in every part by water, without tree or created thing. Immediately after the light and the sun rose in the east there appeared gigantic men of deformed stature who possessed the land. Enamoured of the light and beauty of the sun they determined to build a tower so high that its summit should reach the sky. Having collected materials for the purpose they found a very adhesive clay and bitumen with which they speedily commenced to build the tower... And having reared it to the greatest possible altitude, so that it reached the sky, the Lord of the Heavens, enraged, said to the inhabitants of the sky, 'Have you observed how they of the earth have built a high and haughty tower to mount hither, being enamoured of the light of the sun and his beauty? Come and confound them, because it is not right that they of the earth, living in the flesh, should mingle with us.' Immediately the inhabitants of the sky sallied forth like flashes of lightning; they destroyed the edifice and divided and scattered its builders to all parts of the earth."

The story seems like a new world version of the Tower of Babel, equally destroyed by God and equally resulting in our scattering "to all parts of the earth". The question that intrigues me most for the moment is the question whether this "tower of Cholula" was the pyramid of Cholula. Unlike the Tower of Babel, de Duran's story does not indicate that the Tower of Cholula was destroyed. Was the Pyramid of Cholula the structure that was raised towards the sky, so that man could enter it? It seems that within the local mythological landscape, this could indeed be the case.

Cholula is the largest building in the world, built over more than a millennium, to the glory of Quetzalcoatl, "the Feathered Serpent". That Quetzalcoatl was a serpent is another intriguing parallel to the Garden of Eden and the mischievous serpent. The cult of the serpent in Mesoamerica is equally very old; there are representations of snakes with bird-like characteristics in most of Mesoamerica for close to 2,000 years, from the Pre-Classic era until the Spanish conquest. The civilizations worshipping the Feathered Serpent included the Olmec, Mixtec, Toltec, Aztec (who adopted it from the people of Teotihuacan) and the Maya, the latter who called him Kukulkan. The Maya regarded him as a being that would transport the gods. We regard the Maya as *the* pyramid builders of the New World... did they look to Quetzalcoatl as the deity that was primarily linked with the pyramids?

PYRAMIDS & DWARFS

The Mayan pyramids are spread across the Yucatan peninsula. Today, the Mayans are a well-established civilisation (though when I went to high school twenty years ago, not a single page of our history books spoke about them), but the extent of the Mayan accomplishments only began when a New York lawyer, John Lloyd Stephens, travelled into the Yucatan in the early 1840s and came across a city that was totally buried by the jungle. It was called Copan and contained the remains of a huge step pyramid. Stephens quickly bought the town for fifty dollars, which apparently left the local Indian owner totally incredulous, unable to comprehend why these gringos wanted to have this worthless piece of land and paid so much for it. Though Stephens is unknown, his charitable philantrophy marked the start of the gradual realisation that the Mayans were a true civilisation, their cities showing a level of sophistication that outshone the horror-ridden streets that were visible across Europe during the Middle Ages – when the Mayan civilisation was at its climax. Furthermore, the Mayan calendar was so sophisticated that only recently have scientists been able to interpret it – at a time when most of Western Europe was "calendrically challenged" to the extreme, not helped by the widespread belief that the Earth was flat.

I cannot claim to have visited all pyramid sites in the Yucatan (few people can), but of those I have visited, by far the most impressive is the "Temple of the Dwarf" – also known as the Pyramid of the Magician – in Uxmal. Both names stem from a local legend, that when a certain gong was sounded, the town of Uxmal would fall to a boy "not born of woman". One day, a dwarf boy, who had been raised from an egg by a witch, sounded the gong and struck fear into the ruler, who ordered him to be executed. The ruler promised that the boy's life would be saved if he could perform three impossible tasks, one of which was to build a giant pyramid in a single night. The boy miraculously achieved all the tasks, and became the new ruler.

The Pyramid of the Dwarf is different from any other structure (or pyramid) built by the Maya in that it resembles a truncated

Pyramid of the Dwarf

cone, with an oval base and no corners other than those found on the stairs and on the temples found at the apex of those stairs. Second, it is very tall. Third, it is one of the few pyramids that tourists are not allowed to climb – a tourist indulgence that has been made illegal in Egypt for quite a number of years now; then again, as there are no specific structures to be found on top of ancient Egyptian pyramids, there is no real educational purpose in climbing them – unlike the temples residing on top of the Mayan temples.

Though it appears as a single structure, the Pyramid of the Magician has in fact been built and added to five times in the course of history, this in the known Maya practice of building newer temples on top of older ones, often following the 52 year cycles that dominated their calendar. The original temple has been carbon-dated to 569 AD, with the pyramid receiving its overall completion between 900 and 1000 AD. Mayan chronicles say that Uxmal was indeed founded about 500 AD by Hun Uitzil Chac Tutul Xiu and that his family continued to rule Uxmal for many generations. Uxmal was the most powerful site in western Yucatan and while it was in alliance with that other Mayan town of Chichen Itza, it dominated all of the northern Mayan area, i.e. the Yucatan peninsula.

This is not the only pyramid in the complex; Uxmal has another pyramid, labelled "the Great Pyramid" – sometimes "the Grand Pyramid". It is somewhat tucked behind the Governor's Palace and several visitors are intent on climbing it – having been stopped from climbing that of the Dwarf – though most use it to descend from the Nunnery back to ground level and onwards to the exit, skirting past the other side of the Pyramid of the Dwarf. As few turn back, I believe some people may just consider this pyramid to be a series of steps that they see as a challenge to climb, rather than as a genuine pyramid. Originally nine levels high, the Great Pyramid has been partially restored. It seems that another temple was to be superimposed on the existing structure, but that some demolition had taken place before the plans were halted, leaving the pyramid in bad condition.

Stories of dwarfs and pyramids can also be found at Monte Alban; this is Mexico's version of Peru's fabulous Macchu Picchu, though not as famous and not as impressive – but more than impressive enough. Like Cholula, Monte Alban was built over a period of over two thousand years, but is much older than the other sites – it was started about 900 BC, by the Zapotec people, who were then replaced by the Mixtec people in ca. 1300 AD, who in turn were conquered by the Spanish Conquistadores in 1521, at which time Monte Alban was abandoned.

The site's two pyramids are not its main attractions, even though one contains an internal flight of steps leading to the very top of the building – though off limits to tourists. From here, an underground tunnel passes below the Gran Plaza to the middle group. This enabled priests to reach the Gran Plaza unseen and must have left the audience flabbergasted. The small dimensions of the network have made certain people wonder whether the network was used by dwarfs. The small dimensions may have been merely the result of considerations made during the construction, but we should note how small the corridors in the Egyptian pyramids are – walking through those, while hunching, is physically exertive. In Egypt, corridors such as the Grand Gallery make it clear that the builders could build high tunnels that allowed people to walk upright – but for some reason, they on occassion chose not too. The same seems to apply in Mexico.

TEOTIHUACAN

Though these Mayan pyramids are spectacular, they do not stand out; they are integrated within their ceremonial landscape. Only one pyramid complex stands truly out as being a "pyramid complex": Teotihuacan, the complex visited by the Italian explorer Careri. Teotihuacan sits just outside of Mexico City, though far enough that the city has completely disappeared from sight – something which the Pyramids of Gizeh are unable to accomplish with the modern hotels along the strip to Gizeh and Cairo.

Teotihuacan was the largest-known pre-Columbian city in the Americas. It bloomed between 300 and 600 AD and covered 20 km^2 (7.7 square miles), once holding a population of 200,000 people. The name was given by the Aztec centuries after the fall of the city and is translated as "the place where men became gods"; the original name of the city is unknown. Recently, the glyph that represents the city has been translated as "the place of the precious sacrifice".

The central focus of the complex is, as mentioned, a series of

Teotihuacan Pyramid of the Moon

pyramids: the Pyramid of the Moon and the Pyramid of the Sun, whom together with the Temple of Quetzalcoatl, are the axis along which the city was developed. The actual central axis is the "Avenue of the Dead", running from the plaza in front of the Pyramid of the Moon past the other pyramid and the Temple of Quetzalcoatl, and beyond, originally covering a distance of four kilometres (ca. 2.5 miles). It was named "Avenue of the Dead" because of the archaeological discoveries made alongside it, though the name may also betray a mythical aspect, as Stansbury Hagar suggested that the Avenue may be a representation of the Milky Way – which in mythology is normally seen as a Way of the Soul, taken by the soul after death, to ascend to the Afterlife... Heaven. As Teotihuacan was known as a "place where men became gods"...

To get a proper perspective on the layout of the complex, it is best to climb the Pyramid of the Moon. Even though the first platform of the Pyramid of the Moon does not seem to be high, no single photograph of the complex makes it clear that the plain on which the city was built itself sits at an altitude of more than 2000 metres (6000 feet) above sea level. The steps are also notoriously small and steep, making it a gruelling physical exercise when you add a hot climate (and in some cases jetlag) to the mixture.

Many have stood on this platform, looking out over the complex. And one, Stansbury Hagar, concluded that the entire complex was a map of heaven, reproducing on Earth a supposed celestial plan of the sky world, where the deities and spirits of the dead dwelt. His conclusions were in line with those of Hugh Harleston Jr., who mapped the complex in the 1960s and 1970s and believed that the entire complex was a precise scale-model of the solar system. If the centre line of the Temple of Quetzalcoatl was taken as the position of the sun, markers laid out northwards from it along the axis of the Avenue seemed to indicated the correct orbital distances of the inner planets, the asteroid belt, Jupiter, Saturn (the Sun Pyramid), Uranus (the Moon Pyramid), as well as Neptune and Pluto[11], represented by two mounds further north. Harleston's suggestion fuelled speculation of extra-terrestrial intervention in the Mayan civilisation, as the planet Uranus had only been discovered in 1787 and Pluto as late as 1930. How did the Mayans have knowledge of this? As a consequence, many have shelved Harleston's theory or have conveniently left out the Neptune and Pluto mounds. After all, a mound isn't really a pyramid, right? Seemingly "just sticking to the facts", Hugh Harleston Jr. also concluded that the entire site was constructed according to a system of measurement that he named the STU, "Standard Teotihuacan Unit", which is equal to 1.059 metres. This unit features into the length of a side of the Pyramid of the Sun and the Pyramid of the Moon, as well as in the distance between the two pyramids. Others went beyond these elementary but nevertheless profound observations: Alfred E. Schlemmer stated that the Avenue of the Dead might never have been a street, but was instead a series of linked reflecting pools, filled with water that descended through a series of locks from the Pyramid of the Moon, at the northern extreme, to the Citadel in the south. Author Graham Hancock added: "The street was blocked at regular intervals by high partition walls, at the foot of which the remains of well-made sluices could clearly be seen. Moreover, the lie of the land would have facilitated a north-south hydraulic flow since the base of the Moon Pyramid stood on ground that

Teotihuacan Pyramid of the Sun

was approximately 100 feet higher than the area in front of the Citadel."[12]

The Teotihuacan Mapping Project demonstrated that there were indeed a series of canals and waterways that formed a network between the city, running to Lake Texcoco, now ten miles away – but possibly closer in Antiquity. Was it purely for economic reasons, or was it part of a "religious engineering" task that involved the Avenue of the Dead?

These theories have added to a body of evidence that suggests that the master plan for the site was a visual representation of astronomical knowledge – thus having clear parallels with the Egyptian pyramids, built two to three millennia before, on the other side of the world.

The Pyramid of the Sun is aligned with a point on the horizon where the sun sets on May 17 and July 25, the two days of the year in which the sun sits exactly over the peak of the pyramid at noon (zenith), uniting the heavens with the centre of the world. This orientation explains the 17 degree deviation from the north-south alignment of the Avenue of the Dead. At the time of the equinoxes, the passage of the sun from south to north resulted at noon in the obliteration of a perfectly straight shadow that ran along one of the lower stages of the western façade. The whole process lasts just over a minute. It is possible that the spectacle occurred on all sides. As only the western side remains somewhat intact, it is impossible to draw any further conclusions.

Injecting a dose of "extraterrestrialism", Graham Hancock noted that "the angle of the fourth level of the Pyramid of the Sun is set at 19.69 degrees, the exact latitude of the pyramid itself (which stands at 19.69 degrees north of the equator)" – suggesting that the builders were aware of Teotihuacan's exact position on the globe. But that is not all: many, including Zecharia Sitchin and Graham Hancock, have searched for correspondences between Teotihuacan and Gizeh. The Pyramid of the Sun is 225 metres wide and 65 metres high and constructed out of five successive layers. The floor plan is rather close to that of the Great Pyramid at Gizeh, with sides measuring about 230.4 metres (755.8 feet), though slightly more when the casing stones would still be in situ. The Pyramid of the Moon is much smaller: 42 metres high and 150 metres wide, yet its summit is as high as that of the Pyramid of the Sun, because it sits on the site's highest point. This feature can also be seen at Gizeh, where Khufu's and Khafre's pyramid reach an equal height, even though one is taller than the other. The most obvious comparison, however, is that the layout of both the three pyramids at Gizeh and the three main structures of Teotihuacan represent Orion's Belt, the theory first advanced for Gizeh by Robert Bauval. The Pyramid of the Moon compares with the smallest pyramid on the plateau (Menkaure), the Sun Pyramid with Khafre and the Temple of Quetzalcoatl, which has the largest ground plan, but was never built into a full pyramid, compares with that of Khufu.

Though there are individual differences, it can be argued that the same ingredients have been used, answering to the same general ground plan: to represent the Belt of Orion, the central aspect of a constellation that features in the mythology of both the ancient Egyptians and the Mayans. Coincidence, or design? Is there a Master Plan underlying both complexes? And is that Master Plan the same? And does this indeed hint at some shared knowledge between both cultures, even though time and space separated them?

A POINT OF CREATION

Teotihuacan was a place of pilgrimage in Aztec times; the Aztecs identified it with the myth of Tollan, the place where the sun was created – and a site that popular authors often link with Atlantis. According to another legend, it was where the Gods gathered to plan the creation of man and yet another legend stated that the complex was built to transform men into gods. Like Cholula, the sun, a "tower to reach the gods" and a point of creation seem to be required ingredients in any pyramid package. But Teotihuacan offers us an insight that will allow us to go beyond these initial observations.

When astronomer Gerald Hawkins investigated Teotihuacan, he discovered that the streets were laid out on a grid system, intersecting at angles of 89 degrees, instead of the ninety degrees you would expect to find. This could be a simple design flaw, until Hawkins realised that the grid was not aligned to the four points of the compass, but was instead twisted sideways so that the Avenue

Teotihuacan Pyramid of the Sun

of the Dead ran north-north-east, thus pointing at the setting of the Pleiades. On May 17, ca. 150 AD, the Pleiades rose just before the Sun in the predawn skies. This synchronisation, known as the heliacal rising of the Pleiades, only lasted a century. It is now suggested that it was this event that was at the origin of Teotihuacan and marked its foundation.

The sun and the Pleiades are important in the religious rituals of the New World. The Sun-Pleiades zenith conjunction marked what is known as the New Fire ceremony. Father Bernardino de Sahugun's Aztec informants stated that the ceremony occurred at the end of every 52 year Calendar Round – a calendrical event upon which we already came across in Uxmal. The Aztecs and their predecessors had carefully observed the Pleiades and on the expected night the constellation was supposed to pass through the zenith, precisely at midnight, the New Fire ceremony was performed.

The story is in line with the legend that the gods gathered

together at Teotihuacan and wondered anxiously who was to be the next Sun. The conclave occurred at the end of the previous World Age, which had just been destroyed by a flood. Now, only the sacred fire could be seen in the darkness, still quaking in the wind following the recent chaos. "Someone will have to sacrifice himself, throw himself into the fire," they cried, "only then will there be a Sun". Two deities, Nanahuatzin and Tecciztecatl, both tried the divine sacrifice. One burnt quickly, the other roasted slowly. It is here that Quetzalcoatl's religious importance is explained, for it was then that he manifested himself and was able to survive the fire, ensuring a new World Age – ours.

A subterranean passage leads from a natural cave (another parallel with the Great Pyramid of Giza) under the west face of the Pyramid of the Sun. It is believed that this cave played an important role in the New Fire ceremony. The cave opening points directly to the setting sun on May 19 and July 25, the key dates for Teotihuacan. The cave is seven feet high and was found to run eastwards for more than 300 feet, until it reached a point close to the pyramid's geometrical centre. Here it led into a second cave, which had been artificially enlarged into a shape very similar to that of a four-leaf clover. Each "leaf" was a chamber, about 60 feet in circumference, containing a variety of artefacts such as slate discs or mirrors. There was also a complex drainage system of interlocking segments of carved rock pipes. This is strange, as there is no known source of water within the pyramid.

The story of Teotihuacan fits within a lost Aztec Codex, written down by Martin Matz from Mazatec Indians, who transmitted it for several centuries within their community. The text is known as the Codex Matz-Ayauhtla, or the Pyramid of Fire, and describes a series of legends, from the creation myth to the New Fire ceremony, which is the finale to the initiatory spiritual journey that is encoded into the codex. The text underlines the essence of the Mayan's religious experience, namely that life is a spiritual journey to ascension – a return to God, the One who created the universe. The text states how the supreme deity, Tloque Nahauque, manifested itself as three forces – a duality functioning against a neutral background, from which the four prime elements were created.

Matz made the journey himself; he visited an initiatory site with his shamanic guide, where he took a hallucinogenic substance (in his case mushrooms), entered a cave at a specific moment in the calendar, and consequently was shown a landscape of pyramids, including one that was dedicated to the Moon. The initiate was then taught about the World Ages, the success of Quetzalcoatl, and how ascension and world ages were connected via the New Fire ceremony – and how they were performed every 52 years. The American author John Major Jenkins has described this as "the ultimate self-sacrifice that is the ritual death attending the mystic initiation into divine life [...] in order to merge with Quetzalcoatl, which according to my reconstruction of the New Fire ceremony represents the Pleiades in the zenith with sun at nadir".

It is clear that Teotihuacan formed a site where this New Fire festival was performed: the cave inside the Pyramid of the Sun, with its specific alignment, is primary evidence. But we also need to ask whether the pyramids of Teotihuacan were – could be – a visual representation of the hallucinogenic landscape that the initiates experienced... Was Teotihuacan the materialistic representation of a dream – literally?

Also, let us note that the purpose of the codex and the essence of our existence is the transformation of man into God – which is what the name Teotihuacan signifies. But how was man transformed into God? Was the New Fire ceremony the literal burning of men, who died for ascension? Was it purely a religious, symbolical ceremony, or was some form of technology used in the process? But before trying to answer this question, let us note that it now seems clear that Teotihuacan too is indeed a "Tower of Babel", or a "Tower of Cholula": a place where men tried to become one with the gods – which, to make a quick parallel with the Old World, in Egypt was known through the myth of Osiris.

Technology, if anything, tends to ensure a more methodical approach to a process, guaranteeing a better success of the desired outcome. If a technology was used to aide this transformation, there may be an explanation for the strange sheets of mica that have been found between two of the upper levels of the Pyramid of the Sun. The discovery occurred in 1906, when the complex was in the process of being restored. But the mica was removed and sold as soon as it had been excavated, by Leopoldo Bartres, the man in charge of the project.

More recently, a "Mica Temple" has been discovered on the site, but this time, the mica has remained in situ. The temple sits around a patio about 300 metres south of the west face of the Pyramid of the Sun. Directly under a floor paved with heavy rock slabs, massive sheets of mica 90 feet square were found, placed in two layers, one laid directly on top of the other. As it sits underneath a stone floor, its use was obviously not decorative, but functional.

Mica is a substance containing different metals, depending on the kind of rock formation in which it is found. The type of mica found at Teotihuacan indicates a type that is only found in Brazil, more than 2000 miles away. The same South American mica was found in Olmec sites – another Mesoamerican pyramid-building civilisation from which the Mayans and Teotihuacan seems to have taken its inspiration. It is clear that its presence in Teotihuacan involved a lot of effort – and it thus must have played an important role... like the sand in the Great Pyramid.

In the past decades, a handful of researchers have been able to create a framework that provides a unique insight that has led to a greater understanding of Teotihuacan. It is an accomplishment that Egyptologists have been unable to offer. It is clear that key dates, key constellations and key rituals were performed on the site, rituals that were linked with Quetzalcoatl, but which were equally a transformative event, the initiation of one or more individuals. But making total sense of Teotihuacan will require more mirror gazing, before its total experience is unveiled...

BIRDMEN

Let us return to the Yucatan and listen to the Mayan story of creation, which has survived the destruction of the Spanish invasion. It is contained within the *Popol Vuh*, a 17th century book of the history of the Quiche Maya. The focus is on the activities of the Twin Maize Gods and their family at the time of this Third Creation, which the Maya date to 3114 BC. Many scholars now believe that August 12, 3114 BC marked a significant celestial event – though its exact nature remains elusive.

There are several parallels between the Codex Matz-Ayauhtla, describing the New Fire ceremony and the Popol Vuh. When playing ball, the Twin Maize Gods disturbed the lords of Xibalba, the Maya underworld. The Xibalbans summoned the Maize Gods to the underworld to answer for their disrespectful behaviour. There, they subjected them to a series of trials. When they failed these tests, they were killed and buried in the Ball court of Xibalba. The eldest twin was decapitated, his head hung in the tree next to the ball court, as a warning to anyone who might repeat their offence. It is the Mayan equivalent of the two contenders for the new sun who entered the Fire and perished.

Despite the stern warning not to meddle with the gods, the daughter of a Xibalban lord went to visit the skull, which spoke to her, spitting in her hand and thus making her pregnant. She escaped from the underworld and gave birth to twin boys, the Hero Twins, Hun-Ahaw and Yax-Balam, who themselves were summoned to the Underworld, after they had found their dead father's ball playing equipment. Like their father, they too had made too much noise, but they, unlike their predecessors, were not fooled by the trials of the lords.

After a long series of ballgames, the Hero Twins defeated the Lords of Death and resurrected their fathers, which were reborn as infants. They quickly grew to adulthood, and with dwarf helpers (indeed), woke up three old gods. Two of them became known as the Paddler Gods, because they paddled the Maize Gods to the Place of Creation. The third oldster, God L, was the patron of the merchants and warriors, and destroyed the Third Creation by a great flood. I will briefly point out the many parallels between both accounts: the ballgame vs. the Fire, the destruction of the Third Creation vs. the end of a World Age, etc. But above all, it involves yet another "point of creation".

When the Gods arrived at the place of the New Creation, they sprang up from a crack in the back of a Cosmic Turtle. The crack is identified with the Ball court. But the Maya identified this turtle with the three stars of Orion's Belt – and we thus finally understand why the pyramids of Teotihuacan – if not Gizeh – were laid out in this form.

Once reborn, the Maize Gods directed four old gods to set up the first Hearth of Creation, to centre the new order. This was a hearth made up from three stones. The first stone was in the shape of a jaguar, the second in the form of a snake and the third was a crocodile or shark. The first was set in a place called Na-Ho-Kan, by the Paddler Gods. The second stone was set on the Earth, but by whom is not known. The third was set in the sea by Itzamna, the First Sorcerer.

The Maya saw this hearth in the sky, as the triangle of stars below Orion's Belt (Al Nitak, Saiph and Rigel), with the Orion Nebula as the fire. And it is this hearth that was set up on August 12, 3114 BC – the day of creation – the date of a New Fire ceremony. 542 days later, on February 5, 3112 BC, the Maize Gods completed the Fourth Creation, by setting up the four sides and corners of creation and erecting the central tree – the world tree. This tree was the Wakah-Kan, or "Raise up Sky". It was a great ceiba tree in flower, because February 5, the day of its erection, was also the flowering season for this popular Latin American tree. The tree's stellar equivalent is the Milky Way, leading us back to the Avenue of the Dead in Teotihuacan.

The Mayan story of creation also incorporates a number sequence, from three to four, to five. Three is represented as the cosmic hearth, and the triangle – the shape of the side of a pyramid? From there, the four sides and corners are created; a square – which is the base of the pyramid. Finally, five is the square with a centre: the World Tree, the ceiba tree – and if the centre is raised from a two-dimensional representation to three dimensions, we have the shape of a pyramid.

The most likely location the tourist will run into the Mayan "world tree" is in popular tourist locations, such as Tulum and in front of the archaeological museum in Mexico City, where the Papantla Flyers continue to unwhirl from it. Also known as "bird men", they originally danced in order to please the gods. The spectacle involves a group of men that are attached to a rope hanging from the top of a 50 feet pole. While they descend, one person remains on top, playing the flute, which represents the voice of birds. The descent mimics the World Tree, whereby the dancers are like the motions of the stars, spinning around the pole. The main dancer, the musician, dances on top of the pole and turns first to the East, the origin of the world. Each "volador" eventually turns thirteen times around the pole. Thirteen circles multiplied by four, for a total of 52 circles – representing the 52 years cycle, as well as how it is composed of four periods of thirteen years.

Who was Quetzalcoatl? "The Feathered Serpent" is normally identified with the planet Venus. And it was cyclical relationships between Earth and Venus that established the Mayan calendar. The calendar is, as mentioned, cyclical and uses the specific dynamics between the orbits of Earth and Venus, which cause Venus to appear both as Morning and Evening Star. Every eight Earth years are equal to five "synodic Venus cycles", in essence, the cycles we observe Venus to describe. This 8:5 ratio defines the relationship between Earth and Venus, and is the basic increment upon which the 104-year cycle of Huehuetiliztli is based. The Huehuetiliztli consists of two 52-year cycles, known as Xiuhmolpilli. The beginning of each 104-year Huehuetiliztli cycle is marked by the reappearance of Venus as Morning Star.

The 8:5 ratio can also be expressed as 1.6 and together with other ratios present in the Mayan calendar are reminiscent of Fibonacci sequences, or the Golden Ratio, which describe the mathematical proportions manifest in naturally occurring spirals such as those found in shells, flowers – and the manner in which the "Birdmen" unwhirl from the World Tree?

Connected with Quetzalcoatl through Venus, Quetzalcoatl defines time as a process of creation, and as such embodies the creation process. Many manifestations associated with Quetzalcoatl further connect Quetzalcoatl with spirals. The Caracol (snail) Observatory in Chichen Itza is a spiral shaped structure built originally as a Venus observatory. Figures representing Quetzalcoatl such as sculptures and glyphs reveal subtly placed spirals throughout their structures. Additionally, seashells, which by Nature's design are spiraled structures, are regularly found at the bases of temples and altars devoted to Quetzalcoatl. Coincidence, or design?

MIRROR IMAGES

Chichen Itza. The temples of this complex are amongst the most widely visited in Mexico and its proximity to the holiday resort of Cancun is not solely to thank for this – though it definitely helps. As it sits at sea level, the climbing experiences are less harrowing. But pyramid climbing unfortunately detracts from the tremendous insights that this complex is able to provide us: Chichen Itze is the easiest location where to enter into the mind of its builders – or, to be more specific, where we can answer that all-important "why"-question.

The name Itza itself is derived from Itzamna, the chief Mayan deity that sat on top of the World Tree – like the musician of the Papantla Flyers. Itza functioned as a regional capital of the Maya from 750 to 1200 AD. Chichen Itza's Mayan name means "city on the edge of the water sorcerer's well" and that well is the Sacred Cenote, the path the tourists will best remember for being lined with endless souvenir stands that lead to a round lake – which for some tourists has less appeal that the toilet facilities next to it. Still, it is the Sacred Cenote's presence that may have been the main reason why the town was built where it is – a fact that most tourist guides on the complex fail to underline... some tours leaving out the Sacred Cenote – and toilet facilities – altogether.

Chichen Itza's town plan is divided in two sections. Some believe that one section was built by the Maya, the other by the Toltec, but this version is now being disputed by archaeologists, who have shown that both parts are largely contemporaneous. It is

Chichen Itza the Castillo

Chichen Itza Castillo mirror pyramid in other part of complex.

equally clear that each side is largely a mirror of the other; each
had its own cenote, though one is much more spectacular than the
other. Could we thus have an expression of the "twin" aspect –
connected to the two "faces" of Quetzalcoatl, of Venus, in her form
of Evening and Morning Star, as well as in the Maize Twins, etc.?

The most famous feature of Chichen Itza is its pyramid – one of
its pyramids: El Castillo. The Mayan myths speak of their "place
of origin" as having a Snake Mountain and a Place of Reeds, or
Coatepec and Tollan. El Castillo symbolised the Snake Mountain;
as Quetzalcoatl was a "feathered serpent"… In short, in Chichen
Itza, we finally realise that the pyramid is indeed linked with
Quetzalcoatl, but specifically symbolised the Snake Mountain. The
serpentine connotation of El Castillo is visible through the serpent
carved on its side. On the equinoxes, the sun plays a light and
shadow game, bringing the snake alive, though the effect is
actually viewable for a week before and after each equinox. As the
equinox sun sets, a play of light and shadow creates the appearance

of a snake that gradually undulates down the stairway of the pyramid.

Other calendrical aspects have also been incorporated into the pyramid's design. Each of four stairways has 91 steps, with a final step at the top making a total of 365 days, the number of days in the solar year. This "quartering" of the year further conforms to the 91 days that separate the solstices from the equinoxes.

In one version of the myth, the Aztec built a temple on top of Snake Mountain for their patron god Huitzilopochtli, who then built a ball court at the base of the mountain, and in the centre he placed a hole, called an Itzompan, or Skull Place. It won't come as a surprise to learn that there is a Ball Court next to El Castillo. Indeed, the Ball court of Chichen Itza is both one of the most impressive and one of the best preserved.

The Ballgame had a sacred function, visualising with the Myth of Creation and Origin. Many believe that the Ballgame was a sport, played to life and death. Whereas this cannot be ruled out, the most essential message we should retain from it is that it was the visualisation of the story of the creation of the Fourth World; it thus should be seen as theatre, more than sport. Finally, nearby is indeed the "Skull place" – confirming that Chichen Itza was indeed built following the layout indicated by the creation myth. Tour guides will tell stories that the captain of the winning team was decapitated, whereby his decapitated head was brought to the T-form shaped platform. Perhaps… perhaps… but perhaps the true answer to the enigma of the "Skull place" can be found in the creation myth.

When I walk around Chichen Itza, I can see legends and mysteries come to live, painted against this stone backdrop. Like the inside of the Pyramid of the Sun at Teotihuacan, El Castillo contains a man-made cave, which was believed to be a passage to the Otherworld. On the "mirror side" of Chichen Itza, we find the High Priest's Grave, which was constructed over a natural cave and which has been described as a "smaller version of El Castillo". Pyramids, sitting on top of natural caves, with artificial chambers inside... it sounds so much like ancient Egypt. It sounds like the Great Pyramid.

The chamber inside El Castillo contains a statue of a red jaguar, decorated with flint teeth and jade eyes. A jaguar... almost like a lion? Like the Sphinx? What archaeologists have accomplished in the Mayan world over the past two centuries – and on many sites, in less than a century – is impressive. The buildings have been interpreted within their religious framework, that of the creation myth, which is intimately linked with an astronomical cult, in which key dates to do with the star Venus and its position to the Earth were of extreme religious and social importance. Egyptologists will point out that these archaeologists have it easy: these sites are relatively modern – unlike ancient Egypt. But in most instances, these archaeologists also merely started with a blank pyramid and some myths. But they were able to properly integrate the former into the latter, and arrive at the whole – not merely where pyramids slotted in, but actually how the entire complex should be interpreted. I remember that there is a sacred well on the Giza plateau as well. But no-one has even bothered to look at it, it seems...

MAYAN GENESIS

You may think that Mexico, unlike Egypt, has surrendered all of its pyramid mysteries. But it appears not. The Olmec civilisation is both one of the first and most enigmatic of the New World, prominent from as early as 1500 BC before it disappeared in 100 BC. Their heartland was an area on the south coast of the Gulf of Mexico coastal plain of southern Veracruz and Tabasco. One of its best-known sites is La Venta, which is dated to between 1200 BC through 400 BC. Despite its impressive age, the site was only found and excavated by Matthew Stirling between 1941 and 1943, with several subsequent excavations following through the 1960s.

The site is located on an island of about two square miles, in a coastal swamp overlooking the then-active Río Palma river. Though the Olmec as a civilisation are best remembered for their gigantic stone head (which up front look somewhat African, but from the side are clearly Asian), La Venta itself is best known for its Great Pyramid, which dominates the site – a site which has two pyramids. The Great Pyramid is a huge clay pyramid 110 ft high and is one of the earliest pyramids built in Mesoamerica. The conical shape of the pyramid was once thought to represent the shape of nearby volcanoes or mountains, but recent work by Rebecca Gonzalez-Lauck has shown that the pyramid was in fact a rectangular pyramid with stepped sides and inset corners; the current shape is the result of 2500 years of erosion. The structure has never been excavated, but is thought to contain an elaborate tomb. Within the town's design, the Great Pyramid divided La Venta into northern and southern sectors and it is believed that access to the northern ceremonial precinct of the so-called Complex A was probably limited to the elite.

In 1999, art historian Carolyn Tate stated that La Venta was organized on a centre line which aligned with a 1243 metres high mountain, 100 kilometres to the south of the site, but which despite its distance from the site can be seen from the top of La Venta's pyramid. She wondered whether the pyramid itself might replicate this mountain. She also noted that the Gulf of Mexico, 9 km to the north, can be seen from the top of La Venta's pyramid. Was the pyramid positioned to make a connection between a sacred mountain and the sea? Intriguingly, as we have noted, La Venta sits on an island, and in itself thus represents a mountain (pyramid) sitting on an island, surrounded by the sea.

As in ancient Egypt, the American pyramid seems to have been a development of a platform. Unlike ancient Egypt, the Mayans, from the Olmec period to the Maya civilisation, never neglected to build a temple that crowned the top of the structure. In both centres of the Olmec civilization, San Lorenzo and La Venta, numerous large clay platforms existed. At their top there are believed to have been temples, or perhaps palaces, built of wood. Archaeologists have stated that "the concept of climbing up to a place of religious significance becomes the central theme of pre-Columbian architecture". They thus argue that its natural conclusion was the pyramid, with steps by which priests and pilgrims could climb to the top. They trace this tradition to La Venta, to 1500 BC, a time when ancient Egypt had "just" stopped building pyramids.

We know the ancient Mayan legends and know that the pyramid sits within the landscape that was adapted to depict a divine landscape. The pyramid was "merely" a part of it. But an important part. The centre. Jenkins concludes that "Mayan rulers timed their accession ceremonies to coincide with astronomical events happening in the zenith. Furthermore, these accession ceremonies took place on the top of a pyramid, in the symbolic center of the cosmos, the zenith center."[13] And thus, it seems, that what Rice observed about pyramid building, namely that it was almost genetically coded into the ancient Egyptians, also seems to have been key obsession for the ancient Mayans.

CHAPTER 3
PYRAMID OR PYRAMYTH?

Are there pyramids elsewhere, outside Egypt and Mesoamerica? Were other cultures equally infested with the pyramid virus – or pyramid gene? The answer is yes, and if asked where to look, most will point towards Nubia, south of Egypt. We are still along the Nile valley, in what is now Sudan. In Nubian days, this area was home to three Kushite kingdoms: the first had Kerma as capital and existed from 2400 to 1500 BC; the second centred on Napata (1000–300 BC) and the third was that of Meroë (300 BC–300). It won't come as a surprise to learn that these kingdoms were strongly influenced by their northern neighbours. Eventually, they were even able to invade, conquer and unify Egypt, when the king of Napata ruled as a Pharaoh of the 25th Dynasty, a rule that ended with the Assyrian conquest in 656 BC.

Though the Nubian kingdoms must have been aware of the pyramids that lined the valley further north, it was only during their domination of Egypt that Napata and its successor Meroë devoted themselves to any pyramidal activity in Nubia. That the Nubian kings definitely saw them is known from an account of Pharaoh Piye. After taking control of most of Egypt, Piye set out for Heliopolis to worship the sun god and celebrate his coronation as king of Egypt. He cannot have missed to see the pyramids on his left as he moved down the Nile. In Heliopolis, we are told that he "stood by himself alone. Breaking the seals of the bolts, opening the doors; viewing his father Re in the holy Pyramidion House; adorning the Morning Bark of Re and the Evening Bark of Amun." He then returned to Napata.

Approximately twohundred pyramids were eventually constructed at three sites in Nubia, to serve as tombs for the kings and queens of Napata and Meroë. The first series of these pyramids were built at the site of el-Kurru and included the tombs of King Kashta and his son Piye (Piankhi), together with Piye's successors Shabaka, Shabataka and Tanwetamani, and 14 queens' pyramids. The Napatan pyramids were sited at Nuri, on the west bank of the Nile in Upper Nubia. This necropolis was the burial place of 21 kings and 52 queens and princes. The oldest and largest pyramid at Nuri is that of the Napatan king and 25th Dynasty Pharaoh Taharqa. But the most extensive and best known Nubian pyramid site is at Meroë, which is located between the fifth and sixth cataracts of the Nile, approximately 100 kilometres north of Khartoum, the modern capital of Sudan. During the Meroitic period, over forty kings and queens were buried in that pyramid field.

The Nubian pyramids differ from the Egyptian edifices: they are built of stepped courses of horizontally positioned stone blocks and range from approximately six to thirty metres in height; they are, to all intents and purposes, rather unimpressive. What makes them impressive is the sheer quantity and density of them. What makes them a sad archaeological site is that all were plundered in ancient times, but wall reliefs preserved in the tomb chapels reveal that their royal occupants were mummified, covered with jewellery and laid to rest in wooden mummy cases, revealing that these Nubian pyramids definitely seem to have been tombs.

El-Kurru, about 13 km south from the Gebel Barkal, was

excavated by G. Reisner in 1918-19. The site includes the pyramid of Piankhi, which has a base length of about eight metres and a slope of probably about 68 degrees – much steeper than the 51 degrees of the Great Pyramid – though eight metres is, of course, miniscule compared to the floorplan of the Great Pyramid. Inside, Reisner found a stairway of 19 steps that opened to the east and that led to the burial chamber. Piankhi's body had been placed on a bed that rested in the middle of the chamber on a stone bench. The bench's four corners had been cut away to receive the legs of the bed, so that the bed platform lay directly on the bench.

This is conclusive proof that these pyramids were tombs, but it is in the pyramid of Nuri that is the most elaborate structure. King Taharqa was the first to build in this location and his pyramid is, by Nubian standards, impressive: 51.75 metres square and between 40 to 50 metres high. The entrance was by an eastern stairway trench, north of the pyramid's central axis, reflecting the alignment of the original smaller pyramid. Three steps led to a doorway, with a moulded frame, which opened to a tunnel, widened and heightened into an antechamber that had a barrel-vaulted ceiling. Six massive pillars carved from the natural rock divided the burial chamber into two side aisles and a central nave, each with a barrel-vaulted ceiling. The entire chamber was surrounded by a moat-like corridor, with steps leading down from in front of the antechamber doorway.

The Nuri pyramids were generally much larger than those at el-Kurru, reaching heights of twenty to thirty metres. The last king to be buried at Nuri died in about 308 BC, before construction began in Meroë. It remained the royal cemetery for 600 years, until 350 AD. As at Nuri, the pyramids were stepped and built on a plinth, but now each triangular face was framed by smooth bands of raised masonry along the wedges, where the sides met.

In 350 AD, the Pyramid Age along the Nile had truly ended. The pyramid adventure of the Nubian kings seems to have been a method to integrate their nation with the Egyptians, who themselves had, by 600 BC, long abandoned pyramid building. The Nubian pyramids were clearly tombs, but is that all they were? The pyramids were just one aspect of a larger project, in which the Nubian kings apparently rekindled ancient Egypt's flame. The key seems to have been – once again – the involvement of the Heliopolitan priests, the men behind the original Pyramid Age. In a generalised way, we could state that pyramid building was a particular preoccupation of the Heliopolitan priesthood; temples were the main bailiwick of the Amunite priesthood, who had risen to the forefront of ancient Egypt during the Middle and New Kingdom, when the capital had moved to Thebes/Luxor. It seems that with the Nubian invasion – which had largely only been possible because of the demise in power of Thebes/Luxor – the Heliopolitan priesthood was once again on the rise again.

Excavations at many Napatan sanctuaries, especially at Gebel Barkal, have revealed that the temples were generally built directly over the foundations of ruined New Kingdom (read: Amunite) temples. This indicates that the Napatan rulers deliberately restored religious sites that had been abandoned by the Egyptian pharaohs when they evacuated Nubia some three centuries before. The Nubian kings used "Amunite temples", but converted them to Heliopolitan sun worship. But they did not totally abandon the Amunite beliefs; after all, these Nubian temples had been built according to strict Amunite guidelines, even though the cult had apparently been absent for three centuries and the temples had fallen to ruin. By restoring the old Egyptian cult places, especially Gebel Barkal, they were able to present themselves both within Nubia and especially at Thebes, as the true successors of the pharaohs of the New Kingdom and the direct heirs to their throne – as well as showing their allegiance to the Heliopolitan priesthood.

Taharqa was not only the one who created the most elaborate pyramid, he also transformed the Barkal site into the stage for the celebration of past, present and eternal monarchy, and the perpetual recreation of the world. Why here? Due to the reverse direction of the Nile here, Taharqa's tomb, though still on the "west" bank, paradoxically lay to the east, the place of sunrise and rebirth. Gebel Barkal, on the "east" bank, lay paradoxically to the west, the place of sunset and death.

An important question to be posed is why the pyramid field lay around Gebel Barkal. The first explanation is economic, since the site was seen as an ideal crossing point for the Nile, as well as a crossing point for the caravans crossing the desert from Kawa to Meroë. The second explanation is religious. The sacred mountain Barkal (Barkal is Arabic, meaning both "holy" and "pure") measures 74 metres, made from sandstone and has a flat top. Seen from the west, it looks like the royal Egyptian ureas, topped by the white crown. For the ancient Egyptians, the site must have seen like the Creator God himself having sculpted the site, indicating it should become a royal, sacred site. From the east, it looks like the serpent with the sun disc on its top. The interplay of the tomb and the mountain thus symbolised creation, death and rebirth simultaneously and Gebel Barkal, under Taharqa, was designed to be the ultimate and permanent centre of kingship in the Nile Valley. It was to be the eternal link between the creator god Atum-Ra and Mankind, and between the eternal king and the living king. We therefore find that in Nubia, the pyramid and the sites on which they were built contained far more symbolism than merely a funerary aspect – the sites were directly linked with kingship.

So let us rephrase the question: apart from Egypt and Nubia, and Mesoamerica, are there pyramids elsewhere? We will begin with various "rumours" and small pyramids that were brought into the debate throughout the 19th and 20th century, in the hope to broaden the pyramid debate and take it outside of Egypt and Mesoamerica. But were any of these attempts successful?

SILBURY HILL

The obsession with pyramids is largely a Western preoccupation. In the search for pyramids elsewhere, several English authors focused on Silbury Hill, tucked in a valley in the English countryside near the megalithic ring of Avebury, itself some twenty miles distant from the pride of ancient England, Stonehenge. Silbury Hill does not look like a pyramid and labelling it a pyramid could be deemed as intellectual suicide. Worse: one recent theory has it that Silbury Hill was the pyramid tomb of the leader of an Egyptian scientific expedition, who set up an astronomical centre at Stonehenge, lived at Avebury and was interred in Silbury.

But apart from such pyramidiocy, Silbury Hill looks like a mound, is a "mound", so why think it is a pyramid? The answer is that its interior structure is actually a series of steps, and could thus be classified as a "step pyramid".

Dating Silbury Hill has got much in common with the Great Pyramid, as one series of radio carbon dates gave dates ranging from 4045 BC to 185 BC; a second series resulted in a 2910 to 2340 BC, but which others have corrected to 2800 to 2500 BC, using "a period around 2700 BC give or take a hundred ears [...] for the building of this artificial mountain".[14] This makes it contemporary with the Pyramid Age in Egypt. Like the pyramids, Silbury Hill was a community project. It contains an estimated 340,000 cubic metres of chalk and earth (equivalent to 35 million basket loads of rubble) and rises to a height of 39.6 metres, where the flat top is thirty metres across. The base of the monument is 167 metres in diameter and it is perfectly round – which in my opinion disqualifies it for holding the label of pyramid. Still, inside, there are indeed six, six metres high steps – Zoser's Step Pyramid equally had six steps. The steps are walled with blocks of chalk, which easily deteriorates when left exposed, and hence were protected by the covering layer of earth and grass, which did obscure its interior stepped shape.

Still, excavations have revealed that it is not a burial mound. What is it? Observations by Paul Devereux have revealed that the hill is perfectly implanted within the landscape and is one component of a large ritualistic landscape that involves both natural features as well as nearby megalithic constructions – and thus mimics the implantation of pyramids in the Mayan sacred landscape. As to a connection with ancient Egypt: some researchers have pointed out that there is a "coincidence" between Silbury Hill and the Great Pyramid: the angle of slope of the Great Pyramid is between 51 and 52 degrees and Silbury Hill's location is between the 51st and 52nd degree of latitude. Silbury Hill's 30 degrees angle of slope echoes the Great Pyramid's line of latitude at 30 degrees north. Coincidence? Honestly, I don't really care. Silbury Hill is not a pyramid, and it is not as unique as most popular books about the hill argue. Burl points out that two other huge round barrows were put up within seven miles of Silbury Hill: the Hatfield Barrow at Marden and the Marlborough Mound. The latter is now overgrown with trees and concealed by buildings of the famous College, the former levelled and its location only recently determined by geophysical detection. Perhaps one day we will discover that these three sites form the outline of Orion's Belt, but even if that were the case, Silbury Hill cannot be seen as a pyramid; its floorplane is circular, not square. Any attempt to classify it as a pyramid is in my opinion an unintelligent move by a person who seems to believe that Silbury Hill and the complex in which it resides is only of value if Silbury Hill were to be seen as a pyramid, and not for the monument it truly is.

THE LOUVRE, AND FALICON

"Yes, there are other pyramids. Modern ones." France's most famous pyramid is probably the glass pyramid that marks the entrance to the Louvre museum in the heart of Paris. Since the publication of Dan Brown's international mega-bestseller "The Da Vinci Code", it has become an enigmatic attraction – though the glass panels do not number 666, as Dan Brown hoped for; the Louvre guide lists it as 673 panels – it iss close, but for symbolism to work, of course, it is either hit or miss.

The outer structure was completed in 1989 for the bicenteniary anniversary of France's anniversary, but an "inverted pyramid" was added below the top structure in 1993, at the intersection of two main walkways; the inverted pyramid orients visitors towards the museum's entrance. Both the outer and inner glass pyramids were designed by architect I.M. Pei. The tip of the inverted pyramid is suspended 1.4 metres above floor level, the pinnacle of individual glass panes, 30 mm thick, connected by stainless steel crosses 381 millimeters in length. Directly below the tip of the downwards-pointing glass pyramid, a small stone pyramid (about one meter/three feet high) is stationed on the floor, as if mirroring the larger structure above; the tips of the two pyramids almost touch. It is this specific structure that features so centrally in "The Da Vinci Code", becoming the final resting place of the Grail, or the body of Mary Magdalene.

The pyramid of the Louvre

The pyramid of the Louvre almost wasn't Paris' only pyramid. At the time of the French Revolution, a veritable Egypt and pyramid mania hit France. On July 14, 1792, a "Pyramid of Honour" was erected in the Champs de Mars, where a century later, the Eifel tower would be built, to commemorate the victims of the storming of the Bastille. On August 26, 1792, yet another pyramid was raised, this time in the gardens of the Tuileries, in front of the Louvre and hence near the present glass pyramid, to remember the martyrs of the Revolution. Several other pyramid projects were proposed, though never realised. One idea that never materialised was that of Etienne Boullée, who proposed a "Cenotaph, of the Egyptian kind", which was a pyramid with a missing capstone, to remember the dead. Observers believe that as several of the new rulers of the Republic had Masonic allegiances, they expressed this desire through their love of the pyramid... and other Egyptian-Masonic designs. What is remarkable, is that these French Masons were predisposed to erect pyramids as memorials for the dead... like the ancient Egyptians apparently erected pyramids for their deceased heroes.

Still, France has its own "proper" pyramid, though it is little known, and small in size. The base of the pyramid varies between 5 to 6.5 metres. It sits on the hillside above La Bastide, at the Aven des Ratapignata, to the northeast of Falicon, near the posh Mediterranean town of Nice. Despite its somewhat disappointing size, for a very long time, it was considered to be one of the very rare pyramids to be found in Europe. As it is a pyramid, it almost seems to be an unwritten law that no clear explanation has ever been given for its existence. There are various theories of its origins and some of course include an Egyptian connection. The grandson of the famous archaeologist John Ward-Perkins thought that it might have marked the tomb of an ancient chieftain, possibly an exiled Egyptian. I'll classify that as "imaginative", as for the moment it is totally unsupported by evidence.

On detailed maps, the site is not marked as "pyramid", but as "Grotte de Ratapignata"... for the pyramid does indeed sit over a cave, known as the "Cave of the Bats". Let us note that it is remarkable that this pyramid protects a cave entrance; the Great Pyramid in Egypt and the Pyramid of the Sun in Teotihuacan too sit on top of a natural cave, which was then incorporated into the design of the pyramid. It does suggest that are minuscule French pyramid shares characteristics with its big brothers elsewhere.

While most of its upper section is now missing, the lower section is reasonably well-preserved; fortunately, photographs still exist of the time when the upper part was better preserved. They have allowed for an accurate reconstruction of the site, which had an entrance in its south-eastern corner. The entrance was large enough to permit the passage of one person, suggesting that only one person at a time was allowed to pass towards the cave that opens up underneath.

Today, the site is well-known to the local fire brigade, who often have to rescue people who have descended inside the cave.

France Falicon pyramid

Though the descent is easy enough (for a somewhat experienced climber), the ascent is virtually impossible, as it involves conquering a horizontal ridge; the fire brigade's winch clears it easily, but feet groping in the dark for footholds don't.

Even though the cave was documented from the early 19th century, it lasted until 1898 when Professor Jean-Robert Salifard made a scientific exploration of the subterranean network that was accessible from the pyramid. The end result was a report of 657 pages and 174 illustrations. From the main room, he identified three tunnels, one which continued for "a considerable distance". But when the famous speleologist Jules Gavet visited the site in 1901, he found that these tunnels had been blocked. What had happened between 1898 and 1901? Someone – and apparently not Salifard – had purposefully sealed the tunnels –why? Was it purely for health and safety purposes, to make sure that no souls would wander inside and get lost? Or was it to protect something that was perhaps hidden deeper inside the network of tunnels?

As to the pyramid's purpose: in 1976, author Henri Broch argued that the land sat on former Knights Templar property. Could it be possible that the enigmatic Knights Templar had been pyramid builders? That possibility was also taken up by Maurice Guinguand. But neither author spoke of the work of Jean Carrond. The latter had access to family documents of a certain Baron de Raudie. The very old documents that he consulted spoke of a deposit that was of tremendous importance and which had been owned and protected by the ancestors of de Raudie. In some corners, it has invited speculation that this deposit was part of the Templar treasure, secreted away at the time of their arrest in 1307. But Carrond and others have since discovered that the land on which the Falicon pyramid sits was actually not owned by the Templars, which would actually mean that if any part of their treasure was hidden there, it wouldn't immediately fall to the French crown at the time of their dissolution. Still, it is clear that a Templar connection or even the hiding place of a treasure cannot have been its original purpose. Instead, it seems to have been a site where certain religious ceremonies were performed. The first subterranean chamber shows the best evidence that it was used and adapted for ritual use. There are seven steps, as well as a small platform that originally is believed to have held an altar. Speculation is that the nature of the cult that was practiced here: it may have been the cult of Mithras, popular in Roman times. The cult of Mithras spread across Europe, hand in hand with the cult of Osiris and Isis; sanctuaries of both cults have been found as far north as the border territories of Scotland and England and stumbling upon a Mithras temple in southern France would be the norm rather than the exception. Mithraic sanctuaries were normally – ideally – underground and the cave underneath the Falicon pyramid thus qualifies.

Though that may have been its original cult, in 1922, Etienne Gotteland settled near Falicon and founded a cult that incorporated the pyramid. He nevertheless also made some observations about the structure itself: using the precession of the equinox, he argued that the site of the pyramid (though not the pyramid itself) was 4335 years old, or 2413 BC – roughly contemporary with the Egyptian Pyramid Age. This is of course a controversial dating, and very old. If was indeed a Mithraic sanctuary and the pyramid were to date from that era, then the pyramid would date from ca. 200 BC to 300 AD. But in truth, we have no idea as to its age...

Since 1922, the pyramid has rapidly deteriorated and the French authorities do not seem interested at all in its preservation, let alone researching the site. This has, of course, lead to a certain amount of speculation, with some observers wondering whether the French authorities "want" this site to deteriorate and be forgotten, as its existence somehow inconveniences them. Speculation of another kind was aired by NASA consultant Maurice Chatelain, who argued that the pyramid had been built in 1260 by crusaders returning from Jerusalem. But more importantly, he stated that the pyramid was on the scale 1/288 of the Great Pyramid. He stated: "Why the Crusaders who built the pyramid in Falicon chose this scale of 1/288 is not known, but the precise proportions with the Great Pyramid are surprising because the Crusaders on their way and back from Jerusalem never passed the original one."[15] There is, however, no evidence that Crusaders built it – and no-one has ever performed detailed measurements to argue whether or not it is indeed on the scale 1/288. As such, it is easy to shoot down theories about the possible origins of the pyramid, but extremely hard to identify who, when and why this small pyramid was constructed.

PYRAMIDS ON MARS

So we finally have found a pyramid, however small it is, outside of Egypt and Mesoamerica. Are there others? "Elsewhere" is sometimes defined too broadly – like out of this world – elsewhere in the solar system. And we are thus following in the footsteps of the above mentioned Maurice Chatelain, who is one of several people who believe that pyramids are an extraterrestrial legacy. From the late 1970s onwards, their camp has focused on the question whether, if extraterrestrial beings were present on Earth, there is clear evidence of artificial constructions elsewhere in the solar system, as this would seriously strengthen their argument.

The best candidate for an ancient civilisation is Mars. And, intriguingly, the first potential artificial structures on the planet were thought to be pyramids. Mankind has long been intrigued by Mars and Pyramids, specifically in science fiction circles. It was the title of a serial in the British science fiction television series *Doctor Who*, which was first broadcast in four weekly parts from October 25 to November 15, 1975. The storyline involved ancient

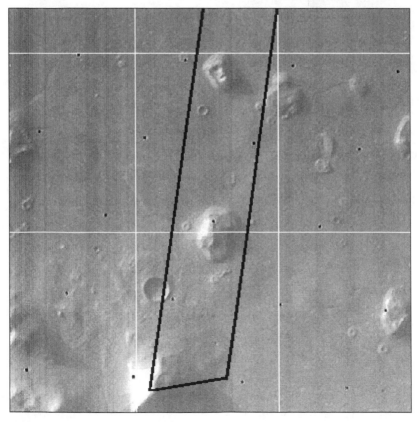

Map of Mars' Cydonia region

Egypt, as well as Sutekh the Destroyer, the last of the Osirians, who was waiting to be freed, imprisoned beneath a pyramid, ready to bring death to all those that are alive; the storyline thus resembles a theory about the Great Pyramid   written down as non-fiction by Zecharia Sitchin in *Wars of God and Men*. A forgotten pyramid-type complex was also at the centre of the movie *Total Recall*, an American science fiction film released in 1990, starring Arnold Schwarzenegger. It was based on the novelette *We Can Remember It for You Wholesale* by Philip K. Dick, first published in 1966.

The first possible "real" pyramid of Mars was discovered in the Elysium Quadrangle of the Red Planet. In 1974, the magazine *Icarus* ran a short article by Mack Gipson Jr. and Victor K Ablordeppy, which reported that "triangular and pyramid-like structures have been observed on the Martian surface". The authors noted that these structures cast triangular and polygonal shadows, suggesting a pyramidal structure. Still, the authors seemed to favour a natural explanation as "steep-sided volcanic cones and impact craters occur only a few kilometres away." The four pyramids were paired, facing each other across a plain. In retrospect unwisely, leading American astronomer Carl Sagan decided to comment on these structures in 1977, initially innocently writing that "the largest are three kilometres across at the base and one kilometre high". What made a connection to an artificial structure was this comparison: "– much larger than the pyramids of Sumer, Egypt or Mexico on Earth. They seem to be eroded and ancient and are, perhaps, only small mountains, sandblasted for ages. But they warrant, I think, a careful look." That was all that was needed to create controversy and generate speculation. In 1996, Robert Bauval and Graham Hancock abandoned Egyptian and Mexican pyramids, devoting an entire book to the Martian anomalies. They wondered: "could they be the first sign, as many independent researchers claim, that Mars is marked by the 'fingerprints' of an ancient extraterrestrial civilization?"[16]

What had transformed the Martian controversy was when an area in the Cydonia region was photographed by the Viking 1 space probe, on July 25, 1976. When the photographs were later analysed by NASA, an area approximately 3 km (2 miles) long and 1.5 km (1 mile) across seemed to resemble a human face. NASA – for some reason, which in retrospect should be classified as unwisely too – decided to announce this "quirk of nature" in a press release six days later. Despite the humouristic tone that NASA tried but perhaps failed to convey in the news release, some people wondered whether it could indeed represent an artificial monument. The suggestion was taken up by Brian Crowley and James J Hurtak in *The Face on Mars* in 1986, but the most notable advocate of this theory became the American journalist Richard Hoagland. In his 1987 book *The Monuments of Mars: A City on the Edge of Forever*, Hoagland interpreted other nearby surface features as remnants of a ruined city and artificially constructed pyramids. In short, he argued for the artificiality of the Face by arguing that other nearby structures could likely be artificial too. As mentioned, in 1996, the debate was brought to a wider audience when Robert Bauval and Graham Hancock decided to write *The Mars Mystery*, which largely was a repetition of Hoagland's theory. But what is of most interest to us (and which appealed to many of their readers too), is that Hoagland, Hancock and

Bauval each drew a parallel between the Martian structures and the pyramids of Earth – specifically the Great Pyramid, though others, such as British author David Percy, also saw a clear overlay between the structures on Mars and... the Avebury-Stonehenge area.

As quickly as the Martian Face became popular, as quickly did it disappear. The Mars Global Surveyor probe in 1998 and 2001, as well as the Mars Odyssey probe in 2002 photographed the feature under completely different lighting than the Viking probe had in 1976 – and at much higher resolution. The new photographs made the structure now look very little like a face, although for some observers, this was "clear proof" either that the images had been doctored, or that, in fact, Earth's powers (the United States of America?) had bombed the Martian surface somewhere between 1976 and 1998, to destroy evidence of this extra-terrestrial civilisation.

The obliteration of the Face on Mars also killed the interest in Martian pyramids. So what to make of the Martian Pyramids? For obvious reasons, we only have – and perhaps only ever will have – photographic evidence at our disposal. These are the same photographs that convinced some that there was a Face – and even sceptics "saw" the Face; they just felt it was a natural anomaly, a trick of light or a photographic illusion – or a combination of all three. When it comes to "seeing" the pyramids, an initial observation that is made is that unlike the Face, these structures seem to have not withstood the test of time. In short, those claiming that there is clear evidence of a pyramid on the Martian surface, argue that the pyramids are partially destroyed – which makes it, in my opinion, extremely difficult to maintain it is "clear

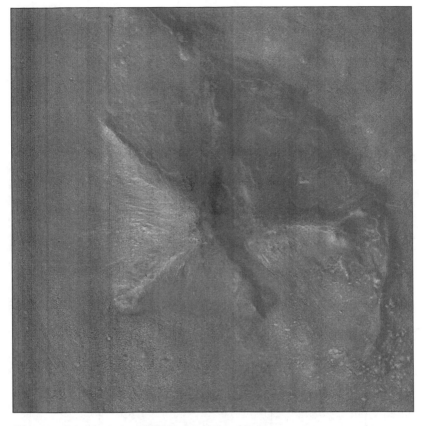

Structure interpreted as D&M pyramid on Mars

evidence", for a heap of rubble or a natural hill are difficult enough to distinguish when you are in front of it, let alone when seeing it from a camera miles up in the sky.

Hoagland and a Russian author Vladimir Avinsky both wrote about pyramidal hills in the Cydonia region; but what for one was a clear pyramid, the other did not interpret as a pyramid at all. Of all pyramid contenders, the most famous is the so-called "D&M Pyramid", which actually looks nothing like a pyramid, if only because it has a pentagram as its ground plan and not a single pentagram-based pyramid has ever been discovered on Earth. The name of this pyramid derived from its discoverers, Vincent DiPietro and Gregory Molenaar, computer scientists working at the Goddard Space Flight Center. What added to the pyramid's fame was its relative proximity to the Face (16 kilometres) and the fact that it was "almost" aligned perfectly north-south, "like the Great Pyramid of Egypt". What few readers of the original material may not have totally appreciated is the fact that it was massive: 1.5 kilometres on its shortest side, its long axis measuring three kilometres, making it 800 metres high – roughly five times the height of the Great Pyramid. This is obviously not a structure built by hands, so if artificial, it was built with elaborate machines – as our extraterrestrial visitors obviously would have had. But if these pyramids were indeed built by the same people that built pyramids on Earth, as most of these authors, Hoagland and Percy foremost, argued, why do we not see such gigantic pyramids on Earth? I would find it grossly unfair that alien visitors build gigantic pyramids on Mars, but just "big pyramids" on Earth…

Anyway: no-one was debating that there was "something" there, but was it a) five-sided b) a pyramid and c) artificial? Neglecting these questions, Hoagland and co. felt that it strengthened their case if they were to point out other possible anomalies or regular shapes on the photographs, then draw lines between the various structures, before to conclude that together, they "proved" the presence of a city. Hoagland even identified a "City Square" in this complex.

In the final analysis, it is impossible to argue that there are no pyramids on Mars – it's impossible to prove a negative. But it is equally clear that any analysis purely based on aerial photography, as has been proven both on Earth and in the case of the Face on Mars, is highly tenuous. As to the D&M pyramid, it is most likely a natural hill, seeing it doesn't really look like a pentagram when you look at it without Hoagland's white-lined pentagram shape drawn on top. And the debate of Martian pyramids will only ever be answered when humans mount an archaeological expedition to the red planet.

Before returning back to Earth, let us quickly note that the Moon also has had its fair share of pyramid fever. A pyramidal structure was seen in the Sea of Tranquillity by Soviet space engineer Alexander Abramov, who claimed that it was positioned exactly like the pyramids at Gizeh. The area was the very region the astronauts of Apollo 11 landed in on the first trip to the Moon in July 1969. In my humble opinion, the article may have been solely intended to create controversy: a piece of Soviet propaganda to argue that perhaps the Americans were hiding a major discovery from Mankind. Several Americans also added to this speculation, including Fred Steckling, whom we single out for arguing that his photographic analysis had revealed possible pyramids in various craters; one image had been shot by the Apollo 8 mission, the other during the Apollo 16 mission. These are indeed all anomalies on photographs, but they are at best indications of anomalies on the ground, and nothing more, until – indeed – we go back to the Moon and do an on-site inspection.

THE UNITED PYRAMIDS OF AMERICA?

With the presence of pyramids in Mesoamerica, could there be pyramids in North America, the United States of America? After all, there is no great natural barrier to stop people migrating north? *The Lost Pyramids of Rock Lake* is the title of a book by Frank Joseph, who has written several books on America's mounds – which some authors tend to relabel as pyramids. Labelling mounds pyramids is bound to cause more interest in your discoveries, and that is exactly what happened in Aztalan, in the northern state of Wisconsin. When Dr. James Scherz discovered that its earthen mound – pyramid – had a deep hole dug at its precise centre, he realised that the structure had served as an alignment marker orientated towards a celestial event. Across the Crawfish River, he then noted the prominent outline of Christmas Hill on the eastern horizon and discovered that alignments between both structures marked the winter solstice (December 21). As an outcome of this discovery, the mound was renamed as the "Pyramid of the Sun", with the smaller structure immediately to the north not wanting to be left behind and hence labelled "Pyramid of the Moon".

In the same category – mounds sometimes labelled as pyramids – is the Monks Mound in Cahokia, Illinois, near the junction of the Missouri with the Mississippi River. The site was first settled around 650 AD, during the Late Woodland period. Mound building did not begin until 1050, at the beginning of the Mississippian period, and the site was abandoned between 1250 and 1400. The original name of the city is unknown and the inhabitants appear to have not employed writing. Around 1000-1400, it covered an area of 9.6 km^2 (6 square miles) and had a population of 20,000 – the largest community of its time in North America.

The city was built around the Monks Mound, the tallest prehistoric earthwork north of Mexico, rising in four terraces to over thirty metres in height. It was the centre point of the "Four

Directions" and the city was constructed along two axes, one running north-south, the other east-west, both meeting at the mound. On the summit of the mound there was once a timber building, over thirty metres in length and perhaps as much as fifteen metres high. Again, it is impressive, but we should continue to refer to them as mounds – not pyramids – and fortunately, the official name continues to be Monks Mount, not Monks Pyramid.

As to Rock Lake and its pyramids: Frank Joseph discovered underwater structures in that lake. Even though they appear to be artificial structures, labelling them "pyramids" is once again stretching the envelope. Fast forwarding to our modern times, the same should be said about the Transamerica Building in San Francisco, which many consider to be a pyramid, and it is often referred to as the "Transamerica Pyramid". Indeed, in its most basic shape, the building itself is a tall, four-sided pyramid. But with the addition of two "wings" on opposite sides of the building, it really has foresaken its pyramidal shape. Still, the name pyramid will continue to be applied to the building, if only because the original Transamerica building, located just down the street, is also a triangular-shaped building. That building is now occupied by the Church of Scientology of San Francisco, which may have chosen the site as its centre because of its pyramidical structure. Still, the structure definitely has inspired someone, for a near-identical structure can be seen as part of the Death Star, in *Star Wars Episode IV - A New Hope*.

For the moment, America's only "true" pyramid remains The Luxor Hotel in Las Vegas. It has an Ancient Egyptian motif and contains a total of 4,407 rooms lining the interior walls of a hollow pyramid. Less known is that contained within are two twin ziggu-rat towers. The hotel opened on October 15, 1993 and was designed by the renowned hotel architect Veldon Simpson. The main portion of the hotel is a 350-foot-high (106 metres), thirty story pyramid of black glass (in comparison, the Great Pyramid of Gizeh tops out at 450 feet, or 137 metres). The hotel is marked by a large obelisk with the name of the property in lighted letters, while the porte-cochere travels underneath a massive recreation of the Great Sphinx of Gizeh. The tip of the pyramid contains a fixed-position spotlight that points directly upward; it is the brightest beam in the world, and is visible from anywhere in the Las Vegas valley at night, and can actually be seen at flight level from above Los Angeles, California, over 275 miles (440 km) away. The beam's output is rated at 41.5 billion candlepower. In the spring, the bright light attracts huge numbers of moths into the light beam, creating a phenomenon that has been likened to snow. It's no doubt ironic that the hotel was named Luxor, after the temple near Thebes, which was the centre of the temple-building cult, which was anathema to the previous Pyramid Age! But then this is Las Vegas...

PYRAMIDS OF ATLANTIS?

There have also been reports of underwater pyramids in the vicinity of the Bahamas, east of Florida in the United States and north of Cuba and the Caribbean. In the late 1970s, Dr. Manson Valentine stated that these submerged pyramids were 420 feet high and 540 feet wide – just thirty feet smaller than the Great Pyramid! The peak was said to rise within sixty feet (20 m) of the surface of the sea, and thus within the capabilities of many divers. Valentine stated that "in the Moselle Reef area, the pyramid causes boat compasses to spin wildly" and added that he was unable to explain this phenomenon.[17] He then linked them to UFO activity that occurred in the same area.

When Valentine first reported on this discovery, no-one – not even he – had seen the structure; no-one had dived; its presence was "inferred" from instrumental data – bringing us in the same domain as recognising pyramids on Mars from satellite photographs. Though Valentine spoke of plans of a follow-up expedition, this never materialised. In fact, some commentators have labelled the Valentine story "an elaborate Atlantis pyramid hoax". The Valentine story appeared in Charles Berlitz's 1978 book *Without a Trace*, the follow-up to his world-bestseller *The Bermuda Triangle*. Intriguingly – and definitely not coincidentally – the location was in the exact area where the American psychic Edgar Cayce had placed Atlantis – the same psychic who had made prophecies about a Hall of Records on the Gizeh Plateau.

The sonar chart, obtained by Captain Don Henry and "authenticated" by Dr. J. Manson Valentine of the Miami Museum of Science, does indeed appear to constitute impressive proof that something sits underneath the surface of the idyllic sea. The tracing shows a cross-section of a distinct, symmetrical pyramid shape rising above an otherwise flat surface. But what few have underlined is that this type of sonar tracing produces a read-out with a greatly exaggerated vertical axis, to make it easier to detect horizontal surface changes. Thus, what appears to be pyramid sides sharply rising at 45° angles is in reality a gentle slope of no more than two or three degrees. The pyramid is thus at most a few feet tall – and not a pyramid at all!

It should therefore not create any amazement that some have labelled the entire story a hoax, though no-one is able to tell whether it was Berlitz himself who spun the story to create another world bestseller, or whether he himself fell for it – making Valentine less than a "qualified expert".

SPANISH PYRAMIDS

We have travelled from France to Mars and the Moon, gone to the States, but all of these forays have been greatly disappointing; for the moment, the Falicon pyramid seems to remain our only "true" – though small – pyramid outside of Egypt and Mesoamerica. But that is soon to change...

In 1991, the renowned explorer Thor Heyerdahl spoke of pyramids on the Canary Islands. He had come across these monuments while he was trying to find further evidence of transoceanic contacts. Of course, many immediately jumped to a "logical" conclusion: pyramids in Egypt, pyramids in Mesoamerica, and now pyramids right in the middle, in the Canary Islands; connect the dots, and you have "clear evidence" of transoceanic contacts, in which the Old World apparently had told the New World to start building pyramids.

There are six step pyramids on the island of Tenerife, located near the town of Guimar, on the eastern shore, about 40 kilometers (24 miles) south of Santa Cruz de Tenerife. The pyramids reach a maximum height of twelve metres. The Archaeology Department of La Laguna University carried out initial excavations and the Canary Islands' Astrophysical Institute looked into possible ancient astronomical relationships. These studies revealed that the pyramids were aligned to the winter and summer solstices, once again underlining that many if not most if not all pyramids have an astronomical component. The pyramids are reported to line up with the sunset which occurs in a distinctive spot on the mountainous horizon. Stairways ascend from a level plaza to the top of each pyramid, where there is a flat summit platform covered with gravel. The stairways are all on the western side, suggesting a ceremonial purpose, because someone ascending to the pyramids' summits on the morning of the solstice would be "welcoming" the rising sun – a very religiously significant act.

Of course, there was controversy. The "opposition" claimed that they were merely terraces or random piles of stone that had been cleared by the Spaniards. But the archaeologists discovered that they were in fact painstakingly built step-pyramids. This "opposition" may have had very selfish economic reasons to say what it did: the land on which the pyramids stand had been earmarked for development in connection with a planned expansion in the upper part of the town and even in 1991, it was clear that archaeology and economy did not easily go hand in hand. Heyerdahl therefore persuaded the Norwegian ship owner Fred Olsen to buy the site, clean up the debris of centuries of disregard and construct a museum. This is now what is known as the "Pirámides de Güímar" Ethnographic Park; the park opened in April 1998 and is attracting 150,000 visitors per year. One of the 'black' pyramids has now been restored. Recent excavations under one pyramid have yielded artefacts identified with the Guanches, the pre-Spanish inhabitants of Tenerife. Still, some refuse to admit that such impressive structures could have been built by the Guanche and suggest that they might have been constructed by the early Christian conquistadores as a time measuring device to know when to celebrate the Catholic festivities of St. John (which occur on June 24, close to the summer solstice). The controversy provides an insight into the type of furore that "welcomed" Careri when published his account of the Teotihuacan pyramids in 1719 who obviously could not have been constructed by the local "devil worshippers".

As to Heyerdahl himself: he believed that these pyramids were remains from pre-European voyagers who sailed the Atlantic Ocean in ancient times. But following Dr. Heyerdahl's express wishes, no theory is forced on the visitors to Guimar. In fact, the symbol of the exhibit is a question mark, asking each person to make up his own mind. Still, the most likely scenario seems to involve the Guanche themselves. If we let go off the idea that they "could not construct such structures" and embrace the possibility that they could, we may have the easiest, most logical and correct attribution as to who built these pyramids. For one, it is known that the Guanche used the Chacona cave under one of the pyramids – indeed, yet another cave underneath a pyramid. Secondly, nearby Guimar was, until the Spanish conquest, the residence of one of the ten "menceys" (kings) of Tenerife, identifying the area as a capital. And as pyramids were related to kingship, why not link the pyramids with Guanche kingship?

GREEK PYRAMIDS

So we finally have found more pyramids. "Are there pyramids elsewhere?" The answer is "yes" and if the follow-up question is "where", that answer is "Greece". Ancient Greece is one of the most revered ancient civilisations – though "modern" by ancient Egyptian standards. What we consider to be "ancient Greece" only started in the last millennium BC. But ancient Greece, so beloved by our 19th and 20th century education system, did not arrive out of nowhere. And when we enter the origins of Greek civilisation, we stumble upon several pyramids.

There are three pyramids in the Peloponnesus, the large peninsula in southern Greece, forming the part of the country south of the Gulf of Corinth. One pyramid is located approximately four kilometres from Argos, in the village of Helleniko; A second pyramid is located outside of the village of Ligouria, near Epidauros; the third pyramid is to be found in Dalamanara, located roughly half-way between the other two, and is worst off.

The pyramids have only recently become the centre of archaeological and historical research, and were immediately hailed by the researching team as the "prototypes" for the Egyptian pyramids. Imagine: an obscure village near Argos in the Greek Peloponnesus could be the origin of the Egyptian Pyramid Age! Immediately, this headline-grabbing statement was also seen as evidence that contradicted "the misguided belief held by many that civilization proceeded from the East". The results of the Athens Academy and the University of Edinburgh had made it clear that the "pyramid idea" had been transferred from Greece to Egypt.

What had happened that made these academic institutions arrive at such conclusions? On February 9, 1995, Pericles Theoharis, the then General Secretary of the Athens Academy, announced the results of a two year study of the Greek pyramids (which excluded the badly damaged Dalamanara structure). The results dated the Helleniko pyramid to 2720 BC, with a margin of error factor of plus or minus 580 years. The Ligouria pyramid, a structure originally measuring 14 by 12 metres, of which very little remains, was dated to 2100 BC, with a margin of error factor of plus or minus 600 years. For the Greeks, this was clear evidence that the Helleniko pyramid was a century older than the Egyptian step pyramid of Zoser (dated to 2620 BC), and 170 years older than the Great Pyramid. In short: the Greeks had been the first to build pyramids.

Controversial claims receive controversial criticism. First line of attack: attack the methodology and the instruments used in arriving at the claim. As the scientists had used the "optical thermo-photo illumination" method rather than the more widely used carbon dating, criticism against this method soon took the format that this method was effective only for measuring ceramics and not on the kind of processed stone used for the construction of these pyramids. Pericles Theoharis disagreed, writing that "this method has been successfully applied on geological substances such as lava, stalagmites, meteorites, cave deposits, and aeolic and oceanic residues" and that it was tested on the "block house" of Mycenae, which had already often been dated using other methods.

To cut a long debate, which occasionally comes and goes, short: the dates seem to be correct enough, but since the debate commenced in 1995, the carbon dating of the Great Pyramid has made the "Out of Greece" hypothesis surplus to requirements once again, underlining that the Great Pyramid – and others – are older than the small Greek pyramids. I want to bypass this controversy, by suggesting that we try to establish whether or not there were links between ancient Egypt and Greece at that time, and leave it aside for the moment who told whom what.

All of the information we have from ancient authors shows that Egypt from the most ancient times was open, known and familiar to the Greeks. It was Herodotus who provided us with the first information on what his Egyptian guides told him about the construction of the Great Pyramid. According to Diodorus Siculus, Menes, the first king of Egypt, constructed his tomb near Lake Moiris and "placed a quadrangular pyramid on it and constructed the much-admired labyrinth."[18] Minos just happens to be the generic name for all Cretan kings of that period, which in the minds of many has suggested a link between that Greek island and Egypt.

Furthermore, there are ancient records about these Greek pyramids. The Helleniko pyramid was known to Pausanias (2nd century BC), who stated that it was built by Acrisius and his brother, Proetus; Acrisius was identified as the grandfather of Perseus, who was said to have been born and have spent his first childhood years near the pyramid, before visiting Africa and Ethiopia. To quote Pausanias: "On the way from Argos to Epidauria there is on the right a building made very like a pyramid... Here took place a fight for the throne between Proetus and Acrisius; the contest, they say, ended in a draw... For those that fell on either side was built here a common tomb."[19] So it seems that these pyramids were tombs... royal tombs.

Greece has more than just these three pyramids. In 1997, author Richard Poe dedicated a chapter to the "Pyramid of Amphion" in *Black Spark, White Fire*, largely arguing that Greece was a child of Egypt – and not the other way around. The "Amphion Hill" or the "The Stepped Pyramid of Thebes" comes closest to being a "real Greek pyramid". The story of this hill is directly linked with the foundation of the city of Thebes. Though some legends say it was Cadmus, others argue that the city's founder was Amphion, the son of Antiope and Zeus. He and his brother Zethus were abandoned by their mother at birth, and reared by a shepherd – a clear analogy with the story of Romulus and Remus, founding brothers of Rome. Together, they, like Romulus and Remus around Rome, built a protective wall around the city that would later become known as Thebes (named after Zethus' wife, Thebe). According to legend, Amphion drew the stones used for building the wall after him by playing magical music on his lyre.

The founder of Thebes met with a tragic ending: Amphion's whole family was struck by a plague, which was seen as punishment from the gods for a wrongful accusation made by Amphion of the Titaness Leto and her children, Apollo and Artemis. Zethus died of sorrow when his mother killed his son by mistake. Whereas in Rome, Remus and Romulus fought to the death, Romulus being victorious, in Thebes, the two brothers were buried in a common tomb north of Thebes, just outside the northern gates.

The story was seen to be as nothing but a legend, until the Amphion hill was discovered to have an interior system of tunnels and chambers, in which one could have been the tomb of Amphion and Zethus. The excavations were done by archaeologist Theodoros Spyropoulos, between 1971 and 1973. Spiropoulos also concluded that the most important aspect about the tomb of Amphion was that it was the only structure in the Greek world in the shape of a stepped pyramid – in short, it was an anomaly. He dated the structure to 2500-2000 BC, coinciding once again with the Egyptian Pyramid Age. Furthermore, the pyramid contained four gold pendants shaped like lilies and topped with papyroid forms, which is classified as a typical Egyptian motif.

The pyramid had been constructed by moulding the sides of the Amphion hill in continuous cone-shaped banks, so that the whole structure became a stepped pyramid, made of four layers. But the true wonder lay inside, where Spyropoulos discovered a system of corridors, steps, passageways and drainage systems. He found a stone-lined chamber with two depressions in the floor. Were these spaces for two bodies? Those of Amphion and Zethus? Unfortunately, Spyropoulos found numerous signs of ancient grave robbing, even though, as mentioned, some fragments of gold jewellery remained. Near the location of the burial chamber is a horizontal tunnel that leads north. Further on, this horizontal tunnel meets a vertical chamber, which leads to another tunnel at a different (higher) level. This area remains to be further explored and may bring further discoveries.

Equally intriguing was the observation that the brick tomb at the top of the hill closely followed the construction of the pre-dynastic Egyptian mastabas. The unique characteristic of these mastabas is that their area is larger than the underground chambers they cover, something which is also true at Amphion. It was this specific correlation with ancient Egypt that made Richard Poe wonder whether the Amphion hill was the tomb of an Egyptian emigrant in Greece...

There is some evidence that suggests that the Amphion hill has an astronomical connotation... as we have now come to expect when standing in front of pyramids. According to legend, the inhabitants of Tithorea (in Phocis, an ancient district of central Greece to the north of the Peloponessos), used to secretly remove earth from the Amphion, but only when the sun crossed the constellation of Taurus. They believed that bringing the earth to

Antiopis' grave would make their land more fruitful than the land of Thebes. To prevent this desecration, the Thebans stationed a contingent of guards at the monument – probably only in the period when the sun was indeed in Taurus.

The connection of the step pyramid with the passage of the sun into the Taurus constellation demonstrates the hill's possible incorporation into an astronomical-mythological landscape. More evidence for this is that the tunnel that leads to the underground burial chamber is in line with the Northern Pole Star. The Taurus constellation is of course the constellation of the Bull, which was the form Zeus took when he abducted the beautiful maiden Europa. She was Cadmus' sister, and he was the uncle of the founders of Thebes. Coincidence?

What does the Amphion discovery mean? Spyropoulos argues that the story of Amphion is an indication that Thebes was founded twice: once in "historic times", but originally by Amphion. Legend states that after the death of his entire family, Thebes was no longer ruled, and Spyropoulos seems to suggest that this was the intermediary period between the first and second (historical) foundation.

The Amphion pyramid is therefore "oop-art": an out of place artefact. It was built at a time when the Greeks did not build such tombs; the typical grave was an urn of funeral ashes, buried beneath a small earthen mound. And Spyropoulos was sure that the people who built it had imported their skills from Egypt, theorizing that Amphion and Zethus themselves could have been Egyptian colonists. Of course, when he first published this theory in a 1972 article entitled "Egyptian Colonization of Boiotia", it was met with scorn and derision. Fortunately, his career has progressed, later becoming Commissioner of Antiquities for the district Arkadia. Though Spyropoulos has shown that the Amphion pyramid is unique, he has also shown that the structure itself is not an isolated phenomenon, but that it was part of a mysterious lost civilisation that appears to have flourished in Greece between 2800 and 1700 BC. He has named this the "Minyan civilisation", named after the legendary people that sailed to Colchis in quest of the Golden Fleece. He believes that this civilisation was ruled by an Egyptian elite. He also argues that such Egyptian colonists may have intermarried in Southern Greece, in the family of the Danaos, a Greek mythological character, twin brother of Aegyptus and the son of Belus, a mythical king of Egypt. The myth of Danaos is a foundation legend (or re-foundation legend) of Argos, one of the foremost Mycenaean cities of the Peloponnesus. In Homer's *Iliad*, the Danaans commonly designate the Greek forces that were opposed to the Trojans. Intriguingly, it is Danaos and his family that is linked with the Helleniko pyramid.

Is the Amphion hill a pyramid? Spyropoulos called it a pyramid, and Poe observes that "with its circular base, the Amphion mound is actually more cone-shaped than pyramidal. Nevertheless, it greatly resembles a stepped pyramid when viewed in profile – almost as if someone had tried to create the impression of an Egyptian pyramid, using the crude materials at hand."[20] As Spyropoulos was a qualified archaeologist, we will agree that, indeed, this is a pyramid.

Doubt, however, does remain about a structure on the island of Crete, to the south of the port town of Chania – from which our word "candy" originates. Though labelled a pyramid, it is more like a cone. Unfortunately, its age has not been ascertained –

in fact, no-one has properly studied the structure. Let us therefore note that the structure "looks" old and "could" be part of the Minoan civilisation that existed on Crete; it could thus be 1500 BC. But it could also be something else... All we know at the moment is that it is located at an altitude of 290 metres above sea level, with a height of 8.5 metres, and a base circumference of 29 metres. The interior of the cone has a chamber, carved out of the solid rock, and measures 2.2 by 2.1 by 1.4 metres in height. Its entrance is to the west and is thus directed towards the sunset. If proven to be linked with the Minoan civilisation, it could lead to the possibility that they too were infected by the pyramid virus. That should not come as a surprise, once we are aware of the fact that the Minoans were seafarers, visited Egypt, but also traded with the Greek mainland. It would be quite bizarre if they had never heard of pyramids! And they may have caught "the pyramid bug" on their travels...

CHAPTER 4

CHINESE PYRAMIDS

Though pyramids are large, and the Great Pyramid very large, they dwarf in comparison to the Great Wall of China, Mankind's largest building project so far. The Wall stretches over a formidable 6,352 kilometres (3,948 miles); if it were reassembled at the equator, it would girdle the globe with a wall eight feet high and three feet thick. It was built to protect the various dynasties from raids by Mongol, Turkic and other nomadic tribes. Several walls have been built since the 3rd century BC, the first by the First Emperor, Qin Shi Huang. The government ordered people to work on the wall, and many people, possibly as many as one million, died while building it. It thus obtained the gruesome title, the "longest cemetery on Earth" or "the long graveyard". This wall, of which little remains, if only because it was mainly built from earth, was located much further north than the current Great Wall of China, which was built during the Ming Dynasty, from the 14th to the 17th century.

Despite whether or not we can see the Great Wall from space (apparently, you can't), in 1920, historian Henri Cordier wrote: "China's ancient past is denied both to us and its population. Its grand past is slowly unveiled, similar to how Egypt's was revealed. Later on, one learned of buildings, standing stones and other monuments that were not mentioned by the Chinese historians (as part of their history)." The largest country in the world was, and is still, largely there to be discovered. Though accepted as a great civilisation, its ancient treasures were barely known to the western world a century ago and in the vast rural areas of China, much remains to be explored.

Throughout the 20th century, there were also rumours of pyramids in China. It was clear that the Chinese definitely had sufficient project management skills to build a pyramid. In fact, whether China had pyramids or not, was not the core of the debate. It was largely accepted that it had. The problem was getting to them, as they were located in forbidden, military zones or zones used for nuclear testing, such as at Lop Nor, which had the largest nuclear test site in the world, occupying an area of over 100,000 square kilometres. 45 nuclear tests were carried out between 1964 and 1996, making the area off-limits throughout the past five decades.

EARLY REPORTS

The Chinese pyramids were largely only known through traveller's accounts of their voyages. In 1912, Fred Meyer Schroder and Oscar Maman travelled to Shensi (or Shaanxi as it is now more commonly written), the province of Xi'an. They dealt in tobacco and candles, but also supplied the Mongolians with weapons. Their guide along the Chinese-Mongolian border was a monk, Bogdo ("the holy one"), who told them they would soon stumble upon some ancient pyramids. Though he himself had never seen them, he knew some could be found around the old town of Sian-Fu (Xi'an): "Mountains as high as the sky. They are no ordinary burial vaults, though emperors or empresses might be buried inside." Bogdo knew that seven pyramids had been discovered.

When he finally saw them, Schroder estimated that the tallest structure measured 300 metres high, its sides 500 metres long. This would mean that this pyramid was the largest in the world, twice as large as the Great Pyramid at Gizeh; the volume was twenty times as large as the Great Pyramid! Shroder noted that it was aligned north-south/west-east, like the Great Pyramid, continuing that "in the past, they were apparently partly covered with stones, but those have disappeared. A few stones lie at the bottom. It is an earthen pyramid, with giant gullies on its sides. They were the reason why the stones loosened and fell down. Its sides are now partially covered with trees and shrubs. It almost looks a natural hill. We rode around the pyramid, but did not discover any stairways or doors." When questioned about its age, Bogdo believed that it was at least 5,000 years old. Chinese ancient records claimed that even then the pyramids were deemed to be "old" – and thus seemed to predate anything that we knew about Chinese history. Evidence of a lost civilisation?

Schroder's account is detailed, but not the first. Before, in 1908, Arthur de Carle Sowerby and Robert Sterling Clark saw the pyramids during their expedition and wrote about them in their 1912 account *Through Shên-Kan*: "The visitor to Hsi-an [Xi'an], as he travels over the rolling plain from no matter what direction, cannot fail to notice numerous mounds of unusual shape dotted about everywhere like immense molehills, often attaining a height of at least 100 feet [30m], and standing on bases of very considerable area. So remarkable are they that he will instinctively seek information concerning them, and will learn that they are the tombs of kings and emperors, and their wives, and of scholars and sages notable in their day. But few indeed have anything in the way of tombstone or epitaph to tell who sleeps beneath the tones of yellow earth; though, concerning some, fantastic legends still linger min the minds of the people."[21]

A third early report originated from the "Segalen mission", a tour of China that the French doctor, ethnographer, archeologist, writer and poet Victor Segalen made in 1909-1914 and 1917 and which brought him face to face with these structures. In 1913, he measured the pyramid's height at 48 metres, encompassing five terraces. One side measured 350 metres in length, a stunning 120 metres longer than the side of Great Pyramid at Gizeh. With 1,960,000 cubic metres of material, it is now the fourth largest pyramid in the world.[22] The Segalen mission also revealed the existence of more pyramids and tombs along the River Wei, the largest tributary of the Yellow River that flows past Xi'an. He also dated the structures to the Han period, following that of Emperor Qin Shi Huang, the man who had built first Great Wall, bringing the entire story once again into the folds of Chinese history.

The Cold War largely placed China off-limits to Western visitors. Throughout, the stories of the early explorers and their reports of pyramids in China fed the imagination of Western pyramidophiles. There were stories of other pyramids located in the Sinkiang province, an autonomous region occupying the northwestern corner of China, and the Takla Makan desert, one of the largest sandy deserts in the world, in the Tarim Basin. The latter area is where the famous "Chinese mummies" have been found. These are Caucasoid mummies, dated to the 2nd and 1st millennium BC. Some tests have found that the mummies contain European genes, confirming the earlier suggestion that the mummies are of Indo-European descent, giving further support to the idea of migrations of Indo-European tribes at a very early period, suggesting the possibility of cultural exchange with the

Chinese world since around 1st millennium BC. But though these are mummies, they have not been found inside pyramids...

New Zealand author Bruce Cathie became interested in the Chinese pyramids and wrote on the subject in *The Bridge to Infinity*, published in 1983. Cathie reported that a member of the Chinese Embassy had officially informed him there were no such things as pyramids in the Shensi province: "There are a few tumuli (burial hills), but no pyramids." Cathie saw this as a clear denial of the Chinese that no such structures existed; the Chinese quickly clarified their statement: a letter from Chinese authorities, dated November 1, 1978, addressed to Cathie, stated that the scientists had learned that the so-called "pyramids" were burial tombs of emperors of the Western Han dynasty: "Records give a different version of the emperors' lives. As the graves have not been scientifically analysed and no markings were seen on the ground, it is difficult to formulate conclusions." So there were "pyramids", but these were "tombs" – not "pyramids"... though they were pyramidal in shape! Confused?

CONFIRMATION

Rules and regulations for travellers were somewhat eased following the death of Mao Zedong in 1976, but change was slow. The American travel writer David Hatcher Childress wrote about Chinese pyramids in 1985, but was unable to visit them. The major breakthrough came only in 1994, after the collapse of the East Bloc, when German travel operator Hartwig Hausdorf was allowed to enter former no-go areas and came away with fresh knowledge of the Chinese Pyramids.

So, in 1994, Hartwig Hausdorf and his company of fellow

travellers landed at the new Xi'an airport, near the neighbouring town of Xianyang, and, driving to the city and their hotel, saw one pyramid which stood along the road. It had been "discovered" a few years earlier, when Xi'an's airport was relocated and a road to the city was built.

Hausdorf was passionate about China's ancient history and had written about its ancient mysteries; he had read and knew Erich von Däniken's work and fate – or the Chinese government's new policy of openness – seemed to have singled him out as the first modern westerner to report back on the existence of the Chinese pyramids. In 1995, he told me: "It's a small miracle I received the go-ahead to enter some 'no go' areas. I was, in fact, the only one who was granted such favours. I assume there are two reasons for this. I regularly visit China with a group of tourists. In 1993, I became acquainted with Chen Jianli, an avid researcher of his country's past. He assured me that he would try and open a few doors inside the Chinese Ministry of Tourism. In fact, in March 1994, I was able to visit some former 'no go' areas in the Shaanxi

Pyramids as seen from road from airport

province. I passed around some copies of my German book, *Die Weisse Pyramide* (The White Pyramid), to the right people. I talked to archaeologists who at first denied any pyramids existed, but finally recognised that they did exist. I was most pleased when the same people gave me further permission to enter other 'no go' zones when I returned in October 1994. I never expected any of this would happen to me. But it seems it had to happen eventually. Following decades of rumour, someone had to clear the picture."

In March 1994, Hausdorf climbed a pyramid and saw a few more from its top. In October 1994, he climbed the same pyramid again and was able to count twenty more pyramids, all lying in the immediate vicinity. It confirmed what had been seen from a US Air Force map of the area around the city of Xian, made with the use of satellite photographs, whichshowed at least 16 pyramids. Hausdorf stated that "it's amazing how the weather in March didn't allow me to see those pyramids. In October it was perfectly clear weather, and more revealed themselves."

But old Chinese habits died hard, it seemed. In March 1994, Hausdorf also met Professor Feng Haozhang, a prominent member of Beijing's academic circle, his assistant, Xie Duan Yu, and three colleagues. At first, they denied the pyramids' existence. But when Hausdorf showed them three photos of three different pyramids, they caved in. Hausdorf described this encounter: "It was as if I had entered a hive. The photographs I took in both March and October 1994 are the proof that squelched five decades of rumour. Most scientists denied the existence of pyramids in China. If any scientist still clings to that, show him my photographs."

Ten years later, in 2004, Chris Maier went to China. He was "just" a tourist and did not have any special permission. There were no longer forbidden zones around the city; in fact, tourists are now welcomed in Xi'an and tourist hotels have been built for those who mainly come to see the terracotta army, which has become the town's main tourist attraction.

Maier first saw the pyramids while his flight was on approach. He saw them again on his bus ride from the airport to the town, as Hausdorf had done in 1994, and so many other visitors have done since. In the hotel, he spoke to his tour operator of his desire to visit these sites and was told that tourists were presented with two tours: one taking in the terracotta army, and a far less popular tour that visited the burial mounds, many of which matched the pyramids that had intrigued the western world since Hausdorf's confirmation a decade before. Maier opted for the least popular tour.

The following day, Maier was on his guided tour, beginning with the largest pyramid, known as the Maoling Mausoleum. "Looking around me, I saw no foreign tourists and Daniel [the tour guide] assured me that most of the people he brought here never took the time to climb the mound, being satisfied with merely

Maoling pyramid

viewing it from a distance. But the pyramid was certainly well known to the locals. Atop the summit, a dozen people walked or sat leisurely and one family was even enjoying a picnic lunch." He also was able to establish its height: a little less than 150 feet, or 50 metres, the same height established by Victor Segalen 91 years earlier.

The Maoling Mausoleum is one of the "The Imperial Tombs", or "The Imperial Tombs of the Han and Tang" – i.e. the Chinese pyramids. As previous visitors had noted, there are two main concentrations: the Han tombs are nearly due west of Xi'an, only 30-40 km away; the Tang tombs are grouped ca. 80-100 km northwest of Xi'an, though Emperor Yang Guifei built his tomb at Mawei, inside the "Han pocket".

The "Xi'an Han pyramids" sit on the northern side of the river Wei, upriver from Xianyang airport (Xi'an being downriver), some 120 km from where the River Wei flows into the Yellow River. There are nine pyramids – referred to as "tombs" – and despite their growing fame as a tourist attraction, none of the imperial tombs has been excavated.

Two tombs are located closely together: The "Maoling Mausoleum", otherwise known as the tomb of Emperor Wudi of the Han Dynasty, who reigned from 157-87 BC, and the tomb of Huo Qubing (140-117 BC), one of his generals. "Mao Ling" originates from the word Ling, meaning tomb, and Mao, taken from Maoxiang, the name of the area in which it was situated. The structure is composed of densely packed earth and is now describes as being 46 metres high, covering 54,054 square metres – conform to the measurements of Segalen and Maier. The surrounding wall that once existed has now all but disappeared. Records reveal that the Emperor began the construction of his tomb as early as the second year of his reign, a practice which was customary. Inside, it is believed to hold his body, dressed in a jade suite made of small pieces joined by gold wire, with a jade cicada in the mouth. Stories state that "jade boxes were buried with the emperor and many animals were sacrificed to provide food for his spirit. It is also said that his favourite books were buried with him."

Nearby is the Tomb of Huo Qubing, a man who died young of disease, which once had a series of stone carved animals lining the approach. These have now been moved into a small museum, which also displays relics of the tombs that have been found in the vicinity. They include decorated bricks that lined the tombs, as well as hollow bricks decorated with dragons and tigers, tortoises and snakes and a range of ceramic models, such as ducks, sheep, farmyards and houses.

This "approach" has been identified as a predecessor of the "spirit roads", which can be seen in the approach to the valley of the Ming tombs, 45 kilometres northwest of Peking. Here, the entrance to the valley is a ceremonial "Arc de Triomphe", or the P'ai-lou, which commemorates the glory of the Ming dynasty. The next structure is the Great Red Gate, considered to be the real entrance into the valley and the official starting point up the road to the tombs. Half a kilometre up the road is the Stele Pavilion, where the deceased were commemorated through inscriptions on stone tablets. The road behind the Stele Pavilion is officially known as the Spirit Road and was built for the spirits of the deceased to serve as an aide to lead the spirit to its final resting place. The beginning of the Spirit Road is marked by two stone beacons, after which the road is lined with 24 animals, as in the

"Xi'an approach". It shows that the pyramid had a Spirit Road as its approach and the question needs to be asked whether there is a correspondence with the Avenue of the Dead that forms the approach towards the pyramids of the Mexican Teotihuacan.

The second "pocket" of tombs around Xi'an sits further west, still along the River Wei. The most impressive of these "Tang tombs" is the triple-hilled Qian ling, 85 km northwest of Xi'an and built for Li Zhi, the Gaozong (Exalted Ancestor) emperor of the Tang and his empress Wu Zetian. Again not excavated, it is the largest tomb of the site and lies on a natural hill that is approached by a spirit road which stretches over the impressive distance of three kilometres, passing between two artificial mounds, making it a "triple hill". The start of the spirit road is marked by two tall towers, conform to the two stone beacons of the Ming Spirit Road near Peking. Whether Han, Tang or Ming, the same animals were depicted along this spirit road.

Unlike the other tombs, since the 1960s, five of the 17 satellite tombs have been excavated. The excavations showed that each site

Maoling pyramid

had been robbed, but only of precious stones and metals; the ceramics and wall-paintings were left undisturbed. One of these structures, the Tomb of Princess Yongtai, can now be entered, leading the visitor down a long sloping corridor with small stepped niches in the walls, filled with rows of pottery tomb figures. The walls are covered with paintings of women, court attendants and servants, carrying offerings and candles and flowers. The corridor leads to a dark stone sarcophagus in the tomb chamber, the ceiling of which is painted with stars. The interior structure is identical to that of the nearby Tomb of Prince Yide and Prince Zhanghuai, the latter which contains a wall painting showing people playing polo. The scene is well-known, if only for its vivid depiction of the game.

The second concentration in this second pocket of pyramids – tombs – focuses on the Zhao ling, the Tomb of Taizong, the second emperor of the Tang dynasty (626-649 AD). It is composed of 177 subsidiary tombs and spread over an extensive 20,000 hectares. But unfortunately, the main structure remains unexcavated.

THE "TERRACOTTA WARRIOR PYRAMID"

There is one more pyramid – mound – in this region: that of Emperor Qin Shi Huang, the man who built the first Great Wall, the first Emperor, but also the man of the terracotta army. And his "pyramid" sits just one mile from where the army was buried. It is believed that Qin Shi Huang's mausoleum once stood almost 330 feet in height, though today it measures to just 150 feet. Its sides measure between 1600-1700 feet, giving the structure a volume that also exceeds that of the Great Pyramid. As the structure remains covered by trees, it is not as impressive as the bare

Maoling Mausoleum. One tourist guide describes the ascent as "it has a stepped path to the top, running through stalls where peasants sell anything from appallingly fragile miniature clay warriors to apples and 'ancient coins'." Like all other "pyramid mounds", it has not yet been excavated and archaeologists should be prudent as one story goes that automatic crossbows and arrows designed to fire are installed inside if the tomb is entered. It may seem a tall claim, but could be true!

Like the Great Pyramid, Emperor Qin Shi Huang's mausoleum has been the subject of endless treasure trove stories. In *Records of the Historian: Biography of Qin Shi Huang*, Han historian Sima Qian describes the automatic crossbows and a burial chamber containing miniature palaces and pavilions with flowing rivers and surging oceans of mercury lying beneath a ceiling decorated in jewels depicting the sun, moon and stars. There could be truth in the latter statement, as the ceilings in some of the excavated satellite tombs did indeed contain stars. Recent scientific work at the site has also shown high levels of mercury in the soil of Mount Li, tentatively indicating that Sima Qian may have provided an accurate description of the site's contents. A magnetic scan of the site has also revealed that a large number of coins are lying in the unopened tomb. A preliminary, month-long excavation was done in 1986 and revealed extensive damage, probably by Tang and Song robbers, which has led some archaeologists to conclude that the interior structure, despite Sima Qian's wonderful description, may be found largely void.

Sima Qian also noted 700,000 workmen laboured on the site. It is a staggering number of people, far in excess of anything Herodotus reported on Khufu's slave force. Other sources instead speak of 70,000 labourers, still an impressive workforce. Like Khufu, Qin Shi Huang was not cordially remembered by his descendents. Still, it started promisingly: he was only 13 when he ascended to the throne in 246 BC and succeeded in uniting the other six states in 221 BC, going down into history as "the First Emperor" He ruled from 221 to 210 BC. But it seems that the "unification" was brutal and the Emperor was remembered as a brutal tyrant for millennia – hence why it took the discovery of his terracotta army to somewhat restore his public profile.

A DIVINE MISSION

Xi'an, the ancient Sian-Fu, translates as "Western Peace". It served as China's capital for most of the Han, Sui and Tang dynasties, when it was known as Chan'an, "Eternal Peace" and recognised as the umbilicus of China's civilisation.

It was the site where the First Emperor decided to be buried. And our First Emperor desired to show that he was no longer a simple king like the kings of old during the Warring States Period; as such, he created a new title, "huangdi", combining the word "huang" from the legendary Three Huang (Three August Ones) who ruled at the dawn of Chinese history, and the word "di", from the legendary Five Di (Five Sovereigns) who ruled immediately after the Three Huang. These Three Huang and Five Di were considered perfect rulers, of immense power and very long lives – echoing stories of the prediluvian patriarchs of the Bible. Though he tried to mimick them, his people obviously felt he failed in that ambition.

But it is not his legacy that interests us; for the moment, we are mostly captivated by his new title, "huangdi". The word "huang" also means "big", "great", while the word "di" also refers to the Supreme God in Heaven, the creator of the world. Thus, by being the first to join these two words for the first time, Qin Shi Huang created a title that identified him with the creator of the world. Is it a coincidence that in Egypt, pyramids are uniquely linked with the cult of the creator god Atum, worshipped in Heliopolis as Atum-Ra? Such identifications with the creator or "the point of creation" was equally found to be present in Mesoamerica. In the case of Emperor Qin Shi Huang, he had indeed created, thus emulating the work of the creator god; the Emperor had created a new China.

The Emperor was clearly greatly intrigued by mythology. Qin Shi Huang died – rather ironically – while on a tour to Eastern China, searching for the legendary Islands of the Immortals (off the coast of Eastern China) and for the secret of eternal life. Reportedly, he died of swallowing mercury pills, which were made by his court scientists and doctors, but which erroneously contained too much mercury. Equally ironic was that these pills were meant to make him immortal. His death occurred on September 10, 210 BC (Julian Calendar), at the palace in the Shaqiu prefecture, about two months away by road from the capital Xi'an. His Prime Minister Li Si, who accompanied him, was extremely worried that the news of his death could trigger a general uprising in the empire, and thus kept the news of his passing secret until they returned to the capital. To make sure there were no leaks, most of the imperial entourage accompanying the emperor was equally left uninformed of the emperor's death, and each day Li Si entered the wagon where the emperor was supposed to be travelling, pretending to discuss affairs of state with him.

The secretive nature of the emperor while alive allowed this stratagem to work, and it apparently did not raise doubts among courtiers. Li Si also ordered that two carts containing fish be carried immediately before and after the wagon of the emperor, in the hope that it would prevent noses from sniffing out what was truly going on inside the imperial wagon: the body of the emperor slowly decomposing. Eventually, after two months of political intrigue, Li Si and the imperial court were back in Xi'an, where the news of the death of the emperor was officially announced.

Qin Shi Huang was buried in his mausoleum, together with the famous terracotta army nearby. That famous Terracotta Army of China was eventually discovered in March 1974 by local farmers drilling a well to the east of Qin Shi Huang's pyramid. The figures were found in three separate pits, with an empty fourth pit also having been discovered. 8,099 figures in all have thus far been unearthed at the site; they include infantry, archers, and officers and are manufactured in a crouching or standing pose. Each figure was given a real weapon, such as bronze spears, halberds or swords, or wooden crossbows with bronze fittings. It is believed that these weapons date to as early as 228 BC and may have been used in actual warfare – perhaps the unification of China itself.

The Qin Empire barely survived his death, for his equally ruthless advisers eliminated his heir in favour of a second, believed to be "less controversial" son; but their choice was nevertheless still overthrown by a series of revolts, installing the Han dynasty in 206 BC, who despite rejecting the previous regime, nevertheless continued to build pyramids, though on the other side of the capital.

The Chinese pyramids are therefore clearly linked with

Emperors; they are labelled "Imperial Tombs" and thus seem to share much with the Egyptian pyramids – at least in their standard identification as "just tombs". Like Egyptian pyramid building chronology, those around Xi'an fall in two periods: the Qin-Han rule, in the late 3rd century BC, and the much later Tang dynasty, in the 7th -8th century AD. Like Egypt, the satellite tombs are known to contain burials. But unlike Egypt, none of the main structures have been properly excavated. And hence, what they will contain and in what state they will be found in, remains a question. But, unlike ancient Egypt, we do have written and largely contemporary written accounts of these rulers and their pyramids; and these documents make it clear that these pyramids are indeed the royal tombs. The main question that remains is whether or not they will have become the victim of grave robbery or not.

THE WHITE PYRAMID

Hausdorf's 1994 book on the mysteries of China was titled *The White Pyramid*. The title refers to a story that started during World War II, when American pilot James Gaussman was flying a routine mission between India and China, when engine problems forced him to descend to a lower altitude. "I banked to avoid a mountain and we came out over a level valley. Directly below was a gigantic white pyramid. It looked like something out of a fairy tale. It was encased in shimmering white. This could have been metal, or some sort of stone. It was pure white on all sides. The remarkable thing was the capstone, a huge piece of jewel-like material that could have been crystal. There was no way we could have landed, although we wanted to. We were struck by the immensity of the thing." He circled around the structure three times, but unable to land the plane anywhere, he continued his flight to Assam, after he had sighted the Brahamaputra River, a marker on his way home.

The report was published by Bruce Cathie in the previously mentioned book. How Cathie came in the possession of Gaussman's report is not indicated and has been the cause of some

Comparison of Maoling to 1945 White Pyramid

intrigue. In an article for the November 2002 issue of the British magazine *Fortean Times*, researcher Steve Marshall offered the possibility that the Gaussman account may simply be an inaccurate retelling of a very real and well-documented sighting made by Colonel Maurice Sheahan, the Far Eastern director of Trans World Airline.

Sheahan's encounter was presented in the March 28, 1947 edition of the *New York Times*, under the headline "U.S. Flier Reports Huge Chinese Pyramid In Isolated Mountains Southwest of Sian." – read Xi'an. As the above described "pyramid tombs" are located roughly north and east of Xi'an, Sheahan's report suggested that he had identified another pyramid – an even more impressive one. In the article, Sheahan is quoted as saying that the pyramid he saw actually seemed to "dwarf those of Egypt": "From the air, Colonel Sheahan said, the pyramid seems to dwarf those of Egypt. He estimated its height at 1,000 ft and its width at the base at 1,500 feet. The pyramid, he said, is at the foot of the Tsinling Mountains about 40 miles southwest of Sian [Xi'an], capital of the province. A second pyramid, he continued, appears much smaller. The pyramid, Colonel Sheahan went on, is at the far end of a long valley, in an inaccessible part. At the near end, he said, are hundreds of burial mounds. These can be seen, he said, from the Lung-Hai railroad." The story also ran in the *Los Angeles Times* ("Gigantic Pyramid in Western China Reported by Southland Air Executive." on March 28, 1947), as well as *The Chicago Daily News*. The English language *North-China Daily News* carried a report on March 31 which added that the size of the pyramid had been calculated by comparison with the size of a nearby village.

Sheahan also noted how "when I first flew over it I was

impressed by its perfect pyramidal form and its great size. I did not give it a thought during the war years partly because it seemed incredible that anything so large could be unknown from the world. From the air we could see only small footpaths leading to a village at the site of the pyramid." The report suggests that he saw the structure several years ago, during the war years.

A photograph appeared in the *New York Sunday News* for March 30, 1947. The published photograph was cropped, so that the sticker of the newspaper photo agency "NEA Telephoto" – which is left on other news photos of the time that were printed later – is removed. But the photograph does not match the description Sheahan gave of the White Pyramid. Furthermore, he placed the pyramid at the end of a valley within a mountain range. The published photo shows a structure on a flat plain. So what to make of this? On the one hand, it seems that what Sheahan saw could have been the pyramid fields near Xi'an, but merely miscalculated their cardinal positions. But it obviously caused intrigue, resulted in the title of one book (Hausdorf's) and the title of an article in *Fortean Times* (Marshall's).

Chris Maier too looked through dozens of aerial images and found several pyramids, but all in the wrong place to be identified as the White Pyramid. They all lay several miles northwest of Xi'an; none of them were in the mountainous territory south of Xi'an, which is where Sheahan was locating the structure. And all lay out in the open, upon flat ground. Worse, he discovered that there were no locations in the area that Sheahan had identified as the site of the White Pyramid that were flat enough to have a pyramid of the size he had described.

When Maier was in Xi'an, he identified, with photograph in

hand, that the Maoling Mausoleum was the famous 1947 black and white photograph that had appeared in the *New York Sunday News*. Maier also found an English tourist book *Xian: Places of Historical Interest*, published in 2002. Under the section describing the Maoling, he read: "In the 1930s, an American pilot, taking photos in the air, took Maoling Mausoleum for his discovery of a 'pyramid' in China." Despite listing an incorrect decade (dates and numbers are apparently often mixed up in this English translation), this book would appear to offer the final bit of evidence required to offer a conclusive identification for the 1947 photo.

But was everything explained? Was Sheahan mistaken? In private correspondence with E Leslie Carlson in 1961, Sheahan admitted that the original published height of the pyramid he saw was incorrect, now listing it as closer to 500 feet tall and thus more in line with the known structures described above. But one problem remained: Sheahan located the structures in the southwest, but those structures are located in the northwest. Did he make a second error? It seems unlikely. Specifically, Sheahan located the structure in the mountains at the base of the Qin Ling Mountains, some thirty miles south of Xi'an. Maier had checked but been unable to discover this structure on the satellite photographs of the area. When he left Xi'an, the plane flew over the area where the White Pyramid was allegedly located; Maier could not make out a valley wide enough to build a pyramid of the size reported. And that seems the end of that?

On April 1, 1947, the *Los Angeles Times* published: "China Giant Pyramid Report Called False": "Nanking, March 31 (AP) - A Central News Agency dispatch from Sikang said today the provincial government had announced following an investigation that the reported discovery of a giant pyramid in Shensi Province proved to be groundless." Was this is an April Fool's joke that had begun too early, or found its climax on its true date? Or was the date of April 1 just a calendrical coincidence? Or was the denial of the pyramid's existence the April Fool's joke? Three weeks later, the *North China Daily News* carried a lengthy report on a lecture on the history of Xi'an, given at the Royal Asiatic Society on April 24. The topic of Sheahan's pyramid was raised during the talk and quickly dismissed – so an April Fool's joke after all? Or evidence of that particular stubbornness that is in evidence whenever claims of extraordinary pyramids are presented?

The story of the White Pyramid remains something of an enigma. It is extremely unlikely that the pyramid can be located where Sheahan located it. It could have been an April Fool's joke, backed up by genuine photographs from pyramids nearby. Cathie then seems to have created, or stumbled, across an altered version of this story, in which Sheahan becomes one "James Gaussman"; the names are somewhat similar when spoken, but close enough to be mistaken? I do not claim Cathie invented it; intelligence agencies are notorious for rewriting newspaper articles, altering details and then submitting them as "top secret report". Why? In short, because intelligence agencies mostly just read local newspapers and transform these stories into "top secret documents", leaving Washington with the impression that rather than sitting at their desk reading the local newspapers, their agents are having secretive meetings with their contacts in the field. If this is the case, a modern myth came about, based on a falsified intelligence report and a possible April Fool's joke – or erroneous observations by Sheahan. But though there is probably no Great White Pyramid, there are at least genuine pyramids in China.

But... there is always a "but". When journalist Julie Byron, writing an article about "Mystery Pyramids", tracked down the son of the late Col. Sheahan – Donald Sheahan – and asked him about his father's sighting, he informed her that his father had indeed seen the pyramid once before the newspapers reported on it, and added that some senior TWA executives were also on the 1947 flight; the purpose of the flight was to establish landing rights for the airline. Don Sheahan believed that his father had taken the photograph, or that it had been taken by someone on the same flight. He had gone through his father's papers, but had been unable to find any photographs of the pyramid. He did find three unlabelled news clippings that specifically mention that Col. Sheahan flew low over the area to take photographs, and two of these clippings say that he has these photographs at home, which is also stated in the *North China Daily News* story of March 31. Some of these clippings collected by his father include the NEA photograph, but he was unable to confirm that his father did, indeed, take this photograph or whether it is actually a photo of the structure in question.

As to NEA Telephoto, or Newspaper Enterprise Association: it is only credited with handling one other photo: the infamous "Roswell weather balloon" photograph, that has been at the centre of the controversy over whether or not an extra-terrestrial space-craft crashed in Roswell, New Mexico, in early 1947. Remarkable coincidence, not?

Hausdorf has been taken to task for making the White Pyramid into more of the myth than it already was. Steve Marshall is quite upset about Hausdorf's listing its height at 300 metres, a statement he made in a radio interview he gave to American radio presenter Laura Lee from a hotel room a few doors down from my room, during the 1997 Ancient Astronaut World Conference in Orlando, Florida. Challenged to verify this statement, which he no doubt made in enthusiasm rather than a scientific spirit, Marshall has continued to haunt him with this statement, rather than label it and classify it and move on. Hausdorf should be classified as the man who heralded the "new pyramid age" of China – a pioneer, with all the flaws and errors that comes with pioneers. Ten years later, thousands of tourists can – though seldom do – visit these structures. A new dawn has broken for these monuments… and it is still early morning.

FURTHER AND BEYOND

China is a big country, with several emperors and several states, spread over a long history. In short: there could be pyramids elsewhere too. As such, on July 6, 2001, the Chinese newspaper *People's Daily* reported on a "Pyramid Built 5000 years ago Found in Inner Mongolia". The story ran that a three-story pyramid, dated to 3000 BC, had been discovered in northern China's Inner Mongolia Autonomous Region:

"The pyramid, which looks like a trapezoidal hill from afar, is located on a hill one kilometer north of Sijiazi Town, Aohan County. The pyramid is about 30 meters long and 15 meters wide at its base. This is considered the best-preserved pyramid built during the Hongshan Culture period that has been found so far, said Guo Dasun, an archaeologist in charge of the excavation. Seven tombs and one altar were also found on the top of the pyramid. Archaeologists also discovered a number of pottery pieces with the asterisk character inscribed on the inner wall. The asterisk character is believed to be related to the understanding of ancient people on astrology. Among the culture relics excavated from one of the seven tombs are a bone flute and a stone ring and a full-sized stone statue of the Goddess unearthed from another tomb. What astonished the archaeologists is a one palm-sized stone genital found on the inner wall of a tomb with a small stone statue of the Goddess below. Guo Dasun said that most of these relics are found for the first time and will shed light on studying the origin of Chinese civilization." What the article shows, is that even though the Chinese pyramids are relatively modern when compared to ancient Egypt, there seems to be have been a native "pyramid cult" that extended back to the same "Pyramid Age" in Egypt, roughly 3000 BC.

China is not the sole Eastern country to have "pyramids". They have also been found on the island of Tonga, in the Pacific Ocean. But, again, this is overstating what is in truth a platform reached by a series of steps. Though they are clear evidence of a forgotten culture intent on constructing stone monuments, they are not "pyramids" – and to readdress this balance, David Hatcher Childress has labelled them "pyramid platforms".

The best candidate for being labelled a pyramid in this region is "the pyramid temple of Marae Mahaiatea" in Tahiti. It is, in essence, a larger "pyramid platform", but there were 11 steps before the platform was reached at a height of 13 metres. "Were" and "was", for even though the structure was seen by Captain Cook in 1769, it was destroyed at some point after 1897. It is known to have measured 21.6 by 81.4 metres, making it a rectangular rather than a square base – and thus not really a pyramid. Another candidate is on the island of Savai'I, where there is Polynesia's largest ancient structure, the Pulemelei Mound. The Lonely Planet guide for Samoa describes it as "this large pyramid measures 61 metres by 50 metres at the base and rises in two tiers to a height of more than 12 metres. It is almost squarely oriented with the compass directions […]. Smaller mounds and platforms are found in four directions away from the main structure. There is a relatively large platform about 40 metres north of the main pyramid and connected to it by a stone walkway." Unfortunately, the jungle there is almost uncontrollable. The pyramid has been cleared on several occasions, but when one visitor arrived there in 1996, it was overgrown and difficult to locate; so much so, that he only found it when he kicked a stone embedded in the top platform!

Probably the one true and uncontested pyramid of the area is in Candi Sukuh, in central Java, Indonesia. This is a veritable step pyramid, believed to have been constructed in 1437 AD and has been described as "Java's Ancient Erotic Pyramid". Candi Sukuh is located on the slopes of Lawu Mountain, about 25 miles east of Solo and is a Hindu temple. Though featured in all guidebooks, it is off the trodden tourist trail. One visitor calculated that only a dozen visitors a week arrived here.

In general layout, the temple conforms to the plan of most other Hindu temples: there are three precincts, consisting of three concentric terraces. But where most temples have a large square shrine, Candi Sukuh has a pyramid. It is the only Hindu or Buddhist temple to have a pyramid – and (of course) nobody knows for sure why the builders chose to incorporate a pyramid in their design.

Perhaps the answer is linked with the temple's purpose: fertility. It is replete with sexual images, specifically male members, which are not abstract phalluses like the Hindu lingam symbol, but "realistic" depictions. Any visitor is warned: carved into the floor of the entrance gateway is a large penis about to insert itself into a vulva. The stone panels along the pathway leading to the pyramid have male figures naked from the waist down. Just to the right of the path near the pyramid is a stone platform, in front of which is a rather well hung dwarf. Less erotic are the stone altars, three in the form of enormous turtles, which stand around the pyramid's western foot. A stone stairway enters the side of the pyramid and leads to its summit. The only object recovered from its summit was a tall linga, which is now in the Jakarta museum.

The pyramid looks Mayan-like, leading visitors to ponder the possibility whether anyone from the Yucatan made their way to Java. But most believe that the pyramid shape was used as an abstract rendition of the inverted female genitalia... which explains the presence of the tall linga – phallus – on top, and also conforms with the carving at the entrance, which warns the visitor to expect a phallus and a vagina.

If the pyramid form here is believed to have been the abstract rendition of the inverted female genitalia, then this is an observation we need to keep in the back of our mind, for it may be an important ingredient in trying to identify the pyramid's symbolism elsewhere... Though this insight may of course simply be wrong...

"Pyramid platforms" have also been found off the coast of

Japan. In 1985, Kihachiro Aratake, a dive tour operator in Yonaguni, Japan was scouting for a new site to view hammerhead sharks. In the amazingly clear water, he saw a megalithic structure that stretched to the limits of visibility and that appeared to be man-made, with expansive terraces interrupted by large angular steps and bounded by flat vertical walls. Though there is potentially an entire complex or town submerged off the coast of Japan, our interest is limited to the "pyramid platform" that measures about 250 metres in length, 100 metres in width and 25 metres in height. It now lies in depths of up to thirty metres of water.

Again, we find that Graham Hancock popped up on the scene and decided to propel these structures to world fame, claiming that they had been above water 10,000 years ago, thus apparently further proving his previously established theory of a lost civilisation that existed 10,000 years ago – in the Zep Tepi of the Egyptians (read: Atlantis).

The first serious scientific studies of the monuments began in 1996 by Professor Masaaki Kimura, a geologist at the University of the Ryukyus on Okinawa. Though he was largely responsible for slapping the 8000 BC date on them, in 1999, Kimura reported that the date of these structures was actually 400 AD – several millennia removed from the 10,000 years old date that "the fringe" had hoped for. Furthermore, whether or not any of these structures are artificial remains the subject of intense debate. For our purposes, we will merely conclude that it may be a "pyramid platform", but that the site definitely does not contain a pyramid. As such, there can be no debate whatsoever whether it would – if it existed – be a remnant of Atlantis or not...

CHAPTER 5

IN THE PATH OF VIRACOCHA

After the passage of the American satellite Landsat II at the end of the year 1975 over northern Peru, there was renewed "pyramid fever" when in May 1976 the Peruvian archaeologist Rodolfo Bragagnini wondered whether the photographs did not reveal a series of pyramids. Near the base of the Pantiacoila Mountains was a curious amphitheatre-like outcropping, encompassing well over one square mile (three square kilometres). Photo enlargements showed ten unexplained structures with elongated shadows, measuring between 150 to 200 yards in diameter. In private, Bragagnini speculated that the site could be a lost city. So, in December 1977, 29-year old Japanese student Sekino Yoshiharu went in search of this mystery. He claimed that he penetrated into the area and returned in the conviction that the structures were of natural origin. Under the assumption that he is correct, it shows the danger in using aerial photography and drawing conclusions based on such photographs alone.

Some may think that the above hope would finally have given Peru a pyramid. The country is indeed mainly known for the Inca Empire, which built sites such as Macchu Picchu. But Peru and pyramids, however close the two words appear to be linguistically, do not appear to go hand in hand in our minds. That, unfortunately, is due to poor education.

MOCHE PYRAMIDS

Trujillo is off the beaten Peruvian tourist track – virtually anything north of Lima is, entranced as tourists are by the Incas, living in the highlands that rise southeast of the Peruvian capital Lima, or the Nazca lines. Lima sits on the Pacific Ocean, but large sections of the capital seem uninterested in the ocean; posh districts such as Miraflores are more interested, though its posh flats and restaurants can be shrouded in the mist coming from the shore below.

Several kilometres north along this coastline sits Trujillo, capital of "northern Peru", homeland of the "Moche civilization", a civilisation that flourished in northern Peru from about 100 AD to 700 AD. The Moche lived principally in the valleys of three rivers: the Chicama, the Viru and the Moche, from which they received their name. They are noted for their elaborate painted ceramics and pottery, gold work and irrigation systems. They were primarily farmers who diverted rivers into a network of irrigation canals to augment the grounds that could be cultivated under the often austere climatological conditions. Their culture was sophisticated, although they had no written language, with their artefacts documenting their lives, with detailed scenes of hunting, fishing, combat, punishment, sexual encounters and elaborate ceremonies. And they constructed pyramids...

West of Trujillo sits the so-called "Chan Chan complex"; to its east sits the Huaca del Sol and the Huaca de la Luna – collectively known as the "Huaces del Moche": pyramids. Chan Chan was the capital of the Chimu Empire, which rose to prominence around 1100 AD – postdating the Moche culture, and its two pyramids which sit on the eastern shore of the Rio Moche.

Once again, we find that pyramids sit in close proximity to a river – though this feature is not prominent for the Mayan pyramids. The pyramids were set apart from the urban centre by a large graveyard.

The Huaca del Sol is the largest pre-Columbian structure in Peru and the largest adobe structure in the Americas. The stepped pyramid is made up of four major platforms that rise from the northeast, where an access ramp may have stood, towards the southwest where there is a fourth, lower and narrower platform. The name "Huaca del Sol" is really a misnomer, as there is no evidence to connect the building with any solar cult. There are, however, no indications as to the original name of the site. The pyramid is an adobe brick temple in a barren desert landscape, one of several ruins near the peak of Cerro Blanco. The nearby Huaca de la Luna is a better-preserved but smaller temple. Archaeological evidence suggests that this temple was used for ritual activity, as well as a royal residence and burial chambers.

The Moche controlled the area from 100-700 AD; the basic huacas – temples – predate this era by approximately a century, before the Moche began to enlarge these structures, turning them into pyramids. By 450 AD, eight different stages of construction had been completed on the Huaca del Sol; each time, new layers of brick were laid directly on top of the old, in the end numbering over 100 million adobe bricks.[23] The number of different maker's marks on the bricks suggests that 93 different communities or groups of builders contributed bricks to the construction of the Huacas, making its construction a major community enterprise. Antonio de la Calancha, a Spanish historian of the early 17th century, stated that 200,000 Indian workers would have been required for its construction and it is logical to assume that these men were not slaves, but worked either on a salaried or voluntary basis.

After the collapse of the Moche civilisation, the site maintained its religious importance, with items of Wari, Chimu and Inca offerings having been recovered. Less reverence was shown by the Spanish Conquistadores. In 1602, the waters of the nearby Moche River were redirected by the Spanish to run past the base of the Huaca del Sol, in order to facilitate the recovery of gold artefacts that were believed to be hidden inside the temple. No such objects were found. It is estimated that approximately two-thirds of the structure has been lost due to this purposeful destruction, as well as erosion due to El Niño and looting. The remaining structure stands to a height of 41 meters (135 feet), though is believed to have originally been about 50 meters (150 feet) high. To preserve of what is left, the pyramid is "off limits", but continues to be an amazing sight, its pyramid edges still sloping at a sharp 77 degrees to the horizon. Virtually nothing of a step pyramid that once sat on its base remains.

Fortunately, the Huaca de la Luna, 500 metres from the Sun

Temple of the Sun, Moche

Temple, has remained largely intact. It contains many colourful murals with complex iconography and has been under excavation since 2004. Whereas the Huaca del Sol is believed to have been a burial mound for Moche rulers, the Huaca de la Luna is believed to have served as a ceremonial complex, though it contains burials as well.

Today, the Huaca de la Luna is coloured by the soft brown of its adobe brickwork, but just after its construction the temple was decorated in registers of murals which were painted in black, bright red, white and yellow. The sun and weather has since faded most of these murals out, but murals used in earlier phases of construction can still be seen inside the Huaca. Many of these depict a deity now known as Ayapec, a Quechua word meaning "Wrinkle-Face", the name given to the deity by the later Inca, because of his physical appearance. He was the master of life and death, the god that kept the human world in order.

The Huaca de la Luna has three main platforms, each one serving a different function. The northernmost platform, at one time brightly decorated with a variety of murals and reliefs, was destroyed by looters. The central platform has yielded multiple high-status burials that were accompanied by a variety of fine ceramics, suggesting that it was used as a burial ground for the Moche elite. The large southern platform was the site of human sacrifice rituals, which are depicted in Moche painted ceramics. After their sacrifice, bodies of victims would be hurled over the side of the Huaca. Some may consider such stories to be based more on tall tales told at the time of the Spanish Conquest than genuine accounts. Though often the case, it is not the case here: in 1995, 42 skeletons of adult males were found at the foot of the

Huaca, all of whom showed signs of grizzly trauma, usually a severe blow to the head. Ayapec, to maintain balance in the world, was believed to require human sacrifice.

Why did they install this complex here? The answer seems to be that it was because Cerra Blanco was a sacred mountain; some of the sites' features actually incorporated rocky outcrops of this mountain, such as in one of the patios of the huacas. Archaeologists thus assume that the site may have honoured the apus, the mountain spirits, of which Ayapec was probably one.

There is also a remarkable similarity between the pyramid's form and the shape of the Cerra Blanco behind it. If you look at the Huaca del Sol sideways, from the Huaca de la Luna, it has the same general outline as the hills behind it. The same interplay between pyramids and landscape is also present at Teotihuacan, where the Pyramid of the Sun, as seen from the Pyramid of the Moon,

Trujillo Huaca del Sol with pyramid-shaped mountain in background

conforms to the shape of the mountain sitting in the distance behind it. Let us however conclude that here too, along the Moche river, there is an intricate interplay between the pyramids and the landscape, as is the case in most if not all of the other pyramid sites.

Two further Moche pyramids are found at the complex of Huaca Rajada, in Sipan, further north, and just outside Chiclayo. The complex of Huaca Rajada ("Split Huaca") derives its name from a large cut made through the site by road-building. This huaca consists of two large, badly- eroded pyramids to the east of the road and a smaller platform on the opposite side of the road, where the Lord of Sipan was discovered. The other two structures, large, badly-eroded, stepped pyramids, seem to have been remodelled in post-Moche times and are still under investigation.

The site is indeed famous for the El Señor de Sipán (The Lord of Sipan) tomb, the tomb of a warrior priest who died around 250 AD. The temple was discovered by Walter Alva in 1987 and has since been heralded as one of the major archaeological discoveries of recent decades. The site was a burial site for the Moche nobles from 200-600 AD. The tomb of Lord Sipan is important as it was found intact. It contained 1200 pieces of gold and precious stones, two young concubines, two guards armed with shields and breastplates, as well as a guardian of the tomb, whose feet were mutilated to symbolise his eternal obligation to keep watch. Also found were ceremonial goblets, necklaces, bracelets, earrings, noseplates, wristplates, rattles and ceremonial knives, all encrusted with precious stones. Like the pyramids near Trujillo, there seems to be a direct relationship between royal burials and the construction of pyramids.

THE PYRAMIDS OF TUCUME

Near Sipan is also one of the major pyramid concentrations of Southern America: the pyramids of Tucume, known as "the Valley of the Pyramids". The beginnings of Tucume are to be found in a legend recorded by Father Cabello de Balboa (1586 AD). It states that Cala, a grandson of the mythical Naymlap, founder of the Lambayeque royal dynasty, went to Tucume to start a new urban centre. The founding of the settlement seems to have occurred around 1000-1100 AD, when the old regional centre at Batán Grande, to the south of the Chancay river, was burnt and abandoned. The pyramids belong to this era and therefore postdate the Moche culture.

Rumours of a vast hoard of gold prompted the famous Norwegian scientist and explorer Thor Heyerdahl, whom we came across at the pyramids on the Canary Islands, to investigate the area. The plains of Tucume are part of the Lambayeque Valley, the largest valley of the North Coast of Peru. Tucume lies on what was once the southern margin of the valley, but thanks to the Taymi irrigation canal (over 43 miles long), which brings water northward from the Chancay river, it is surrounded by fertile agricultural land.

The Taymi canal is not a modern canal: it seems that construction coincided with the foundation of Tucume, around 1100 AD. It is a formidable effort of engineering and while at it, the people had time and energy to erect no less than 26 major pyramids. Though there are 26 structures in total, archaeological work is focused on the three main structures: the Huaca Larga, Huaca 1 and the U-shaped "Temple of the Sacred Stone". The Huaca Larga, or the Long Pyramid, is the longest adobe structure known to date. It measures around 2,300 feet in length, from the foot of La Raya

Mountain to the short, straight access ramp on the north end. Originally, it was a freestanding platform, but it was remodelled into is current shape by adding the step pyramid on top. Long corridors and dividing walls partition the complex, and researchers have identified a northern, possibly public, ceremonial area and a southern area devoted to cooking and manufacturing.

All buildings of this period, which marks the Chimú domination of the area, were painted in the colours red, white and black. Like the Moche pyramids, the walls were decorated; one mural depicting flying birds in the "Temple of the Mythical Bird" stands out from the rest. Apparently, the Chimú tried to convert Huaca Larga into a structure that resembled Chan Chan, found near Trujillo.

Heyerdahl and his team opened forty tombs. So many artefacts were uncovered that a museum was built at Tucume. Four burial chambers were found in the 600 meter long Huaca Larga pyramid. Inside these chambers, the bodies of 16 female weavers sacrificed to the gods were found. These date from the Inca period (1470-1532 AD).The weaving of delicate textiles, an activity that the Inca often entrusted to consecrated women, was therefore practiced at Huaca Larga and may well date back to Chimu or even pre-Chimu times. It once again underlines that though we have neatly divided Peruvian history in various "cultures", the sites show continuity in use, with one culture not abandoning a sacred site and constructing its own, but merely "taking over" the management of the site.

In a different room atop Huaca Larga, archaeologists discovered three male burials, one of them of a mature, robust man with insignia, suggesting he may have been the Inca governor of Tucume. Shortly after these burials took place, all standing structures on Huaca Larga were razed and huge fires were lit on top. Oral history recalls that enormous fires were lit by the Spanish colonists to convince the local population that Tucume was the gate to purgatory. Purgatorio (purgatory) is still the name by which the local people refer to the complex today. But despite this "Christian warning", local shaman healers ("curanderos") continue to invoke the power of Tucume and the central La Raya Mountain in their rituals, assisted by shamanic techniques and the psychoactive San Pedro cactus, holding weekly rituals which researchers believe have been going on since Inca times – if not before.

Like the Cerra Blanco at the Chan Chan complex, the Cerra La Raya forms the focus of this site. All 26 structures are built around this circular and cone-shaped hill, which rises 197 metres high and which is also known as "El Purgatorio", or Cerro Purgatorio. Its official name, Cerra La Raya, is derived from a ray fish that according to legend lives within the hill. It is clear that this hill was held sacred – and continues to be held sacred – and is at the core of why these structures were erected here. Access to the sacred mountain was originally restricted, as many cultures felt that humans should not enter the domain of the "apu", the mountain god, though there is evidence of later Inca constructions on the hill, such as an altar site.

To understand this complex, we need to look at the "Temple of the Sacred Stone", which is a small, unpretentious, rectangular U-shaped structure to the east of Huaca Larga. It is considered a major temple that pilgrims had to pass by before entering the complex. The walled roadway system of this section of the Lambayeque valley leads straight to this temple, and then onwards to Huaca Larga. The revered object of this temple appears to have been a large, upright boulder in the middle of the one-room building: the "sacred stone". Archaeologists "officially" do not know what it represents, but in my humble opinion, it represents the "navel of the world", identifying this site as a sacred centre. Such navel stones have been found in various religious centres throughout the ancient world, with the navel stone of Delphi probably the most famous example. As the Cerra La Raya was off-limits for humans, the "sacred stone" was used as the mountain's physical presence in the sacred precinct, the only part of the apu they were allowed to come close to, if not touch. The small "Piedra Sagrada" represented the larger omphalos of "Cerro Purgatorio".

The identification of the site and the mountain with Purgatory is probably not a coincidence. The Spanish conquerors probably understood the local rituals and compared them with their Christian upbringing. Purgatory and fire go hand in hand in the Christian tradition, where purgatory is a state of existence, the domain of the dead who were with sin and where the fire purges the soul of its sin. There are clear references to Purgatory in both the Old and the New Testaments. In 2 Macchabees 12: 43, 46 the Jewish practice of praying for the dead stated that "it is therefore a holy and wholesome thought to pray for the dead that they may be loosed from their sins." The sins of these dead were removed by what was believed to be a long, slow "simmer" of fire. St Cyprian and St Augustine spoke of purification by fire, which "purges away all sin by suffering." Is it coincidence, or design, that elsewhere, pyramids – by their very name – are linked with fire? I specifically refer to the New Fire festivals in Teotihuacan in

Mexico. Could it be that similar rituals as in Teotihuacan were practiced here, in northern Peru?

NOT JUST LINES...

Say Nazca, and you say lines, made famous by Erich von Däniken. They were first spotted when commercial airlines began flying across the Peruvian desert in the 1920s. Passengers reported seeing mysterious primitive landing strips on the ground below – and von Däniken turned this observation into speculation, capturing Mankind's imagination at a time when we went to the moon and wondered whether someone else had once come down to Earth. If so, was Nazca a spaceport?

Though the "landing strips" theory works from the air, on the ground itself, the land is definitely unable to accommodate a smooth landing. Furthermore, the lines exist mainly because its builders exposed the underlying soil; in this desert landscape, with no rain and hardly any wind – conditions similar to our Moon – any trace made, can remain visible for centuries.

There are more than 800 uncannily straight lines, some running for many kilometres. They are interspersed with spirals and other geometric shapes and trapezoidal spaces covering many square metres, as well as animal depictions, like a monkey with a curved tail, a spider and a humming bird. Some researchers have argued they have an astronomical component, but others doubt this interpretation, saying stellar alignments could be purely by chance – based on the gigantic numbers of lines that exist, some must be orientated towards an astronomical event. British author Tony Morrison subscribes to the theory that the lines formed sacred "spirit lines", aligned to various hill and mountain peaks surrounding the Nazca plain. The Nazca lines would therefore be a gigantic "soular map"[24], in which sacred centres were connected by straight lines (linked with spirit flight), themselves aligned with the mountains and their apus; in short, a complex where man could interact both with the ancestors and the mountain gods, performing rituals and/or acts of remembrance at the various sanctuaries that were normally located at intersections of two lines. If Morrison is correct, then the Nazca plateau was a "landscape of the Otherworld" and could thus be seen as another example of an otherdimensional landscape portrayed on Earth. We have come across this already at Teotihuacan, but we also note that Zitman's interpretation of the Egyptian pyramids equally concludes that they depict the form of the Hennu bark, the boat taken by the soul to reach the Afterlife.

Few know that the Nazca culture also built pyramids, at Cahuachi, which overlooks some of the Nazca lines. Italian archaeologist Giuseppe Orefici has been excavating the site for the past few decades, bringing an archaeological team down every year. The site is made up of six pyramids, the highest reaching to about 70 ft, overlooking a walled court of 4050 square yards and sitting in the centre of the ancient city. The town itself is split in half by the river, with the six pyramids constructed around a small natural hillock, which we could argue was therefore held sacred – and thus fitting in the template of where people in the region implanted their pyramids.

Is there a connection between the Nazca lines and the city of Cahuachi? At first, it was felt not to be the case. When the site was first excavated in the 1950s, it was thought to be the centre of an expansionist military empire, though its population was known to have been small. In the 1980s, archaeologists like Giuseppe Orefici began to overturn these ideas. They could find no evidence for a bustling urban centre and certainly no sign of military activity. Instead, the city seemed to have been dedicated solely to ritual and ceremony. They concluded that the city was the destination of many pilgrimages, which meant that the population greatly increased at times of these ceremonies. Orefici also believed that the pyramids, lines and the "Great Dune of Nazca" formed part of one, huge ceremonial landscape.

Nazca lines

Rather than a military complex, Orefici interprets Cahuachi as a city of priests who were the guardians of the Nazca culture and religion – if not the lines. On the other side of the pampa lay the big, urban settlement of Ventilla. It is between Ventilla and Cahuachi that the Nazca people created their lines. Could the template that we have identified elsewhere not only apply to where the pyramids were built, but to the entire Nazca region as a whole? If so, we know that at Trujillo, the urban settlement and the pyramids were set apart by a large graveyard; should we interpret the Nazca lines as a giant graveyard too? I will merely note that it does coincide with the conclusions reached by Tony Morrison.

Despite its present fame, the period of most activity at Cahuachi is believed to have been short lived, about 200 years, and the site was abandoned around 200 AD. What happened at Cahuachi that made its existence so short-lived? At the moment, no-one knows for sure. But what is known, is that between 300 and 350 AD, two natural disasters struck the region: a great flood and an earthquake, whereby the latter cataclysm split the temples in two. Archaeologists actually found dead bodies under the fallen walls. Still, this disaster occurred one century after the city is believed to have been abandoned. Why… is a question that the future may help to answer.

CARAL

These Moche, Chimu and Nazca pyramids are impressive centres, proving without a doubt that Peru has its rightful place on the Pyramid Map of the World. The pyramids were often built over successive "cultures", covering a period of roughly 1 AD to 1400 AD. Built in bricks – like the Zoser Pyramid at Saqqara – they fit in the overall "pyramid template", which has been, as everywhere else, slightly adapted in certain details, but overall, applied. It would be pyramids that would illustrate a recent breakthrough in

Peruvian history: it occurred with the discovery of the Caral complex, 22 km inland and 160 km north of Lima. In total, there are 18 ancient complexes along the Supe Valley, of which Caral is one. Dated to the 3rd millennium BC – indeed – it has overthrown the Peruvian chronology, pushing it back by several millennia... but also pushing the presence of pyramids in the New World back to the 3rd millennium BC – the same millennium when the Egyptians erected their pyramids along the river Nile.

The Caral complex was initially noticed in 1905, but apparently forgotten afterwards. Archaeologist Ruth Shady, of the Archaeological Museum of the National University of San Marcos in Lima, began excavations at Caral in 1994 and has continued since, since 1996, co-operating with Jonathan Haas, of the American Field Museum. In decades to come, Caral will be largely seen as Shady's legacy. For our debate, she made two major contributions: first, Shady felt that the "pyramids" were just that: pyramids; before, they were considered to be natural hills. Secondly, her research led to the announcement of the carbon dates of the site, published in the magazine *Science* on April 27, 2001. The article stated that the complex dated from 2627 to 1977 BC, making, as mentioned, the Caral complex contemporary with the Pyramid Age of Egypt, but also predating any other pyramid in South America by about two to three millennia. Caral was thus identified as the earliest of the sophisticated civilizations in the Americas.

The heart of the site covers 150 acres and contains six stone platform mounds – pyramids. The largest pyramid measures 154 by 138 metres, though it rises only to an altitude of twenty metres; two sunken plazas are at the base of the mound and a large plaza connects all the mounds – pyramids. It was terraced with a staircase leading up to an atrium-like platform, culminating in a flattened top, housing enclosed rooms and a ceremonial fire pit – evidence of a New Fire ceremony?

All pyramids were built in one or two phases, which means that there was a definitive plan underlying their construction. The design of a central plaza would later also be incorporated in similar structures across the Andes, thus showing that Caral was indeed a true cradle of civilisation and not an "oopciv", an "out of place civilisation" that predated but did not influence its successors.

Around the pyramids, many residential structures were found. One house revealed the remains of a body that was buried in the wall, though it appears to have been a natural death, rather than evidence of human sacrifice. Amongst the artefacts that were recovered were 32 flutes made from pelican and animal bones, engraved with the figures of birds and monkeys. It shows that though situated along the coast, its inhabitants were aware of the animals of the Amazon – and this suggests that they had entered that jungle.

Caral is hard to accept. It is very old. Still, its dating of 2627 BC is beyond dispute, based as it is on carbon-dating reed and woven carrying bags that were found on the site. These bags were used to carry the stones that were used for the construction of the pyramids, thus proving that the pyramids date from that era too. Furthermore, the material is an excellent candidate for carbon-dating, thus allowing for a high precision.

How did this culture begin? Before Caral, there is no evidence (yet?) of an earlier civilisation in the region. All that has been found is the existence of several small villages. Some may argue that aliens or ancient Egyptians landed ashore and "brought" civilisation to the region. But more arcanely, it is suggested that these villages merged together in 2700 BC, quite possibly based on the success of early agricultural cultivation and fishing techniques. The invention of cotton fishing nets must have greatly facilitated the fishing industry and it is believed that this excess of food might have resulted in trade with the religious centres, i.e. Caral. As the economy thus had a surplus of workforce, it either meant unemployment, or using the workforce in a new endeavour – such as pyramid building, or, more specifically, enhancing the religious complex of Caral? If this scenario is correct (and it probably is), we should draw yet another parallel with ancient Egypt, where the pyramid building is believed to have been the result of an excess labour force, following social and economic changes (see chapter

Caral, Peru

7). It is a remarkable coincidence that the same social situation existed, at the same time, on two opposite sides of the globe and that pyramid building was apparently the only or most logical solution the "Employment Agency" could come up with. Is it coincidence, or evidence of design? Alternative researchers will certainly soon reopen this debate, but archaeologists steer well clear of it.

For an unknown reason, Caral was abandoned rapidly after a period of 500 years (ca. 2100 BC). The preferred theory as to why the people migrated is that the region was hit by a drought, forcing the inhabitants to go elsewhere in search of fertile plains. The harsh living conditions have since remained in place. Though they went, we do not know where these people went to; perhaps towards the coast, perhaps towards the Amazon, perhaps elsewhere. Wherever they landed, they did not immediately begin to construct new pyramids, suggesting that in their new settlement, times were once again tough and they could not devote themselves to religious building projects. But the knowledge of the pyramid somehow was kept alive and would, like a rekindled fire, begin to relive after 1 AD.

Caral was at first believed not have had a written system of communication, which made its existence as an advanced centre, both religious and specifically economically, all the more remarkable. But since 2001, archaeologists have recovered an artefact that may represent one of the earliest forms of communication in the world, roughly equivalent in age to the cuneiform script of Mesopotamia.

The Inca civilization, three millennia later, had quipu, a complicated system of knotted cords of different colours. Many of these quipus were destroyed by the Spanish Conquistadors, but approximately 200 of them dating no earlier than about 650 AD have been recovered. Although archaeologists do not all agree about the function of the knotted strings, one fairly compelling argument is that the quipu was a method of record keeping – essential for traders, which for the Supe Valley culture is believed to have been its transformative element.

The recovery of quipu from Caral, if the context and dates are correct, suggests that there was a continuity between Caral and the Inca civilization, underlining our previous observation of a continuation between the "various" Moche, Chimu and Inca civilisations. It also means that quipu as a tradition is at least 2000 years older than previously assumed. Thirdly, and most importantly, if quipu were indeed a form of written communication, they are among the earliest forms of writing in the world, only slightly younger than cuneiform, which has been identified at the Mesopotamian site of Uruk, in approximately 3000 BC. As a very recently identified civilization of the world, Caral has the potential to help rewrite human history – and the Pyramid Age.

Caral had a population of approximately 3000 people. But there are 17 other sites in the area, allowing for a possible total population of 20,000 people for the entire Supe valley. All of these sites in the Supe valley share similarities with Caral: they had small platforms or stone circles as part of local religious life, but it seems that Caral was the religious glue that monitored and dictated the religious life of the civilisation as a whole.

A December 2004 article by Haas, Creamer and Alvaro Ruiz reported on the results of an additional 95 radiocarbon dates from

13 sites along the neighbouring Pativilca and Fortaleza river valleys. A total of twenty sites with large platform mounds found in this survey vary from 10 to 100 ha in area, and have stratified house floors, sunken circular plazas and irrigation works. Approximately seventy radiocarbon results from eleven of the sites support a date range of about 3000 to 1800 BC, nicely framing the carbon dates of Caral and thus cementing its place on the timeline. Like Caral, they had a mixed economy of irrigation-based agriculture and marine foods from the nearby coast.

Caral has offered new insights, a new dawn; but the site itself may soon have an unhappy ending. According to the World Monuments Fund (WMF), Caral is one of its hundred important sites under extreme danger. Shady argues that if the existing pyramids are not reinforced, they will disintegrate further. The environmental conditions are so extreme that this will not be an easy task. The task is further complicated by the fact that thieves roam the area, in search of archaeological treasures. Though the Peruvian government has given half a million dollars in aide, Shady argues that it is simply not sufficient – and the WMF even argues that the Peruvian government is a contributing factor to the site's decay. Private donators have stepped in to help, such as Telefonica del Peru. But Shady is hopeful that the main source of income will be tourism. For a long period of time, tourists were shunned from the site as they might inhibit the ongoing archaeological excavations. But as of 2006, the site has been opened for tourism and the hope is that the site will soon become part of the tourist route, on par with the enigmatic Nazca lines and the idyllic Machu Picchu. Though much less famous than those two sites, it is much older and offers the traveller the possibility to see pyramids – in South America.

LIMA PYRAMIDS

Few people on visits to Peru will have seen these pyramids; it will take several years before the main tour operators will see a need or desire to go off the beaten track and take in the Moche, Chimu or Caral sites. There is, however, one pyramid in the capital Lima that is incorporated in the tourist route. I had seen and photographed it myself, and I did not even remember I had visited it until I started research for this chapter. I had indeed seen the "Huallamarca pyramid" and taken some photographs. That I had forgotten about it, implies that it is not very impressive; but in retrospect, I do wish I paid more attention to it at the time.

The pyramid sits in San Isidro, a suburb of Lima, which prides itself on being home to many Peruvian artists. But it is the Huaca Huallamarca, a pre-Inca burying temple which dates back to the 4th century, which is where our bus stopped, where we got out for ten minutes to take a few photographs, and return on the road – I assume to the Gold Museum, but can't remember. Huallamarca is a stepped pyramid, with a slope ascending to the top; the structure is surrounded by streets and high rise buildings, but we should be grateful it was not demolished, as it most likely would have been in the western world. What is disappointing, and what did not make it stand out at the time of my visit, is that the pyramid looks as if it was constructed yesterday. That is the result of extensive restorations, so much so that the site is now used for concerts and exhibitions, illustrating the cultural spirit that roams through the district.

Another "Lima pyramid" is the Pachacamac Pyramid, sitting

about 30 km to the south of the capital, along the beach. It is mainly seen by those having opted for a Peruvian beach holiday. Pachacamac means "the Earth's Creator" and immediately reveals the emerging link that seems to exist between pyramids and the "creation of the world". Pachacamac was the creator god of the people who lived along this stretch of the Peruvian coastline in about 500 AD.

The site had at least one pyramid, cemetery and multicoloured fresco of fish – reminding us of that other fish which was supposed to live in the central mountain of the Tucume pyramid complex. Like the Nazca pyramid complex, Pachacamac was also a centre for mass pilgrimage. Later, the Huari (ca. 600-800 AD) sponsored the construction of the city, probably using it as an administrative centre. Later, the Inca maintained it as a religious shrine and allowed the Pachacamac priests to continue functioning independently of the Inca priesthood, as at other pyramid centres further north. This complex included an oracle, which the Inca consulted for important matters affecting the State. Pachacamac was actually taken into the Inca pantheon, being worshipped along with the sun. The Inca constructed five additional buildings in the complex, including a temple to the Sun, on the crest of the hill above Pachacamac's precinct.

In 1533, Francisco Pizarro sent his brother to seize Pachacamac's treasure, but only seemed to find a wooden idol. This was found to be sitting on a snail-shaped platform, with the wooden carving stuck into the earth inside a dark room, separated from the rest by a jewelled curtain. The setting may imply that the statue itself may have been the oracle, kept inside a labyrinth and behind guarded doors, allowing access to the high priests only.

Pachacamac-pyramid in Lima, Peru

Myths about Pachacamac are sparse and confused: some accounts, for example, identify him as Manco Capac's cowardly brother Ayca, while others say that he, Manco Capac and Viracocha were the only three sons of Inti, the sun god. Another story says that he made the first man and the first woman, but forgot to give them food and when the man died and the woman prayed over Pachacamac's head to his father Inti to make her the mother of all the peoples of earth, Pachacamac was furious. One by one, as the children were born, he tried to kill them, only to be beaten and to be thrown into the sea by her hero-son Wichama, after which he gave up the struggle and contented himself by becoming the supreme god of fish. Just as these deities promised to return one day, we will return to these deities later on too.

THE INCA HOUSE OF CREATION

The Inca themselves do not appear to have been great pyramid builders, though they took over the management of several existing pyramids along the Peruvian coastline. As impressive and beautiful as Macchu Picchu or Cuzco are, there are no pyramids, though sites such as Sacsayhuaman, on top of Cuzco, are clear evidence that the Incas were able to work with gigantic stones. Such accomplishments goes against the notion that the Spanish called the Inca culture "diabolical" and until recently, it was deemed to be "primitive". The Inca civilisation was therefore often not included in school curriculum in Western Europe. But in recent decades, pressure from "sensationalist authors" such as Erich von Däniken has forced the archaeological world to look at these monuments. Von Däniken posed the central question as it stood in the 1960s: if the Inca were primitive or stupid, how had they been able to create their often complex buildings, such as Sacsayhuaman or Ollantaytambo? If indeed stupid, who aided them? If no-one could be identified, did we not need to look towards extraterrestrial beings? Today, it is clear that the Inca were not "stupid" – nor diabolical. And thus, we no longer need to look towards the sky for answers. It is now clear that the Inca built upon centuries of knowledge accumulated by their predecessors, available to them from across the enormous area they united. They were the last in a series of indigenous group of rulers who had toiled the land for hundreds of generations, for thousands of years; they did not "just" appear out of nowhere.

I can't blame the Inca for not building pyramids: building pyramids at altitudes sometimes in excess of 9000 feet may stretch the notion of fun – most people have problems walking at their normal pace from the hotel to the boats moored on the shores of Lake Titicaca, at 3821 metres (12,536 feet) the highest navigable lake in the world. But there is always a but...

Ollantaytambo

This "but" is not well-known and only found "locally", in Peru itself. The local archaeologists are beginning to offer a new understanding about the Inca's religious framework. It is written down in a book that is on sale only locally and frequently used by the local tour guides. Walking back from the impressive Ollantaytambo complex to the bus, I got my copy, trying to fight of souvenir sellers I did not need, trying to make my way to the only female souvenir seller who was also selling the book. The book's cover has a photograph of the sacred valley, between Cuzco and Macchu Picchu. The authors are Fernando and Edgar Elorrieta Salazar and they focus on Cuzco and the "Sacred Valley" – a valley that is devoid of pyramids, but harbours the sites which are the destinations of most tourists that have come to Peru to see the Inca civilisation. The sacred valley continues south of Cuczo, towards Lake Titicaca. It was on an island in this lake, the Island of the Sun, that the Inca legends state that the creator god, Viracocha, appeared on Earth. It is from here that Viracocha's voyage began, walking through this sacred valley that became sacred as a result of this voyage. Amidst spectacular scenery that is quite similar to the barren mountains of my adopted Scotland, the valley descends to an altitude of 3400 metres in Cuczo and 2800 metres in Macchu Picchu. It is said that Viracocha continued on this path, walking in a southeast-northwesternly direction, until he reached the Pacific Ocean... promising that he would return... one day.

The legend of Viracocha and how he "walked" the sacred valley brings us face to face with the enigmas of the Incan civilisation: Tiahuanaco, Cuczo and Sacsayhuaman, Ollantaytambo and Macchu Picchu. They designate key sites on his voyage, the "Holy Road" travelled by the Creator Deity. The recent fame of Macchu Picchu has somewhat upset the importance of this "path" as a whole, but the Salazar brothers clearly identify that Ollantaytambo was in Inca times much more important. Though at first apparently much less impressive than Macchu Picchu, its siting within the landscape is nevertheless complex – and contains more symbolism than Macchu Picchu. Again, though there is no pyramid at Ollantaytambo, it is a sacred site and it has been carefully positioned with the natural landscape, with which it interacts.

Research has identified that the Inca civilisation had specific preferences of alignments to certain mountain tops, evidence of which can be found in Macchu Picchu. These mountains were the residences of the apu, the mountain gods and every year, a major procession still makes it way up one mountain top, to come face to face with the divine abode of god. But the pilgrimage is hard and only fit men dare to go on it. Many – most – both now and in Inca times, had to experience their religious life in the valleys below.

At Ollantaytambo, most guides point out how the impressive megalithic structures were placed on the side of the hill and the effort that went into them. But the Salazars point out that what gave the site its sacredness was the profile of a human being, identified with Viracocha, which can be clearly distinguished in the mountain side opposite. They have further identified that the temple at Ollantaytambo is aligned to certain notches in that hill, the alignment of which coincides with important sunrises in the calendar. In Ollantaytambo, it is the stone face of Viracocha towering over the site that is part of the Inca legend; it is this presence that shows that the creator god is still present, literally "watching over" his people… and the modern tourist.

There are more such solar alignments incorporated in this area's sacred layout: the Salazars identified that in the valley below Ollantaytambo, the first beam of the sunrise falls on the so-called Pacaritanpu ("House of Dawn"), where the gods became divine and which they identify as the site of the Inca's mythic origin – a place of creation. When you look upon this "House of Dawn" from Ollantaytambo, it is hardly identifiable and definitely does not look important, unless it is looked upon with the "right eyes". At first, there appears to be nothing but a cultivated field. Though dating from the Inca time period, the question why an ancient field should be so important, is a good one. But a second glance will reveal that the entire field portrays a gigantic pyramid. So, rather than build an actual pyramid, the Inca have used an "optical illusion" to create a pyramid out of delineating fields. It is a pyramid, but it's a pyramid in two dimensions, though when viewed from the right location – which was marked as sacred – it looks like a three-dimensional pyramid.

Am I to take this seriously? Is it just their imagination? No. The Salazars have identified such "optical plays" in other Inca structures, identifying various animal forms in the hills and designs of Macchu Picchu. The design of the capital Cuzco was ingeniously created to form the image of a puma, the "royal animal" – the southern American equivalent of the African lion and the Mesoamerican jaguar. And many of these constructions were a mixture of natural shapes, augmented – "stressed" – through human intervention.

The Salazar brothers say that the Incan legends identify the Pacaritanpu as the site from which the first Incas came into the world after the Flood, the end of the previous age and thus the point of creation of the new world. "So wrote Cabello Balboa in 1586 without understanding the magnitude of the monument he was describing, because this place [...] was not built to be seen from the dwellings of man [...] but rather from the heights where the mountain powers have their abode." [25] This abode is a place called Intipuncu, or Gateway of the Sun, and is located five hours of continuous ascent from the valley floor. Climbing this mountain would be suicide (and I "of course" did not have the time... and it rained at the time as well...), so I will let the Salazars describe what all tourists can see on the pages of their book: "the succession of nine terraces used for cultivation (and provided with irrigation canals and founts of water) appears to the observer to make up the two main faces of a pyramid [...] Recent studies carried out in the area agree with a tradition that says that the soil for these terraces

House of dawn - Ollantaytambo

was brought from far away in order to build them."[26] This sand thus sits in the same category as the mica of Teotihuacan and that other sand inside the Great Pyramid; "out of place materials" incorporated into the pyramid shape.

The Salazars draw specific attention to two areas on one "side" of the pyramid, which they describe as "two enigmatic 'windows'": "In Inca mythology these 'windows' symbolize the doorway through which one gains access to the world of the unknown." So it seems that these windows were like a gateway, an entrance – a stargate? – into another dimension. "They also represent the sacred receptacles with which, by means of light from the sun, the upper world communes with the interior world in the cycle that activates the principle of generation that give life to man and the Earth." So, once again, the sun and stories about

(re)generation of man and the Earth – linked with floods and creation, as we saw before and elsewhere.

Whereas an astronomical component hasn't been identified (yet?) for the pyramids along the Peruvian coastline, this two-dimensional pyramid does have an astronomical connotation. "In accord with this cosmology, at dawn on the winter solstice (June 21) the day on which they commemorated the appearance of the Incas, a ray of light filters through the high mountains to enter the place where tradition said the Incas first entered the world as gods." That site is this pyramid – or to be more precise, one of these two "windows". "Later the sunlight defines one of the edges of this pyramidal construction with astonishing precision, evidence that it was purposely aligned with the sun. Thanks to the information given to him by the astronomer Inca Juan Yumpa, the native chronicler Guaman Poma (1613) described this characteristic: 'And so in the planting, on the month and on the day, they look at the high peaks through which the sun rises and by the clarity of the ray of sunlight that gives onto the window, they plant and harvest food in this kingdom.'" Finally, the pyramid, or "House of Dawn", also has a solar spectacle at the summer solstice (December 22), when sunlight falls on the west face of the Pacaritanpu.

Though the Inca did not build an actual pyramid, they incorporated their mythologies in more ingenious ways into the landscape, resulting in an intricate play between the mountains, the stars (the sun) and the calendar.

What does it mean? Modern research suggests that the Sacred Valley of the Vilcamayu and Urubamba rivers symbolised the Milky Way – further parallels with the Avenue of the Dead in Teotihuacan and other pyramid and religious centres. William Sullivan reports on the intentional flooding of Cuzco, when in January, at sunset, they opened the floodgates and let a torrent of water rush through the streets of the capital: "As the floodwaters scoured the streets, they washed along the ashes of all the burnt offerings from the previous year. Runners waited at the bottom of the city, at the point where the Tullumayu and Huatanay rivers convened, and swept the offerings into the Vilcamayu River. As the flood approached them, the runners began a race of more than thirty miles along the banks of the Vilcamayu, all the way to Ollantaytambo, where the river begins to drop off steeply toward confluence with the Amazon."[27] Sullivan and others have seen the Vilcamayu as the "River of the Sun", taking on the form of the Milky Way. The inhabitants of Cuzco, it seemed, remembered the Flood of the previous world by creating one annually. It clearly signified a renewal of life, the New Year, and washed away the "ashes" of the previous year. And, in what should now be unsurprisingly, as the flood washed away the ashes of the old fires, a new fire was lit – a New Fire Ceremony. At Ollantaytambo, "at a bridge spanning the river, [others were waiting] and threw a final offering of coca into the torrent. Throughout the night, innumerable torches, stationed along the river bank, lit the runners' way. [...] The river, then, was meant to carry the offerings right out of this world. [...] According to Molina, this event began at sunset in the month of January, that is, when the southeast/northwest branch of the Milky Way was up and moving toward the zenith." [28]

Why is there this connection between the Milky Way and the soul? Because it was seen as the path the souls took on their way from this realm to the "Otherworld". Did the lights along the runner's course represent both the stars and the souls of the deceased, along which the runners raced towards Ollantaytambo, the site near the "Pyramid of the Dawn", where the gods became gods – like at Teotihuacan, where a ceremony involving water and fire equally seemed to "make gods"?

On an astronomical level, John Major Jenkins believes that the answer as to why there is such a connection can be found in the Galactic Centre, the centre of the Milky Way. He believes that ancient cultures, across the world, saw this celestial region as the origin, and goal, of the soul's travel, a stargate into another dimension. He has argued that this knowledge was incorporated into the calendar of the Maya and that the same knowledge was depicted on the landscape of Peru.

In this vision, Cuzco, the capital, which is known to have been labelled the "navel of the world", is situated between the two previously mentioned rivers. This corresponds with the dark "gate", north of the constellation Sagittarius, which Jenkins interprets as the "gate" or "window" to this other dimension. He further argues that the point of creation was underlined by having the sun standing in the centre of this Galactic Centre – an event that will occur again on December 21, 2012 AD. Of course, one of the rivers, the Vilcamayu, was the "River of the Sun". But more intriguing is that within this interpretation, Lake Titicaca is the location of the Galactic Centre – a point of creation, which corresponds with the ancient Incan legends. So let us quickly set course to this lake… as fast as the lower levels of oxygen allow us to.

LAKE TITICACA

For most, Lake Titicaca equals Tiahuanaco and its famous Gateway of the Sun, on top of which we find a depiction of Viracocha, as if anyone who would step through it, would become like the God. It could indeed be interpreted as a veritable stargate.

Modern borders have placed Tiahuanaco in Bolivia, not Peru. But despite this modern reorganisation, it is clear that the "Gateway of the Sun" continues the knowledge that we have come across in Peru; we are, once again, in front of a "window" of the sun. And there is a pyramid… or mound.

Part of this complex is the Akapana platform – sometimes

labelled a pyramid, or by Alan Kolata as "the sacred mountain of Tiahuanaco". The Akapana measures 688 feet on a side and is 49 feet high, orientated towards the cardinal points, as all good pyramids do. The earthen interior was shaped like a seven level stepped pyramid and faced with fitted andesite stones. Still, because it was tehn covered, it is now more like a large mound than a pyramid.

The Akapana was part of a set of twin "pyramids" with Puma Punku. Both terraced mounds have their doorways facing the rising sun – dawn. Both Puma Punka and Akapana possess twin staircases on their east and west sides. This east-west axial design is repeated throughout the Tiahuanaco site. Still, the Akapana was not original to the site. It seems that around 700 AD, three centuries into the existence of Tiahuanaco as a powerful city, there was a sudden change in direction, with all construction efforts turned towards building what would become the largest structure in the Andes: the Akapana pyramid. In the end, the project seems to have required too much effort; the pyramid lay unfinished when the city was abandoned.

Little remains of the Akapana, as – alas the fate of so many pyramids – it was used as a quarry by builders, even from as far as Bolivia's capital La Paz. Only about ten percent of its facing blocks remain. Inside, archaeologists have uncovered a network of zig-zagging stone channels linked with fine ashlars. These were meticulously angled and jointed, and served to sluice water down from a large reservoir at the top of the structure, through a series of descending levels, to a moat that encircled the entire site and that came to the pyramid's base on its southern side. Tour guides, point out that the pool was used by the ancient astronomers to study the stars from reflections in the pool – I wonder why they couldn't just as easily look up towards the stars directly. Indeed, archaeologists believe that instead the site was connected with a cult of the rain, or river – in short, with the element water. I would argue that the site was connected with the story of the Flood, and that it was linked with the story of the creation of the new world.

We have arrived in Tiahuanaco from Ollantaytambo and Cuzco; we have travelled up the sacred valley. During my stay in Peru, I took the train from Puno (on Lake Titicaca) to Cuzco, watching the landscape slowly move by – and this train goes slowly, much slower than a car. On my way to Cuzco, I reminded myself of a myth, recorded by the Spanish priest Cristobal de Molina, in ca. 1573: "In the province of Ancasmarca, which is five leagues from Cuzco, in the Anti-suyu division, the Indians have the following fable. They say that a month before the flood came, their sheep [llamas] displayed much sadness, eating no food in the daytime, and watching the stars at night. At last the shepherd who had charge of them asked what ailed them, and they said that the conjunction of stars showed that the world would be destroyed by water. When he heard this, the shepherd consulted with his six children, and they agreed to collect all the food and sheep they could, and go to the top of a very high mountain called Ancasmarca. They say that as the waters rose, the hill grew higher, so that it was never covered by the flood; and when the waters subsided, the hill also grew smaller. Thus the six children of that shepherd returned to people the province." The story seems hardly different from Noah and his Ark that strands on Mount Ararat. That story originated in Mesopotamia and is equally believed to have recounted the end of one age and the arrival of a renewed earth.

This renewal is what was expressed in the New Year and its various festivals; in ancient Egypt, the New Year began with the flooding of the Nile; in Cuzco, with the opening of the sluices; in Teotihuacan, the possible water system that was installed along the Avenue of the Dead may equally have been employed for such a New Year festival, which involved the extinction of the old fires, to culminate in the New Fire ceremony.

Whereas some may argue that Molina merely reported stories that the Indians had already learned from previous priests – which seems unlikely, given Molina's scathing comments that follow the above excerpt – it is clear that the stories were indigenous. It means that here, in Mexico, or the Middle East, at varying times in our history, we have the same recurring myth: creation, renewal and transformation, both of the earth and of men, involving two of the four elements: water and fire.

BECOMING VIRACOCHA

Viracocha was said to have created the world at Lake Titicaca: he created the sun, moon and stars and commanded them to rise above a cliff of black rock looming out of the lake, known today as Island of the Sun. Then, Viracocha was said to have created Mankind, all the tribes of the Andes, each already with its distinctive dress, language and customs. This underlined the notion that each tribe formed part of a larger whole and that true understanding would only occur if one looked at the totality, rather than individual tribes in isolation. Each tribe possessed a statue, commemorating the creation by Viracocha of the tribal ancestor. Each ancestor had arisen from a particular sacred site within their territory, whether it was a cave, spring, tree trunk, or other structure. Each such site was known as a pacarina, literally "place of dawning" – a memory to the place of their creation. But above all, there was one "sacred centre", more sacred than all secondary sites of creation.

There is a clear continuous line going back from sites such as Caral to the Inca cities that these were deemed to be sites of creation, but also of transformation; the emphasis was on transforming oneself in Viracocha, who is in essence just like Quetzalcoatl. Many scientists, authors and archaeologists have noted that there is little to distinguish Quetzalcoatl from Viracocha and that both seem to have a common origin.

As elsewhere, Peru has a clear connection between the landscape, the stars, the gods and the "process of transformation", from man into god. The name Akapana is derived from "Hake" and "Apana", two words in the ancient Aymara language, still in use in the area. Hake means "human" or "man", while Apana means "to die". Akapana could thus mean "Place where humans die". We could ask whether it was a place of sacrifice, or a site where death was conquered; where Mankind could become a god, like Osiris in Egypt, or Quetzalcoatl in Mesoamerica... as in so many other pyramid sites.

As elsewhere, new evidence of this connection continues to be uncovered almost on a daily basis. In early 2006, archaeologists discovered the oldest known celestial observatory in the Americas: a 4,200 year old structure marking the summer and winter solstices was found at Buena Vista, about 25 miles inland in the Rio Chillon Valley, just north of Lima. "It is on a totally barren, rock-covered hill looking down on a beautiful fertile valley," said Robert Benfer of the University of Missouri. The observatory was built on the top of a 33 feet tall pyramid with precise alignments and sightlines that provided an astronomical calendar for agriculture. As to who built it, archaeologists so far have got not a single clue.

This discovery pushed the envelope of civilization farther south and inland from the coast, as well as showing that they, even then, had an important place in astronomy in their life. The summer solstice marks planting time, as the Rio Chillon begins its annual flooding, fed by melting ice higher up in the Andes. The flooding deposits fresh soil on the land, fertilizing the crops and eliminating the need for manure from domestic animals – all very similar to the Nile, all very similar to stories of floods that marked a new era; a new creation, a transformation both of the land and the people. The local hero who accomplished this act of creation and transformation was Viracocha... What's in a name?

CHAPTER 6

EUROPE'S PYRAMIDS

A pril 2006 was a busy month for pyramids. On Thursday April 6, 2006, the international press reported the discovery of a Mexican pyramid. The Hill of the Star (Spanish: Cerro de la Estrella) at Iztapalapa, on the outskirts of Mexico City, had just surrendered its secret: it was the site of a 1500 year old earthen pyramid of the Teotihuacan culture, which, like the pyramid of Cholula, was now located under a Roman Catholic church.

Ceramic fragments and ceremonial structures convinced archaeologist Miriam Advincula to begin mapping the area in 2004, while archaeologist Jesús Sánchez said that "when they first saw us digging there, the local people just couldn't believe there was a pyramid. It was only when the slopes and shapes of the pyramid, the floors with altars were found, that they finally believed us." Their work resulted in a 22 metres (60 ft) tall, 150 metres (500 ft) wide pyramid that was originally carved from the hillside in 500 AD and which was abandoned in about 800 AD. The discovery underlined that pyramids, despite what many people would think, can easily disappear from sight and can, over time, become overgrown and "forgotten".

The following week, the world press went into overdrive, this over the possible discovery of a pyramid in Bosnia. It was the follow-up to a news item that ran on October 31, 2005, when certain news feeds (including the Associated Press) ran the story that a "Bosnian explorer finds 'Europe's first pyramids'." This statement, as so many headlines need to be, was erroneous. We have already come across the Greek pyramids, but even leaving those aside, there is another contender for the title of Europe's "first" pyramid… and it can be found in Italy.

THE OLD MOUNTAIN

Rome has a pyramid; one of its subway stations is even named after it. It is the "Piramide Cestia", the tomb of Caius Cestius, who died in 12 BC. Cestius spent time in Egypt and ordered

Pyramid of Cestius, Rome

that his slave should be freed upon his death, but not before they constructed his pyramid in the final 330 days of service to their master. The structure is 36 metres (120 ft) high and may be a familiar sight for anyone who has taken a taxi ride between the airport and the centre of Rome – the route normally taking you past this pyramid, which is illuminated by night. It is built of a very firm composition of mortar and small stones, faced with tablets of white marble. The original entrance was by means of an inclined shaft about halfway up the northern side of the Pyramid. This shaft (opened in the 7th century AD) led straight to the centre of the vault, covering the grave-chamber. The interior walls were decorated with stuccoes and fresco paintings divided in panels by means of painted candelabra that framed female figures. Impressive as it is and intriguing as it is to find a pyramid in the heart of Rome, unfortunately, the pyramid itself is not displayed to its full potential; part of it sits lower than street level and a wall has been built right onto two sides of the pyramid, to enclose the park area behind.

But the pyramid of our interest is not in Rome. In early 2003, the "pyramids of Montevecchia" ("Old Mountain"), only ca. 30 miles from the Italian city of Milan, were discovered through the use of satellite and aerial imagery. These pyramids are now completely covered by ground and vegetation and appear to be natural hills, but the possibility of something more was enough for the Czech WM magazine and their editor in chief Georg Wojnar to visit the area. They arrived on May 8, 2003, in an effort to locate and survey the site. The team soon learned that discovering their location from the ground proved more difficult than imagined, with the team becoming "impressed" with the driving abilities required to negotiate the roads that lead towards the hills. After two days of failed attempts, they finally succeeded in locating the pyramids and carrying out an initial survey.

The team's conclusion appeared in the June 2003 issue of WM. They had come to the conclusion that the first pyramid was estimated to have a base of 100 metres, with a height of fifty metres. In total, three potential pyramids were surveyed, with one pyramid showing clear signs of stones worked into the structure, close to the surface. A platform with an oblong superstructure with a size of 18 by 9 metres was also discovered. All three structures had an inclination of 42/43 degrees. The sides of all pyramids were aligned and were offset from the cardinal points by approximately 7 to 12 degrees northeast. The team wondered whether this was an error in design or a sign of something more intriguing. From the initial aerial surveys, there was speculation that their layout compared to the pyramids of the Gizeh plateau – and thus to the

Montevecchia second pyramid © Bill Ingle

Belt of Orion. The Czech team stated that their on-site research had showed that the pyramids actually aligned with the passing of Orion at the sunrise of the summer solstice. The Czech team felt that the site should be known as "the Italian Gizeh".

After I wrote an article on the Italian and Bosnian pyramids for *Nexus New Times*, Bill Ingle wrote to me, wondering whether I was familiar with the fact that he had been involved in an expedition (a somewhat grandiose term to use, but still) to the Montevecchia site. I was not. "The Great Coordination Point Expedition" had, like the Czech team, located and inspected the site during two fall 2004 visits.[29] Before Ingle's arrival, he had discovered that the three hills were located in the Parco Regionale di Montevecchia e della Valle del Curone. I will quote from Ingle's expedition notes: "We found Montevecchia without difficulty, then continued through Alto Montevecchia. [...] The hills are immediately behind the villages of Monte and Cereda, a small parking lot carved out of the base of the first hill, 'la collina dei cipressi' (Hill of Cypresses)." Ingle and team explored the area and the site, but after three days on site, felt disappointed. A second visit occurred in November 2004, at the end of which Ingle came away with the feeling that "for anyone wondering whether actual stone pyramids will be found lurking within the hills, I suggest this is not the case. In my opinion these are natural hills that were shaped and augmented long ago, but only archaeological spadework will provide a definitive answer."

Despite this initial on-site investigation, several questions remain, including whether these are manmade, natural or artificially elaborated structures. Amongst the other outstanding questions are the questions who and when these were built. To try and provide an answer, the Czech team asked the Italian archaeologist professor Gregoria for his input. He provisionally dated the structures to 3000 BC, making them largely contemporary with the Egyptian pyramid building age. But no remains in the vicinity have been found that can shed any further light on these structures and there is no known civilisation in the region that built similar structures at the time. As a consequence and despite the findings by the Czech team, some have argued that the Montevecchia structures may be nothing more than a terraced hill with stone supports.

THE VISOCICA PYRAMID

When the Czech article became known outside of the Czech language, several people commented that "You would think every archaelogist and film crew would be racing to Montevecchia to investigate..." But the Italian discovery failed to excite the media, if only because no archaeologically led investigations were – and have been – carried out. Europe might have a pyramid... but no-one was too sure... and not many seemed to care. Two years later, all that had changed.

In late October 2005, an emigrated Bosnian explorer Semir "Sam" Osmanagich believed that he could announce the first uncontested, ancient and large pyramid in Europe. The story ran in the leading Bosnian newspaper *Dnevni Avaz*, reporting matter of factly that "the 45-year-old is so certain two pyramids are hidden in Visoko valley that he has spent some 16,000 euros (20,000 dollars) researching the area, located either side of a river about 30 kilometres (18 miles) from the Bosnian capital. Residents of the nearby town of Visoko have long known about the presence of the two structures they always referred to as 'pyramids' but none of them was ever intrigued enough to investigate further." Let us note how the suspected pyramid site sits in a valley, next to a river… and by these facts alone fits into the "pyramid template".

Osmanagich lives in Houston (Texas) and his fascination for ancient cultures had made him visit many ancient structures of the New World, resulting in the publication of several books, mostly for Bosnian consumption. In April 2005, he was promoting his latest book in Sarajevo, when Senad Hodovic, director of the Visoko Historic Heritage museum, came up to him during the event and invited him to Visoko, to see "the pyramid". Osmanagich remembers that "while I was on the top of the Visocica hill, I noticed that the shape of the hill is a symmetrical geometric form, aligned to the cardinal points of the compass and with a flat top. Across the valley, there was another hill called Pljesevica, with obvious triangular sides. Even though the hills were covered with forest, I immediately 'recognized' the pyramids."

An initial survey showed that the main structure measured ca. 70 metres (230 feet) high, with a square base of 220 by 220 metres (730 by 730 feet). The survey also confirmed that it aligned precisely with the cardinal points of the compass – as did the second pyramid nearby. A postcard made from aerial photography from 1954 also showed the obvious pyramid-like structure of the hill, which looks anything but natural. Again, all the indications suggested that the hill could indeed mask a pyramid underneath.

This is where the investigation in Montevecchia had stopped two years before. But Osmanagich did not want to leave it at that: "Three months after my initial visit, I gathered all necessary permits and started with a geological survey in order to confirm my hypothesis. The first survey, conducted by geologist Nadja Nukic, was performed in August of 2005 and geological tests of the soil, penetrating 17 metres (56 feet) into the structure, showed 15 anomalies, suggesting that some layers of the hill were man-made. I had solid proof that the hill was not a natural formation." Specifically, Nukic herself was most impressed with three layers of brown polished stone that lie an equal distance from each other underground. It was at this point that Osmanagich decided to invest.

Osmanagich returned to the site in October 2005, to carry out further geological and initial archaeological research, with fascinating results. He thus found that the walls of the Visocica structure were found to be built from Breccia stone blocks. When these blocks were cleaned, it was found that they were placed like bricks in a brick wall: the upper block was moved inwards in relation to the lower one. Some of the stones were removed and were found to have a flat and smooth surface... all indications that these structures were built, not natural geological features.

The team also used probing wells, the results of which showed that the structure was indeed a stone step pyramid: a flat plateau, approximately 2.5 metres wide, is followed by a steep slope of thirty metres, then another plateau, then another steep slope with the same angle, a pattern that is repeated to the top of the pyramid, which has a plateau. The team also discovered that "the entrance causeway is paved with manufactured sandstone blocks. They are ten centimetres thick, cut by human hand, polished and then transported to this area." Amazingly, the length of this paved causeway is an enormous 420 metres (1/4 mile).

Small-scale excavations continued until early November, when winter set in, with the work focusing on what may have been the entrance to a pyramid-shaped temple on the top of the structure. Intriguingly, the team had also found underground tunnels: "There are a number of 'intersections' along the way. Most of them are covered with dirt and rocks, but we will begin to clean them from the spring of 2006 onwards", Osmanagich concluded.

Originally, Osmanagich believed that an existing hill had been reshaped into a pyramid shape and then coated with a type of primitive concrete. But by November 2005, after larger areas had been unearthed, the team concluded that the whole hill was actually a stone structure. Within a period of six months, the Bosnian team had carried out an amazing amount of work, resulting with an unambiguous statement that "Visocica hill could not have been shaped like this by nature", the statement given by lead geologist Nada Nukic. "This is already far more than we have anticipated, but we expect a lot more from further analysis."

Osmanagich believed, based on his travels, that pyramids came in pairs, one symbolising the sun, the other the moon. It is indeed a conclusion that could be drawn from the available evidence, though I personally would not yet subscribe to the theory that pyramids "have" to come in pairs. Still, he had seen such "twin pyramids" guarding the entrance to a valley in the New World and believed that the Bosnian pyramids conformed to this model. The Visocica hill was thus labelled "the Bosnian pyramid of the sun"; the "Bosnian pyramid of Moon" was believed to be under the neighbouring hill of Pljesevica. Osmanagich stated that "beside these two artificial structures, several other mounds exist in the same valley, and they tend to have very geometric (triangular) sides and clear, linear breaks. Dr. Amer Smailbegovic (Reno,

Nevada) has applied remote sensing techniques that showed that the Bosnian pyramid of the Sun and Moon exhibit flat, triangular sides with clear geometric brake-lines between the flat sides. The observed phenomena are not to be confused with triangular facets naturally occurring in a tectonic setting, for those occurrences only exhibit single-side triangulation and are uneven in appearance, whereas the observed anomalies exhibit two or more, even triangular sides. The results of thermal inertia suggest that the pyramids are composed of less consolidated material and tend to cool faster than the surrounding mounds (which are presumed to be denser). This finding is congruent with what would be expected from an artificial structure – lesser density materials, porosity, internal cavities all contribute to increased loss."

In short, it seems that the valley was potentially littered with pyramids, a possibility that is actually not too difficult to accept: it is known that pyramids often come in clusters, and are often "heaped" together in single valleys. Furthermore, all these mounds

Bosnia 1954 postcard

are mutually equidistant and all align to the cardinal directions. Three structures are of an approximately same height, but differ in overall size. Osmanagich believed that we could thus "freely speak about the Bosnian Valley of the Pyramids."

These two initial probes, in August and October 2005, had pushed the Bosnian pyramid beyond the Montevecchia structures. It was also enough to create a media frenzy. But newspapers want conclusions, so Osmanagich gave in to the pressure and felt that he had to provide an interpretation of these structures, though archaeological excavations had only just begun. "Who built them? How old?" Osmanagich stated that in his opinion, the hills were reshaped by the Illyrian people, who inhabited the Balkan peninsula long before Slavic tribes conquered it around 600 AD. Little is known about the Illyrians, but Osmanagich suggested that they were more sophisticated than many experts had so far suggested – evidence for which would be the pyramids themselves.

But Osmanagich's books also spoke of Atlantis and civilisations that could have existed 10,000 years ago. In an effort to whip up the frenzy, he was "unfortunately misquoted" about the possible age of these pyramids: 27,000 years. What Osmanagich had said, was this: "It's very well known that a medieval Bosnian town existed on the top of the hill between the 13th and 14th century. Artefacts that show traces of small Roman and Illyrian observation posts (2000 and 2500 years old, respectively) have also been found. It is a classic example that a later culture built their villages on top of earlier structures. […] These findings show that it is more than 3000 years old. We know that Bosnia has continuously been populated for 27,000 years. So, the pyramids must have been built in between these two dates." So the date of their construction could be anywhere between 1000 BC and 27,000 BC – though he personally favours the Illyrian period, thus providing much more conservative dates than those quoted by the media. But conservatism has never made for good headlines...

UNEARTHING A PYRAMID

Considering the importance of the discovery, the original team established a foundation called "Archaeological park: Bosnian Pyramid of the Sun", which was ratified by the Bosnian Justice Department and which had a number of Bosnian archaeologists, geologists, geophysicists, historians and other experts amongst its members. Osmanagich observed that it was "very interesting that for the first time in a long period, Bosnian politicians on all political levels have united to give support for this project." Like the building of pyramids had been a community project, in Bosnia, investigating one had equally united the country.

Osmanagich was named project director and his team started a five-year archaeological project on April 14, 2006. Shortly before, he told me in an interview that "hundreds of experts and students, cleaning crews and enthusiasts, will come to the middle of mountainous Bosnia to take part in a fantastic archaeological event. We plan to once again work until the first snow comes at the end of October."

The media's interest exploded as soon as the first shovel was dragged up the hill. The start of excavations on April 14 2006 was widely reported and when the two excavation sites scheduled for the Pyramid of the Sun (on the eastern and northern slope) almost immediately found that some of the blocks had been laid on top of each other, to a depth of four blocks, the media was invited back. This time, the media not merely ran a news item: they sent television crews and reporters on the scene, all demanding an interview with Osmanagich, all reporting back to their newspapers and radio and television stations about what was happening just north of the Bosnian capital.

Most of these reports included an update of the state of excavations, statements from Osmanagich, normally supported by a member of his scientific team, especially some of the geologists on his team. After all, the primary question which had to be answered was whether or not this hill was natural or man-made. Providing an answer to that question was the bailiwick of geologists, not archaeologists; and the Bosnian geologists on site remained firm in their conviction that this structure was man-made.

But in the western world, these reports seemed to upset

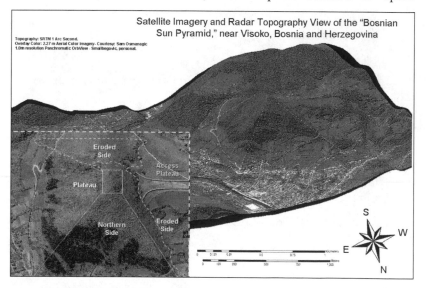

Aerial map of Sun Pyramid, Bosnia

western-based archaeologists. For some reason, they felt left out. It has indeed grown customary in the western media to seek "an alternative point of view" in any report, which is often highly critical, if only so that a controversy can be created out of nothing. When newspapers ran their initial stories, most had not contacted western scientists on this topic, if only because none had visited the site, none were involved in the excavation and no-one seemed to feel their input was required, as Bosnian experts were on site and on hand to provide a scientific opinion.

But it was clear that the western scientists did not want to be left out, and tried their utmost to wriggle their way in. Thus, Penn State University Professor Garrett Fagan aired his opinion that "they should not be allowed to destroy genuine sites in the pursuit of these delusions[...] It's as if someone were given permission to bulldoze Stonehenge to find secret chambers of lost ancient wisdom underneath." Boston University's Curtis Runnels, an expert in prehistoric Greece and the Balkans, commented on Osmanagich's misquoted opinion about the age of the pyramids, which, as we noted, some newspapers had placed at 27,000 years old. Runnels stated: "Between 27,000 and 12,000 years ago, the Balkans were locked in the last Glacial maximum, a period of very cold and dry climate with glaciers in some of the mountain ranges. The only occupants were Upper Palaeolithic hunters and gatherers who left behind open-air camp sites and traces of occupation in caves. These remains consist of simple stone tools, hearths, and remains of animals and plants that were consumed for food. These people did not have the tools or skills to engage in the construction of monumental architecture." And he was, of course, correct. Seeing Osmanagich had given me the correct setting of that statement, identifying it as an error made by the journalist, I tried to highlight this correction in certain circles of the Internet where these people occasionally gather. I was astonished how deadset this group of scientists was to "kill, kill, kill" Osmanagich and the Bosnian pyramids. Some even questioned what my source was, and whether I had actually published the article containing the rectification! Pointing out to these people that the article had appeared so far in three continents and soon in more than five languages, I also argued that they should perhaps make direct contact with Osmanagich, to verify that what the written media had reported, was factually what he had stated. That fell on deafmen's ears and many continued to critique Osmanagich solely on what they read in the media. That, of course, is not a scientific approach at all from these "respected scientists", but the media seemed to be able to let them get away with it.

The critics have not only zoomed in on the misquote of a date of 27,000 years old, they equally used Osmanagich's previous statements against him. Osmanagich, as I reported already, had written books on ancient civilisations, in which he spoke of Atlantis and structures as old as 10,000 years ago. Some newspapers reported that Osmanagich had claimed that the Bosnian pyramid was 10,000 years old. I knew that Osmanagich had not been drawn to date these structures in any radio or television interview – which one can easily verify. I asked him directly whether he had at any point given an interview in which he dated the pyramids to 10,000 years old. His response was a clear "no". Call me stupid, but I accepted Osmanagich's denial. Furthermore, I had seen an interview from a Bosnian newspaper, syndicated to a Belgian newspaper, in which the

Bosnia Pljesevica, Pyramid of the Moon

reporter specifically noted that Osmanagich could not be drawn into an opinion there.

But the main attack came in a letter to the editor of *The Times* on April 25, 2006. It came from Professor Anthony Harding, president of the European Association of Archaeologist. He referred to Osmanagich's theories as "wacky" and "absurd" and expressed concern that insufficient safeguards were in place to protect Bosnia's "rich heritage" from "looting and unmonitored or unauthorised development". He specifically criticised the media, in this instance *The Times*, for airing Osmanagich's viewpoint without advising the likes of him and his western colleagues. Indeed...

The instrument used to attack Osmanagich was that "his" excavations were "destroying" the medieval village on top. His opponents stated that it was "sacrilege" that he was digging in search of fantasy evidence that this was a pyramid, endangering the archaeological remains on top. The "medieval village" referred to was a fort, used by the medieval Bosnian kings. It had been burnt down in the 16th century by the Turks and little remained, if only because over the past few decades, not a single archaeologist had been interested in preserving the site. Statements such as that of Enver Imamovic of the University of Sarajevo that the excavations would "irreversibly destroy a national treasure" were therefore largely made to eradicate his profession's neglect of this "national treasure", blaming any potential damage to the "national treasure" on Osmanagich. Unfortunately for Imamovic, his colleagues came to inspect the site soon afterwards and concluded that the excavations in no way had or were harming this "national treasure".

Just a few days after the initial upheaval, a team of miners were sent into the tunnel system located under the mountain and which had been identified as a priority for exploration. The miners reported to have found 3.8 kilometres of tunnels, several of which crossed each other at 90 degrees. Though the team had been equipped with oxygen, they had had no need to use it; every thirty metres, they had felt a breeze, suggesting that despite the extent of the system, ventilation had been incorporated into its design.

The tunnels also yielded objects. The first object discovered was a "great monolithic plate of 7 or 8 ton, with 90 degrees edges." Elsewhere in the system, inscriptions were found, but whether these have a direct relationship with the pyramids remains unclear, as part of the system was known to the local population and may have been explored, if not used as a site of graffiti.

CONTROVERSY 2

Next event: the Bosnian president, Prime Minister and several other politicians visited the site. These visits themselves were used by the critics to argue that the Bosnian government was trying to create a pyramid out of a natural hill, to put itself on the world map. In short, the critics were arguing that the Bosnian government were supporting an archaeological fraud – which needs to be classified as a "conspiracy theory", rather than a "scientific opinion". And it requires extra-ordinary evidence, which the critics have not provided... at all.

Next: on June 1 2006, the excavation of the Pyramid of the Moon opened. As at its sister site, almost immediately, at a depth of only 40-80 cm, blocks and slabs (15 cm thick) were found, as well as a type of "pavement".

Next: Dr Aly Abd Barakat, an Egyptian geologist, visited the two excavation areas, on the north and east faces of the structure. He concluded that the blocks on the eastern face are of a similar construction to those found in Egyptian pyramids: handmade and polished. Barakat stated that the ancient Egyptians polished their stones to reflect the sunlight and wondered whether perhaps the same effect was aspired to by the Bosnian pyramid builders; if so, this would indeed be a "Pyramid of the Sun". Barakat also agreed that the blocks, four metres by 1.5 metres in size, were brought from a different location. These sandstone blocks obviously had to come from quarries, but no-one was sure which one exactly. There were some quarries near the river Neretva (in Herzogovina), suggesting once again that some of the raw materials for pyramids were often sourced from distant locations.

Studying excavations on the north side of the pyramid, Barakat concluded that the blocks were equally handmade, using a mould to form the blocks, which consisted of an ancient 'concrete'- like mix. He also noticed a white line, some 0.5 cm thick, between the blocks, indicating a cement-like substance had been used to adhere the blocks together. Finally, Barakat visited the third excavation site, located at the base of Pljesevica Hill, and concluded that the "steps" that form the sides of this pyramid were also manmade. Some twenty metres above this excavation, he noticed a large number of blocks placed symmetrically, suggesting they were equally manmade.

Barakat had barely left the site, before the critics attacked him. Indeed, they attacked him, not his observations; they wondered "whether he was indeed a geologist" and "whether he had the proper scientific credentials". Such questioning is particularly obnoxious. In short, when someone states that "he is not sure that Barakat has the proper credentials", he implies that Barakat has not, whereas the problem really lies with the person uttering the statement, who has obviously not tried to validate whether or not Barakat has the proper credentials. Throughout, characters like Osmanagich and Barakat were attacked at such a personal and obnoxious level, rather than debating their findings.

Hostilities reached a crescendo on June 8, when Professor Anthony Harding, who six weeks before had written his letter to *The Times*, apparently visited the site. I say "apparently", for no-one on site had seen or spoken to him during his visit. On June 10, however, Harding spoke to the media. He claimed that he had visited the site and had "rejected claims that a hill in central Bosnia is a man-made structure that many local residents insist is a pyramid." "Not any evidence at all has been found", he stated. He argued that "no pyramids are known in Europe, and there are no records of any ancient civilization on the continent ever attempting to build one." That, of course, is totally wrong, as we know – and we will merely to the Greek pyramids as evidence that Harding is wrong. Harding stated that he visited the site "briefly" and "looked at the same stone block Barakat said were manmade", which he identified as "a natural formation". "I've seen the site, in my opinion it is entirely natural." His "opinions" got reported across the world, but what also got reported was the statement by the leading scientists on site: they noted that they were unaware of Harding's visit; he had not identified himself and as such had not been given "site access" to inspect the excavations closely. Furthermore, he himself stated that his visit had been "brief". Furthermore, Harding had to concede that he did not visit any of the other sites in the area, had thus not observed the stone pavements nor seen the tunnels. Soon, it was learned that Harding had spent no more than fifteen minutes on site, and this between nine and ten o'clock in the evening! But that did not stop him from concluding with this statement: although he had not seen the stone pavement, by looking at photographs, "I would not believe it to be archaeological. It looks to me as a natural stone pavement."

Here was a classic standoff: one scientist who had "briefly" visited the site and had spent radically less time there than most of the 10,000 tourists that came to the site each weekend, that scientist stated that it was all "natural". On the other side of the ring, a geologist who had inspected all sites, personally, closely and not "briefly", who argued these were manmade. In this contest, Harding was furthermore unlucky that Osmanagich was not in

Bosnia during the period of his visit, which meant that instead, Mario Gerussi, a "proper scientist" and the director of excavations, had to comment about the behaviour of his colleague, which slightly backfired on Harding. Though Harding could criticise Osmanagich for being "not a scientist", though he attacked Barakat whom was "possibly not a geologist", what Gerussi was saying was clear: Harding had aired an uninformed opinion, seeking no dialogue with his fellow scientists on the site. This made the media realise that Harding could be on a personal vendetta here. To seek resolution in this standoff, they quoted how just days before, Prof. Dr. Dario Andretta, Rector at the Italian University of Lumuci in Rome, a geologist and sedimentologist, had visited the site. The visit had occured in cooperation with the University of Zenica. The media stated that "accompanied by the Project Leader Mrs. Nadja Nukic, [...] Andretta verified the drill shafts [...]. They have discussed and analysed the exhibits and their opinions were in accordance to the conclusions drawn from the scientific studies." Andretta had used the proper scientific channels, had spoken to the archaeologists on site, and agreed with their conclusions: that this was a manmade structure. Victory therefore seemed to be for the "manmade" camp and the victory seemed about to be consolidated when Andretta said that after his return to Italy, he would ask the Italian Government to investigate their requests about future co-operation and to provide necessary resources for the research. He also proposed to proclaim an International Conference in order to unite groups of qualified experts for present and future projects. Finally, Andretta accepted the Foundation's invitation to be the Leader of the Geological Committee. He declared: "My impression is that what we have to do is of high importance for today's research. We are convinced that what has been discovered is of the highest interest for the geological and archaeological field of research. The different [...] structures are man-made. The first impression we have is that those structures have been well thought out, in order to be adapted to the morphology of the geological zone. As for now, we don't have indications on how the structures have been exactly build, to which civilization those structures belong, nor for which usage they were destined. However, we have an important starting point for further in depth research." That was a proper scientific opinion, which was so sadly lacking from Osmanagich's critics.

If you think Harding had a go at Osmanagich... a man named Mark Rose attacked the discovery with what seemed to be vile and hate. Rose, who continuously refers to debate as "the Ice Age Bosnian pyramid story", was invited by Osmanagich to inspect the site personally, but it seems Rose never took up the offer. When it was pointed out to Rose that Osmanagich, though he had spoken about Atlantis, but that this should not be held against him and that he had never dated the pyramid to anything as extreme as 10,000 years old, Rose rather desperately tried to find – and failed – first hand evidence that Osmanagich had indeed said as much. His statement that "we are still awaiting any credible evidence that these hills [...] date to the end of the Ice Age" and that "the burden of proof is on those making it", are perfect examples of a man solely out to create controversy, and cast himself in the role of chief whip. Anyone can create controversy and the techniques used by Rose are very basic, but equally sad.

Another example of Rose's attitude: in early June 2006, Rose was already looking for "a report" on the excavations.

Archaeologists are famous for turning in reports at best one to two years after the excavations and sometimes taking as long as twenty years. Still, Rose – and some inspired by his line of thinking – was demanding that two months and thus not even half-way through the first season, "reports" were produced? Though to give Rose some credit: other critics were actually calling, six weeks in, for a "detailed map" of the complex – something which has taken Egyptologists mapping the Gizeh plateau more than a decade! Either time passes more slowly in Egypt than in Bosnia, but if not, it is clear that not everyone is judged equally.

The rollercoaster ride continued. On June 12, Agence France-Presse stated that "Barakat said that he had sent a report on the site to one of the world's leading Egyptologists, Zahi Hawass, who had recommended him to the foundation leading the excavation work." Rose commented that "I have not been able to confirm the claim he was recommended by Hawass", which surely is purely his own fault and problem: it is his inability that has caused this, yet he injects it into his article apparently to cast doubt over Barakat's claim. It gets worse: "So Harding, an archaeologist, says it's natural. Barakat, supposedly a geologist familiar with pyramids, says it's a 'primitive pyramid'." "Supposedly a geologist"! What would happen if someone wrote: "So Harding, apparently an archaeologist who claims to have excavated Bronze Age site but has never worked on a pyramid site, says it's natural. Barakat, a geologist familiar with Egyptian pyramids and various natural formations, says it's man-made."

A further bodyblow to the "natural" camp came when yet another group of scientists and experts, sent by the Federal

Ministry of Culture, arrived, to inspect once again that the "medieval town" was not damaged. The committee was accompanied by Mrs. Dr. Zilka Kujundzic-Vejzagic, one of the biggest opponents of Osmanagich. After the inspection, Kujundzic-Vejzagic declared: "The works of the foundation Archaeological Park Bosnian Pyramid of the Sun did not damage [the site] nor [have] the new excavations compromised the integrity of the medieval site." And so another stick to beat Osmanagich with had just been taken from his attackers.

LEGENDS

Part of the Bosnian project was also to map local knowledge. One local legend stated that when the Turkish Empire invaded Bosnia in the 14th century, the Turks heard a story from an old woman who was living at the bottom of the Visocica hill. She said that "nobody is allowed to live in the ancient town located at top of the hill unless they are prepared to guard its secret, hidden under the town, with their life." She said that the town hid a secret "that wears two layers": "One layer has been brought there and is getting worn off by the rain (the earth layer). The second layer is an 'eggshell' layer which is thin and fragile. If the eggshell gets damaged and its contents are taken away by water (flood), this will cause bad luck for the people of the Valley." What the woman seemed to be saying, was that the local people knew the structure on which they lived was a man-made structure, which could easily be damaged. It seems that the Turks were impressed by the story and at the time decided against invading the town, even though it was the capital of the Bosnian state at that time.

It was not the only strange event that occurred in the valley. One story involved a local family which in 2004 started to dig the foundations for their family home. However, they could only dig to a certain depth, where they discovered massive slabs that stopped them going any deeper. They tried again and again to get through the rock, chipping away at the slabs with tools for several days and well into the nights, but found they were having little success. Eventually, they had to stop their work due to complaints from neighbours – on the other side of the "mountain", who claimed that the hammering at night had been keeping them awake. The noise from their digging and hammering had been echoing through the chambers and tunnels inside the pyramid.

Where does this leave this pyramid? Unexpected help came in September 2006, when archaeologists in Ukraine announced that they had unearthed the remains of an ancient pyramidal structure near the city of Lugansk. The stone foundations of the structure, probably in the form of a step pyramid, were thought to have been built around ca. 3000 BC. The complex, which covered three-quarters of a square mile and was around 60 metres (192ft) high, was probably used for 2,000 years.

Investigations are only in the infancy, but it is thought that they were built by animists who worshipped a sun god. The "pyramid" is in fact a complex of temples and sacrificial altars topping a sculpted hillside with steps on its sides.

Viktor Klochko, head of the excavation, said that the discovery was "the first monument of its age and kind found in Eastern Europe. It changes our whole conception of the social structure and the level of development of the cattle breeders and farmers who were the direct ancestors of most European peoples."

Although graves have been found at the Lugansk site,

archaeologists think it was used for sacrifice by burning, rather than as a burial ground. According to Klocho, "People lived in the surrounding valleys and climbed up it to carry out their ceremonies. They had a pagan cult that bowed down to the sun, as did the ancestors of the Slavs."

His conclusions are, in my opinion, in line with what we should expect to find, some years down the line, for the Bosnian complex. At present, it is too early to provide a clear answer. We can, of course, speculate and some, including Marco Guido Corsini, have: Corsini believes that the pyramids are of Egyptian origin. Corsini had studied the Greek pyramids, felt by many to have an Egyptian dimension, as well as the palace of Phaistos, best known for its so-called Phaistos Disc. But Corsini was more intrigued by a document that had been found in the same palace, the so-called "Apotheosis of Rhadamanthys". This is a record of the funerary ceremonies of Rhadamanthys, who was massacred in about 1570 BC and buried in Thebes. But a cenotaph for him was erected at Phaistos, in Crete. Corsini believed that Rhadamanthys was the Egyptian pharaoh Seqenenra Tao II, whereas the legendary king Minos of Crete was his son Ahmose, the founder of the 18th Dynasty. He believed that these kings were Cretan, not Egyptian, and were thus foreign invaders on the throne of Egypt – that concept itself is not so special.

It is in the Greek Thebes that we have indeed already seen a potential link with Egypt, at a time when the Egyptian capital was equally named Thebes. For Corsini, this is not a coincidence. In fact, he argues that Rhadamanthys and other "European rulers" of Egypt decided to establish Egyptian colonies in Europe, such as on mainland Greece... and specifically in Thebes. Cadmus, the legendary founder of Thebes, is thus seen as a member of this "European ruling elite", but Corsini states that Thebes was not the only European colony. He believes that they founded a new Greek kingdom in the land of the Illyrians.[30] The Illyrians, of course, are the people who lived in the "Bosnian Valley of the Pyramids". And for anyone not familiar with European geography, Bosnia sits largely north of Greece and east of Italy. Anyone travelling between Italy and Greece, by land... will pass through Bosnia. So when we know there are pyramids in Greece, and possibly a pyramid in Italy, a pyramid in Bosnia suddenly seems a logical expectation to have.

The "Valley of the Pyramids" is therefore potentially just that: a valley whose flanks are dominated by pyramids, which may have identified the valley as sacred: its northern limit is delineated on the western side of the river by the Pyramid of the Sun and in the east by the Pyramid of the Moon. Further south and on the eastern side of the river, we find the Pyramid of the Dragon. Some of these structures may turn out to be natural; that in itself is not important. If a single pyramid is eventually ratified as a pyramid, than it shows that this valley was an important religious location – and it may be the very reason why later, the Bosnian capital was established here. But if this is a sacred region, then it is equally clear that the pyramids are but one aspect of a larger whole, in which further work, elsewhere in the valley and beyond, needs to be performed. Unearthing pyramids is one thing; identifying them as manmade another; interpreting their function as to the "why here" and "what for" is an altogether different matter. Only time will tell, and research in Bosnia is only in its infancy. Demanding to know the "why" of the pyramids takes an awfully long time...

as we know it took – and takes – in Egypt. In fact, we need to return to Egypt, in an effort to address that very question over there.

CHAPTER 7

BACK TO EGYPT

It is clear that in most locations, the pyramids have surrendered several of their secrets – though some discoveries have obviously been made too recently to have conveyed their final message. When we compare our understanding of the Mesoamerican pyramids and set this against that of the Egyptian pyramids, it is clear that there are certain things amiss. But the Egyptian position is not so much one of despair, but rather one where the few bright sparks that might lead us to an understanding have been obscured by ridiculous or more popular theories. Egyptology is a minefield and the preponderance of "pyramidiotic theories" have had a negative effect on the general public's understanding. Let us try to get through the minefield, in the hope that on the other side we will find understanding.

So who built the pyramids? Were they a work of a united labour force, or a slave labour force… or aliens? Egyptologist Christine El Mahdy has done extensive research on this question. She found a stela at Dashur, placed by Sneferu, the man who built three pyramids, which read how "the settled Nubians working on the two pyramids of Sneferu are given tax exemption". El Mahdy read this inscription as a clue why pyramids began to appear. Though Imhotep had shown the way, after his death, pyramid building had become largely unsuccessful, with projects abandoned before their completion. For El Mahdy, "this, it seems likely, could have been caused by labour shortages."[31] She agrees with Davidovits that the 4th Dynasty had quarries beyond Egypt's border, which contributed to the country's economic prosperity, which in turn resulted in an enormous immigrant workforce.

Excavations on the Gizeh plateau that have occurred since 1984 have uncovered massive bakeries and workshop areas, as well as two cemeteries. According to Zahi Hawass, the Lower Cemetery contained burials of workmen for the site and their foremen, while the Upper Cemetery contains tombs for the artisans. The remains of the former category showed immense wear and tear on all of their joints; fractures were numerous, as could be expected, but the evidence also suggested that medical service was present for the injured and that, in general, these people lived normal lives. With the discovery of these cemeteries and the stela at Dashur, it is now the consensus that the building of pyramids was seen as a community project, in which the excess labour force was directed towards building pyramids, rather than sit along the river Nile and watch the boats pass by. As we noted previously, the same surplus in labour was probably what lay at the origin of the Caral complex in Peru, Silbury Hill in England... and many other pyramids. Some pyramids seem to have been the work of dictators (such as that of Qin Shi Huang in China), who forced their subjects to build their mausolea. Though Khufu has for centuries been seen as a dictator who used slave labour to erect his pyramid, this new evidence suggests that the Great Pyramid, if not all Egyptian pyramids, were a community project – not the whims of dictactors.

THE ARCHITECT'S PERSPECTIVE

How was the Great Pyramid built? The French architect Gilles Dormion has given an architect's perspective on the construction of the Great Pyramid. When he gave this opinion, it did not sit well with many Egyptologists, if only because Dormion was considered to be an outsider, whose insights rocked the boat, for it seems that Egyptologists had seldom consulted architects to have their input. And as they had never invited any architect, why welcome them when they show up unannounced?

Dormion's book is remarkable, for it approaches the Great Pyramid for what it really is: an architectural challenge. He first looked into the ramp theory, trying to settle the debate whether one long ramp was used, or instead an enveloping ramp. Dormion argues that the Great Pyramid – as well as all other "true pyramids" – were in a first phase nothing more than step pyramids, such as Zoser's. On top of this, a smooth "envelope" was constructed (phase two). Dormion states that the existence of a first phase radically changes the debate as to how the pyramids were built –

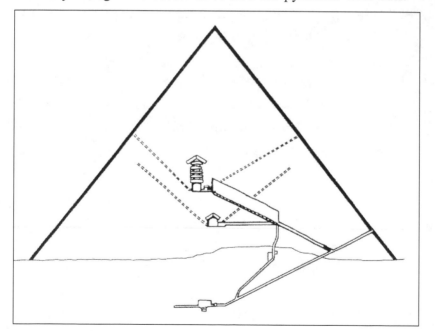

Cut Great Pyramid

and makes the entire enterprise less challenging. The presence of this interior structure also allowed for a clear "sightline" to be established to the top, which would have been the only method that allowed the pyramid builders to work this accurately on the smooth and perfect outer casing. Finally, the "two phased" approach also conforms to certain statements made by ancient authors, who argued that the pyramid was first built with a ramp, then with machines, as the guides told Herodotes. A ramp would have been used for the construction of the step pyramid, with remains of the ramp then easily incorporated and obscured when the casing stones were placed into position (or cemented if you accept Davidovits' approach) by machines (levers, pulleys, perhaps even kites?).

Next point on his agenda: the ventilation shafts that have caused so much debate since 1993. Are they aligned to the stars? Will they lead to unexplored chambers? In his opinion, they are just ventilation shafts: he argues that those of the Queen's Chamber, featuring so prominently in *The Orion Mystery*, were used as ventilation shafts, until they were blocked when the outer casing was applied. He does not believe that they were directed to any star or constellation. He reaches this conclusion based on the fact that the Queen's Chamber's shafts are perpendicular to the side of the pyramids, i.e. aligned with the other slope of the side of the pyramid. That is the primary cause of their alignment and any resulting alignment to a star or a constellation should be seen as accidental. As to the ventilation shafts of the King's Chamber, these have dissymmetric axes: one at 45 degrees, the other at 32 degrees 30 min. Why? Dormion notes that both exit at virtually the same height (80 metres 72 cm and 80 metres 73 cm), suggesting that exiting at the same height was the builder's prime requirement

– and not any astronomical alignment, which, if present, should once again be seen as coincidental.

It should by now be clear that Dormion is an independent mind, who tells it as he sees it. Thus, he did not mince words when he noted that Egyptologists had made it unnecessarily difficult for all of us to accept that the Great Pyramid fit within the "Pyramid Age" of Egypt. Indeed, he suggested that it were the Egyptologists who were partially to blame for theories that the Great Pyramid was 10,000 years old. Dormion felt that the sequence of pyramid building preceding Khufu should be reordered. His proposed timeline was Meidum, Dashur North, then Dashur South, then Khufu, showing a clear line of more ingenuity in each one; Egyptologists place Dashur South earlier than Dashur North. He underlined that Sneferu built three pyramids with a total of 3,300,000 m^2, or 600,000 m^2 more than Khufu. Though it makes the Great Pyramid "great" as it is a single pyramid, from a project resource point of view, it was less than the work that went into building Sneferu's three pyramids and was therefore within the comfort zone of the project managers.

What about the three chambers in the Great Pyramid? Were they planned from the start? Dormion accepted the theories of Ludwig Borchardt, who explained that the existence of the three chambers in the Great Pyramid was because the building plans were repeatedly changed. The original plan only seems to have catered for a subterranean chamber. Details in the construction of the ascending passage and the manner in which it interacts with the descending passage suggest that it was not part of the original plan. Dormion also tries to explain why the King's Chamber is not perfectly in the middle of the pyramid, which he believes has an entirely practical explanation: the King's and Queen's Chamber would be separated by less than one metre if the King's Chamber did sit in the middle of the pyramid. That space, obviously, is not much – and it would probably take an architect to notice it – who would then decide to move the King's Chamber further along, to guarantee the chamber's integrity.

He also noted that the top of the relieving structure that sits above the King's Chamber is located at mid-height of the pyramid. The top of the relieving structure of the Queen's Chamber is located at one fourth of the structure, whereas the floor of the King's Chamber is at one third of the height of the pyramid. These are clear and simple ratios, obviously deliberately incorporated into the pyramid architect's plans. Why did he place the floor at mid height? Because it was clear that there would be less stress on the structure of the chamber, guaranteeing that the interior of the chamber – the King's coffin – would remain intact.

In the series of relieving chambers above the King's Chamber, no less than 2000 tons of granite were used; they are located at a height of 50 metres, showing the labour and effort that went into placing them. But these slabs have cracks. In some explanations, it is the result of an earthquake, but if so, why did this earthquake not damage the structure elsewhere? Dormion believes that the problem occurred very early on, when the pyramid was settling – as any new building does. When it did, the hard granite tried to adjust its balance, but somehow was inhibited. Dormion blames the proximity of the relieving structure of the Queen's chamber, which sits on one side of the floor of the King's Chamber, but not the other. So, on one side, the hard granite of the relieving chambers underneath meant that no settling occurred there; but on the other side, limestone, cement and various other "soft" rocks did settle. This resulted in one side settling, the other not, and the slabs above cracking as a result of the one-side displacement.

The cracks meant that the granite slabs probably had broken. All of them? From inside the King's Chamber, only the granite slab that formed the ceiling of the chamber could be seen – and that was clearly cracked. Was it broken? To inspect further, an opening was made in the Grand Gallery, to inspect the first relieving chamber. Some attribute this hole to a grave robber, but it is clear (even to non-architects) that the person digging this hole knew where he was going and what he was doing; a grave robber would never suspect that there were relieving chambers above. That inspection would have confirmed that the slab had indeed broken. And broken is broken; it could not be mended – it would only have been possible to replace it with a new slab, but as the pyramid was finished, it would literally have meant breaking down the top half of the pyramid, replace that slab, and rebuilt the pyramid... an impossible task. Instead, the sad conclusion was that the crowning glory of the pyramid, the King's Chamber, had become a failed structure. Why is the Great Pyramid alone in having chambers inside the pyramid itself? For Dormion, the answer is that it was unique because the experiment failed.

Dormion believes that as the chamber's structural integrity had gone, it meant that the king could not be buried inside this chamber. He suggests that there is a hidden chamber. For after abandoning the King's Chamber, where was Khufu buried? Elsewhere... but where? Outside of the pyramid, or in some undiscovered chamber inside? In Antiquity, Diodorus Siculus stated that both Khufu and Khafre were not buried in their pyramids. His statement was disregarded, for he also wrote that both structures were being built at the same time, which Egyptologists of course "know" cannot be correct. Where does Dormion think it is? He made a detailed study of the floor of the Queen's Chamber and concluded that it had been replaced; he also focused on the nearby niche in the Queen's Chamber, which showed signs of having become victim of treasure hunters. Why did treasure hunters think that there could be something hidden behind this niche? Because of the presence of an enigmatic stone, which could have indicated that something had been consealed behind it, which had then been closed off by positioning into place a single stone. When they removed the single stone, they dug for about 15 metres behind it, obviously convinced to find something there, and only giving up after ten metres past the stone of the wall. The treasure hunters in their haste did not see what Dormion saw: he found that there is a small hole in the floor behind the niche, which together with the refitting of the floor, suggests that something occurred underneath the floor of the Queen's Chamber. That something, he believes, is another room... the final resting of Khufu... which he assumes remains inviolate. With suggestions of hidden chambers, Egyptologists had a stick to beat him with... and have thus talked themselves into the belief that they can thus also "safely" disregard all of his other findings. After all, he is an architect, not an Egyptologist...

A LARGER FRAMEWORK

Why did pyramid building reach its climax in the 4th Dynasty? Why did it then rapidly decline? It is a central question for Egyptologists, which have been unable to answer the question convincingly. If pyramid building merely required a labour force and stone-hewing techniques, you would expect to see an ever-increasing capability in creating pyramids, resulting in pyramids with greater complexity. But that is not the case. Why?

For Davidovits, the answer is a problem of resources: minerals. The pharaohs are known to have sponsored expeditions into the Sinai, to mine minerals. Davidovits sees these as the essential agents in the creation of geopolymers. If the mines failed to produce sufficient minerals, than the pyramids would no longer be built. But there was a second problem, possibly more important: the construction of the pyramids specifically used an enormous amount of wood. Palm trees were cut down at a tremendous rate to satisfy the need. But the newly planted trees took sometimes as much as 100 years to achieve the height of its cut-down predecessors. But the pyramid projects were using up many trees, in a period of only 50 to 60 years. This meant that at the time of the annual flooding of the Nile, because of the absence of mature trees, the soil consistency became altered; as a consequence, the soil became less fertile, even the path of the Nile began to change. Suddenly, famine or at least the threat of famine became a fact of life. As such, the pharaohs had to make sure that the welfare of the nation was guaranteed, which he could be making sure that never again buildings on such a massive scale would be constructed. In retrospect, the Pyramid Age may be seen as Egypt's crowning accomplishment, but it also almost killed it.

A lot of attention has gone into the Great Pyramid, both in this book and elsewhere. But little attention has been paid to place the Great Pyramid within its context – if anything, the Great Pyramid has always been taken out of context. We have already seen that a larger framework for the Egyptian Pyramid Age has been provided by Willem Zitman. Any interpretation needs to see the pyramids within the context in which it sits. Let us now look at the Great Pyramid and how it sits within its immediate landscape.

We have already noted that Robert Bauval walked this path, resulting in his Orion Correlation Theory, which fits nicely within Harleston's interpretation of the pyramid complex at Teotihuacan. But he is not the only one who has come away from the Gizeh Plateau with observations on how the pyramids interplay and play with the surrounding landscape.

Author Robert Temple observed that Kahfre's pyramid is placed in such a manner that on the winter solstice (December 21), it throws its shadow on the south face of the Great Pyramid.[32] Maurice Chatelain pointed out that Khafre's pyramid was built "in proportions of 3:4:5 in strict adherence to the sacred triangle and the theorem of Pythagoras."[33] We merely note the presence of this 3:4:5 in the creation mythology of the Mayans too.

Edgar D. Wilson in *MEVS: Creator of the Pyramids* suggested that distances around the Great Pyramid could be related to astronomical distances. Though his reason (that the pyramids were designed by extraterrestrial beings) is most likely erroneous, it does no change his findings. Wilson drew circles whose radii are equal to the distances that Mercury, Venus and Earth have as measured from the Sun. I report his findings because of the incorporation of Venus – Quetzalcoatl. The circles he drew were centred on the mid points of the bases of the pyramids of Menkaure, Khafre and Khufu. The three circles actually intersect in one location, inside the Temple of Khafre, located near the Sphinx. To be precise: the circles converge in a pit in which a statue of Khafre was once found. To underline this finding, Kenneth McCulloch explained: "It is important to note that the fact that the circles intersect at any point is important; there is no mathematical reason why three circles should intersect at the same point. Normally, three randomly selected circles which intersect will do so, two circles at a time, in three different points."[34] When Wilson then centred the circles on the tops of the pyramids instead of the mid-points of their bases, the radii are measured at different elevations. This time, they intersect inside the Temple of the Sphinx, immediately next to the Sphinx. Wilson notes that "there could be three very good reasons for selecting the south central part of the Temple of the Sphinx as a place where all three measurements come together. First, according to legend, the Sphinx represents the Sun; second, due to the position of the Sphinx this is the only place in its Temple where all three pyramids can be seen at the same time."[35] It is the second observation for which Wilson should be congratulated.

Another scholar who has seen the three pyramids of Gizeh as a whole is Stephen Goodfellow. Like Bauval, he believes that this could mean that there was an original plan, or that all three constructions were erected so that a cohesive whole existed at the end of the individual projects. Goodfellow drew one straight line through the southern corners of all three pyramids, then an arch connecting all three northern corners. The circle and arch meet to the west of the pyramid of Menkaure, and Goodfellow has labelled this "the vanishing point" and is nothing more than a "point" which underlines that elementary geometrical considerations were incorporated in the positioning of the three pyramids; their placement was not random, but conformed to an overall plan.

Chatelain, Wilson and Goodfellow's conclusions have had little impact in Egyptological circles, where the theories of two leading researchers, Zahi Hawass and Mark Lehner have equal problems of becoming the new standard interpretation, despite the scientific standing of these two gentlemen. Why is there such reluctance to accept the theories of these qualified men? Because their opinions diverge from the Egyptological dogma. According to astronomer EC Krupp, Mark Lehner has been "tempted [...] to speculate, at least informally, that some Old Kingdom pyramids were not even true tombs where the body of the deceased pharaoh was interred, but symbolic tombs, magical houses for the spirits of the dead kings."[36] This is a radical conclusion, which coincides with statements from Kurt Mendelssohn which we quoted in chapter 1. We know that Mendelssohn was completely disregarded and if it had come from anyone else but Lehner, it would have again been disregarded. Let us note that Krupp points out how even Lehner has only dared to suggest this "informally".

Let us note that Goodfellow identified a "vanishing point"; we see vanishing points in daily life, namely at the horizon. A key question is why the the Great Pyramid was originally known as Khufu's Horizon. Lehner wondered whether there was an intentional solar alignment at Gizeh and thus focused his attention on the summer solstice sunset. He observed that from the Sphinx (an important location, as identified by Wilson), the northernmost sunset of the year lodges the sun midway between the silhouetted pyramids of Khufu and Khafre. Together, the two pyramids and the sun form the Akhet symbol, which is the solar disk framed within a pair of stylized mountains – pyramids. The ideogram is connected to the root akh, "to shine".

Ziggurat of Ur

The summer solstice also corresponds to the time of the year when Sirius reappeared in the predawn sky, to signal the annual flood. The necropolis of Gizeh thus became a stage on which the sun died at the horizon, before its rebirth was signalled by the heliacal rising of Sirius in the east. With this in mind, the original name of the Great Pyramid – Khufu's Horizon – can finally be understood.

Of course, this equally identifies the Gizeh complex with the activation of the great cosmic cycles of death and rebirth, and this is similar to Mayan concepts and the role of the pyramid in their cosmology. But unlike Mayan scholars, so far, Lehner and co. seem unwilling to tackle the subject of cycles of time – Egyptian chronology. However, I note that in his analysis of the pyramids, Willem Zitman has done as much.

But let us remain within the hallowed walls of Egyptology and see what Zahi Hawass has to say about the Gizeh complex. He argues that Khufu equated himself with the divine sun and may even have considered himself to be the living incarnation of the sun. The identification of the king with the sun is indeed made in the Pyramid Texts. So that statement in itself is nothing too controversial. The controversy is that Hawass states that Khufu contrived the Great Pyramid not so much as a tomb and a site for the royal funeral, but as a monument intended to consolidate and preserve the continuity of royal power. He saw it as a temple for a cult of the divine king, who was returned by death to the deity, whereby the pyramid told the primary myth of kingship: the command of celestial forces and cosmic order. And that conclusion may be absolutely correct... it also absolutely "coincides" with the conclusions reached about the role of the pyramids within the Mayan cosmology... which in turn coincides with the role of the pyramid in several other civilisation's cosmologies.

THE TOWERS OF BABEL

In Teotihuacan, "men became gods"; they ascended. The Egyptian hieroglyph for "ascent" is a step pyramid. Was the pyramid therefore a stairway to heaven, to help the king ascend to the sky, to the abode of the gods?

Before answering that question, let us note that a stairway to heaven sounds like the Tower of Babel, a comparison we noted upon before. The Tower of Babel was supposedly located in Babylon, the land of ziggurats. The ziggurats of Mesopotamia are an endangered species – and it is Mankind that is responsible. Of the 32 known ziggurats, 28 are in Iraq. In the past two decades, they have seen an eight year long war between Iran and Iraq in the 1980s, followed by two Gulf Wars, one in the early 1990s and the other in 2003. Saddam Hussein parked jet fighters right next to them, in the hope that American troops would be unwilling to bomb his Air Force, as they could potentially destroy the ziggurat in the process.

But what's in a name? In any overview of pyramids, the Mesopotamian "ziggurats" are seldom included. And why should they, for, after all, they are labelled "ziggurats", not "pyramids" – or "mounds". Even though they are different in name, in shape, they are clearly step pyramids. The definition of a ziggurat is normally "a temple tower of the ancient Mesopotamian valley and Iran, having the form of a terraced pyramid of successively receding stories" – betraying that key word, "pyramid".

The "pyramid vs. ziggurat" controversy is intentionally created, as Egyptologists have broken every speed record on the books in informing everyone that pyramids are tombs and ziggurats are temples. But we note that Hawass in his vision of the Great Pyramid is referring to the pyramid more as a temple, rather than merely a tomb. But his colleagues have argued for the "tomb vs. temple" distinction, as they see Egypt's creation in isolation to the cultures around them – this in sharp contrast with their critics, who claim that ideas floated freely between Egypt and Sumer, one such idea being the step pyramid. Hawass has made it clear that this controversy should now be abandoned. As such, pyramids and pyramidal temples, i.e. ziggurats, have more in common than previously thought.

It is therefore intriguing to observe that the earliest examples of the ziggurat date from the end of the third millennium BCE – in the middle of Egypt's Pyramid Age. Like the Egyptian mastabas, the ziggurat was built in receding (ranging from two to seven) steps upon a rectangular, oval or square platform, thus confirming they were a step pyramid. Like Zoser's pyramid, the ziggurats were made from bricks; sun-baked bricks made up the core of the ziggurat, with facings of fired bricks on the outside. The facings were often glazed in different colours – not unlike the Northern Peruvian pyramids several millennia later.

The ziggurat is believed to have been a symbolic representation of the primeval mound upon which the universe was thought to have been created, which thus makes it conform the pyramid template. The ziggurats were also built as a bridge between Heaven and Earth – a stairway to Heaven. But they were not only a cosmic axis between Heaven and Earth, it also penetrated into the Underworld. Furthermore, it created a "horizontal" bond between the various lands, thus unifying the Earth. Its seven levels represented the seven planes of existence, as well as the seven planets and the seven metals, hence perhaps why each tier was coloured in a different colour, corresponding to the colours of the various sacred metals. As such, we may also have come face to face with the basics of alchemy, which tried to unify the various metals to create the "primeval atom" – a substance that seemed to

Reconstruction of Ziggurat of Ur

transcend time and space and brought Mankind in contact with the gods. Intriguingly, the Mesopotamian ziggurats were not places for public worship or ceremonies; they were dwellings for the gods. Through the ziggurat, the gods could be close to Mankind and each city had its own patron god. Only priests were permitted inside the ziggurat and it was their responsibility to care for the gods and attend to their needs. We can only wonder whether the same concept – that pyramids were houses for the gods – existed in Egypt. If so, it may explain Kurt Mendelssohn's reference as to what the coffin in the Great Pyramid could contain: a "divine essence".

It is also known that part of the rituals performed inside the zigurrats was an initiatory encounter with death. This ritual was central to the Akitu, the Babylonian New Year. We note the literary resemblance to the word Akhet, "Khufu's horizon". Akitu translates as "power making the world live again" and therefore fits the description of the New Year, as well as corresponding with the established pyramid template. During this New Year festival, the death and resurrection of Marduk – the Mesopotamian equivalent of Osiris – was re-enacted. This involved his descent into the Underworld and his resurrection three days later. The role of Marduk was played by the king, who was ritually disrobed and "confined in the mountain", i.e. the ziggurat. Only one person, the king, went through this experience, on behalf of the community.

The ziggurat was a tower reaching skywards – like the Tower of Babel, which was built somewhere in the land where ziggurats rose at the same time. The best candidate for the biblical Tower of Babel may be the Marduk ziggurat, or Etemenanki, in ancient Babylon – Babel. The name itself, Etemenanki, is Sumerian and translates as

"The Foundation of Heaven and Earth" – a connection between Earth and Heaven, built by Mankind. It is an extensive and massive ziggurat, of which remarkably not much is left, not even of the base.

Archaeological findings and historical accounts put this tower at seven multicoloured tiers, topped with a temple of exquisite proportions. The temple is thought to have been painted in an indigo colour, matching the tops of the tiers. It is known that there were three staircases leading to the temple, two of which were thought to have only ascended to half the ziggurat's height.

Is this the Tower of Babel? If it is, then we know that it was most likely built by Hammurabi, the sixth king of Babylon and the first king of the Babylonian Empire, who reigned from 1792 BC until 1750 BC. It was he who made Babylon the capital of an empire and his ziggurat – his tower – must have underlined the city's newfound importance. It is known that Babel was the native name of the city called Babylon by the Greeks, the modern Hilla. It means "gate of the god" – a good clue as to what we come across in chapter 11 of Genesis. After the Deluge – which we now should read not as a natural cataclysm, but in line with the other mythological accounts found elsewhere in the world, such as in Cuzco – Mankind attempted to build a city and a tower whose top might reach unto Heaven. The project failed because God "confounded the languages" of those who were working on the project, so that they could not understand each other. Hammurabi indeed conquered various regions and his influence stretched as far as the Mediterranean Sea. His capital Babylon must have been a powerful magnet and must have attracted individuals from all of these foreign regions, who recently had been made citizens of the

Babylonian Empire. It is clear that they must have spoken different languages – and were some employed in the ziggurat project? And did the project fail because communication was poor? If so, it is well-known in project management that communication is central to its success and that most projects fail as a result of it. In fact, more projects fail because of problems in communication than because of resource problems. And Khufu's constant change of scope in where he wanted his burial chamber to be located is another well-known example of how projects can fail. There is nothing new under the sun...

Why did the story of this ziggurat make it into the bible? The Jews were ill-disposed towards the Babylonians, who, like the Egyptians, overran their area almost cyclically. The cults of Egypt and Babylonia were also anathema to Jewish monotheism and hence, failures on gigantic building projects such as the Tower of Babel were no doubt used by its opponents to illustrate how these "pagans" did not obey the command of God.

What do we know about the fate of the "Tower of Babylon"? It was started by Hammurabi, and added on by several of his successors. It seems that Hammurabi never completed the project himself – which is probably what the Bible hints at as the curse for not obeying God's command. We need to underline that the bible does not say that God destroyed the tower (as popular opinion believes); rather, it suggests that after the various people "babbled" in different languages, the building fell into disrepair. The Book of Jubilees does state that God – at some point, later in time – did overturn the Tower with a great wind. According to the Greek scholars Lucius Cornelius Alexander Polyhistor and Abydenus, the tower was overthrown by the winds – suggesting that the tower was no longer maintained and that as a result, the winds slowly eroded the structure; it seems that Time did not fear this ziggurat!

BUILDING THE AFTERWORLD

Back to Egypt. The Great Pyramid may be void of any texts now, but in the past, its cover stones were said to contain inscriptions. Several other pyramids still have texts: the so-called Pyramid Texts, renditions of the so-called "Book of the Dead", which were not inscribed on the casing stones, but on the walls of the interior corridors and chambers. Several Egyptologists have written about the age of the Book of the Dead and several have argued that it was much older than ancient Egypt. In the 19th century, Gaston Maspero stated that "the Pyramid Texts carry us so far into the past that I have no way to date them but to say that they were already old five millennia before our era. As extraordinary as that figure may seem [...] those texts already existed before the First Dynasty, and it is up to us, in order to understand them, to place ourselves in the consciousness of those who wrote them down over seven millennia ago."[37] Others agreed, including the German scholar Adolph Erman, as well as Wallis Budge.[38] Wallis Budge added that the texts themselves were correctly called "The Coming Forth Into Day", which were "powerful guides along the road which, passing through death and the grave, led into the realms of light and life, and into the presence of the divine being, Osiris, the conqueror of death."[39] In short, the Book of the Dead – "The Coming Forth Into Day" – is a manual for the dead, to find their way through the perils of the afterlife, towards Heaven; it is a manual for ascension, "for men to become gods".

The Pyramid Texts state how "I am a soul... a star of gold". In

Egyptian mythology, the deceased's soul was placed on a boat, sailed by a navigator: the boat would be the instrument for the soul's voyage through the Duat, the Afterworld. When I was first confronted with this symbolism of a boat, I was slightly perplexed and wondered why it was necessary. Yes, Egypt was a gift of the Nile, but why compare a voyage on the Nile with a voyage through the Afterlife? A boat seemed ill-equipped to describe such an otherwordly voyage. Soon, I felt it was a perfect symbol, for it offered a logical setting for what the challenge of the soul was in the Afterlife. First, the boat could endlessly, without a specific goal, float around. The role of the navigator of the boat would in this instance be minimal. Second, the boat could row back to shore. The navigator would have to do some work, but nothing out of the ordinary. The third option was for the boat to go on a voyage of discovery, towards a "mythical place", which the ancient Egyptians visualised as the "extreme West"; a country in the extreme West meant a country very far away from the "start" of death. It would thus be a perilous journey, but if achieved, the soul would arribe in a land of Eternal Bliss, where the gods lived too.

From this perspective, the image of a boat makes perfect sense: every ancient Egyptian knew about sailing. They realised the dangers and the fears that sailors had to conquer, specifically if faced with decisions to sail to distant places; and they compared this to the fear the soul would no doubt experience in his voyage through the Duat, towards the gods. The Egyptians portrayed this boat in the sky as the constellation Argo and its navigator was the star Canopus – the second brightest star in the sky (after Sirius) and the southern polar star for the ancient Egyptians. As The Book of the Dead was a map – an itinerary – for travel in the Duat, mythologically, the Book of the Dead would therefore have to be present in this boat (Argo) and should also be visible to the helmsman (Canopus) who took the soul of the deceased to the Afterlife. The Papyrus of Nu, dating from the 18th Dynasty, does indeed say that the original text was indeed present in the Shrine of the Sacred Boat.[40] Could this also explain the presence of the gigantic boat pits next to the Great Pyramid? Furthermore, as we know that the Pyramid Texts were painted on the walls of the pyramids, were they seen as the instrument – boat – that enabled or aided the king in his ascension? All the available evidence, from the likes of Hawass and Lehner, but from other cultures as well (if only the ritual that the Babylonian king performed during the New Year festival in the interior of the ziggurat)… all that evidence, suggests that the answer is "yes".

But what was the Duat? What could be expected after the threshold of death? Eastern religions speak of a state following death that they have called this "bardo". Christians are familiar with a state of Purgatory, which we have already come across. So what did the ancient Egyptians think the Duat to be? To explain, we need to indulge in a bit of comparative theology. The Egyptian Book of the Dead is not the only map for the travel of the soul after death: the Tibetan Book of the Dead is a similar manual. The Tibetan Book is called the *Bardo Thodol* and is a guidebook to help the soul in the review of its previous life and the planning of the next life. It is clear that this body of knowledge was arrived at through a series of "paranormal experiences" that Mankind must have experienced since its beginning. Of primary importance must have been what we now call near-death experiences (NDE), which since the 1960s has achieved some scientific attention. But it is all too often and easily forgotten that people have died for tens of thousands of years and thousands must have come back from the brink of death, telling their "near-death experiences" millennia before Western doctors decided to document them within the clinical setting of a hospital. These near-death experiences, no doubt enlarged with the experiences from drug-induced trances (as practiced by the curanderos on El Purgatorio) can thus have been at the origin of what a culture believed happened to us upon death. The Tibetan Book of the Dead thus describes the various stages that the soul will have to pass through at death. But it is a book for the living as well: it aims to concentrate the mind of the living on their continual preparation for the Afterlife. For the Tibetans, the ultimate goal of the soul's (repeated) incarnations on Earth is to liberate ourselves from the cycle of life and death, upon which we can rejoin (the Creator) God. As this task of the soul is challenging, reincarnation is deemed to be the most likely outcome for the majority of human beings who have not yet attained   sufficient spiritual advancement during their life – and preceeding past lives.

The Egyptian Book of the Dead was therefore the manual for the deceased person to find his way in "death". So what did the ancient Egyptians think happened to the soul after death? Was it similar or different to the Tibetans?

It is clear that the Egyptians, like the Tibetans, had a vastly defined concept of "the Afterworld" – the Duat. Wallis Budge and others have noted that the ancient Egyptians' notion of the Afterworld bears striking similarities with the African shamanic worldview, from which Egypt evolved. When Maspero and Wallis Budge stated that the Book of the Dead predated ancient Egypt, they did not see it as a legacy of Atlantis, but saw it as a body of knowledge that had been accumulated by the shamanic tribes that lived in and near Egypt before the unification of the various tribes into the First Dynasty. Throughout these Dynasties, Egypt never forgot its magical past. But, equally, as they believed in magic, they also believed that the knowledge of certain formulae themselves would allow them access to a divine realm, where they would be met by the ancestors, deities, and remain there forever. In short, the ancient Egyptians largely agreed with the Tibetan model, but it seems that they equally believed that the entire system could be shortcut through magical formulae.

I say I "believe" and I have not used a reference to back up this belief. There is a simple reason for this: debates on the contents of the ancient Egyptian religion are – to say the least – scant. It is largely discussed only by "New Age" authors, who often approach the subject from a preset agenda and whose thinking should best be qualified as "barely touching the subject"… or harsher conclusions along those lines. One of the exceptions was the American author Charles Muses, who was equally inclined towards providing a New Age interpretation. Nevertheless, Muses was a scholar and was able to substantiate parts of his thinking. He realised that in the museum of Torino (Italy), there was a coffin from the Egyptian village of Gebelein ("Two Hills"), which depicted the plan of the Duat, as written down in the Coffin Texts, spell 650.[41] The plan visualises the three paths of the soul, as I have outlined above: floating about in the Afterworld, a return to the land of the living or a voyage towards a "Blessed Realm" – ascension. It is depicted as a fork in which the central path leads to ascension and the other two paths diverge from it, postponing ascension for another lifetime – or another death.

A divinity guards the entrances, the gateways (windows?), and has the final say over which path the soul shall take. Muses further identified each path with the types of couch, or bier – or coffin – on which the deceased pharaoh (imitating the god of the Afterworld Osiris) was placed. The central path (ascension) was identified with the lion couch, the hippopotamus couch with reincarnation and the cow couch with the floating about in the Duat – a state of "nothingness", as the Tibetans considered "life" in the Bardo to be.[42]

Egyptologists have discovered various depictions of the "lion couch", as this was the path obviously favoured for the pharaoh. After all, if the pharaoh did not go on this voyage, who within the Empire could? Examples of a hippopotamus and cow bier were nevertheless found in the tomb of Tutankhamun, and his tomb shows that each couch was furnished, as to a large extent, what would happen after death could only be confirmed once the deceased pharaoh was dead. It is furthermore known that Tutankhamun was very young when he died and hence his initation/preparation to successfully walk the "central path" – or Lion Path – upon death may not yet have been completed. But the preparation during life, whether in Tibet or Egypt – or elsewhere, was clearly aimed towards chosing and successfully walking the path of ascension – climbing the stairway to heaven.

The state of the bardo is therefore identical to the encoffined Osiris: though dead, he is not "dead dead": there is still potential, not for a return to earthly life as he was, but for a life "elsewhere". The "soul" is in a "land of nothingness", a gateway, a crossroads, where the soul is also in need of a guide, which in the sky was identified with Canopus, the navigator of the boat Argo. In this Celestial Boat, the pharaoh now had to set course on the right path.

Let us go through each path in detail. At death, the easiest path was the path of reincarnation (the hippopotamus): one body was exchanged for another and the cycle of life continued. In nature, this cycle was visible in the snake shedding its skin, the sun rising and setting, the seasons, the deer renewing its antlers – symbols and "physical evidence" that has been found at many sacred sites, whether or not there are mounds, pyramids or ziggurats. It was the path chosen by most souls, it seems for a variety of reasons: the soul might have too much fear to go on a voyage or even dwell in the Duat for too long; the life review that quite a substantial percentage of the near-death experiencers report might have been specifically negative: life was not led properly, i.e. in accordance to some divine guideline, and hence a successive incarnation was required for the soul to grow before it might be ready to return to the "Creator God".

The "path of the Cow" was to sail about in the Sacred Boat in the Duat. It is believed that this was literally "biding time": the soul was undecided what to do. It is this state that in folklore seems similar to that of being a ghost: the soul is literally in a state of "nowhere", it has not gone on. But at some point, the soul seems to have been expected to either reincarnate, or the boat could set sail towards the "Lion Path's Gateway".

This was the challenge of the Egyptian pharaohs and may be symbolised in the image of the Sphinx: a mixture of lion and man. We also note how the Sphinx was a central feature of

Gizeh's sacred landscape and how it formed a vital site from which Lehner realised the importance of the Akhet. But the Sphinx itself – "man as a lion" – looks towards the east, towards the sunset, specifically on the equinoxes (March 21 and September 21), though generally each morning. Are we to see the Sphinx as a visual interpretation of the myth that the king had died, but would, the following morning, be reborn, not as a mere mortal, but as a companion of the Creator God, as a soul who had successfully completed his voyage to the divine realm of the Creator God – a man who had become a god, who had been transformed into a god... a man who had walked the Lion Path?

CELEBRATING THE HEB SED FESTIVAL

Ancient Egypt was a concretisation of tribal shamanic knowledge. The tribe's shaman not merely focused on death, but also on the world of the living, which many cultures saw as preparation for death. The notion that life and death are not mutually exclusive but should be seen as an integrated whole can also be found in the innovative approaches of Lehner and Hawass. They are slowly abandoning the old dogma that the pyramids were nothing but tombs. They may have been tombs, but it is now also more and more obvious that they performed a function for the living king – they were temple, as well as tomb.

This forces us to see the pyramid as places of initiation, rather than gigantic mausoleums. Such an interpretation was very much in vogue a century ago, mainly by people of Masonic ideology. But Freemasonry is, in essence, a stylised rendition of a voluntary death during the lifetime – an initiation. Before Hawass and Lehner, the "pyramid as temple of initiation" debate – which makes the Egyptian pyramids conform to the pyramid template –was revived in 1982 by the Egyptologist Edward Wente and has been discussed by British author Jeremy Naydler. Naydler stated that "while scholars generally accept that this 'voluntary death' was one of the central aims of the Greek and Hellenistic mystery cults, Egyptology has resisted the idea that any such initiatory rites or experiences existed in Egypt."[43] In my opinion, this would make Egypt unique amongst all ancient civilisations – by the absence of such practices. It would mean that Egypt, of all ancient cultures, did not have a religion that allowed for the spiritual development of the soul... which would be extremelyodd, for all ancient accounts argue that Egypt was precisely the world's authority on such practices. But, Egyptologists argue, where is the evidence? What, apart from ancient travellers' account (which for Egyptologists somehow do not seem carry any evidentiary weight whatsoever)... what is there?

The answer is once again the Book of the Dead, in their first written format of the Pyramid Texts. That they have been overlooked at the obvious solution is because these Texts would

Imitation of Heb Sed run in front of Zoser pyramid

become a victim of their own child, the Corpus Hermeticum. The Corpus Hermeticum was a concise and clear synopsis of the religious framework of ancient Egypt, codified in the 3rd century BC, following the Greek conquest of Egypt. They inspired the alchemists of the Middle Ages, lay at the foundation of the Italian Renaissance, may be a key to explain the symbolism in paintings by Leonardo da Vinci and Sandro Botticelli and even contain the earliest reference to the Grail... The Pyramid Texts were believed to contain the true – native – ancient Egypt's own – message; unlike the Corpus Hermeticum, which had been written for a Greek audience. The decipherment of the hieroglyphs had created the expectation that the Pyramid Texts would soon reveal ancient Egypt's true doctrine. But when Gaston Maspero, the first to publish the Pyramid Texts, summed up his effort to translate these Texts, he confessed that despite trying, he was unable to discover any profound window in ancient Egypt's religious doctrine.[44]

The disappointment came because the Pyramid Texts did not contain the doctrine (like the Corpus Hermeticum), but "just" the rituals, the "manuals", used in that religion. A manual of your television does not reveal what programs it shows or what you watch and what the experience of "television watching" really is or feels like. The manual will never reveal the joy you experienced when Goran Ivanisevich finally won Wimbledon, only how to increase the volume on your site during those agonising last few minutes of his final against Australian Pat Rafter. The Pyramid Texts were just such a manual, for in ancient Egypt (as elsewhere), the doctrine itself was apparently never confided to print – if they did, it has never been discovered. But in Ptolemaic times, when the Greeks ruled over Egypt and when most scholars now accept the

Corpus Hermeticum was written, there was a need for Jews and Greeks to learn the religious doctrine of the Egyptians, to understand the religious life of their neighbours and compatriots, and hence the doctrine was finally written down – though the Greeks and the Jews had no need for the rituals itself, and hence the Pyramid Texts were not incorporated into the Corpus Hermeticum. Millennia later, when the mystique of the hieroglyph had lifted, the disappointment of not seeing the true breadth of the Egyptian doctrine led to a major disappointment, which hung over Egyptology as a black cloud – and which is only slowly drifting away.

Naydler has shown that the Pyramid Texts in no single instance seem to imply that the king is actually dead. We note that the ancient Egyptians saw death as a potential – a decision of which path to take. But Naydler has seen phrases in the Pyramid Texts that suggest that the king is very much alive – physically alive – at the time when that section of the texts is read. Though it is therefore without doubt that the Pyramid Texts focus on the king, Naydler argues that they focus mainly on his role as ruler – not as deceased head of state. The Texts thus become records of the rituals that the king performed, at key times of his rule, which Naydler has identified as his coronation and the Heb Sed festivals, which was a renewal of his kingship that occurred at thirty year or less intervals. These rites confirmed the power of the king over this and the "otherworld", the union of which was accomplished by the king, through which he established his divine rule over the land. Let us note that in this interpretation, the pyramid becomes a temple, and the inscriptions on its wall were not meant to be read by the funeral cortege, or by the deceased soul of the pharaoh, but by the living pharaoh, as he performed these rituals in the interior of the pyramid.

The Heb Sed festival is named after the short kilt with a bull's tail that the king put on for the culminating rites of the festival. The festival lasted five days in total and took place immediately after the annual Osiris rites, at the time when the Nile's Flooding retreated, at the moment of the rebirth of the land, mimicking the creation of the world – an a new age. It is yet another clear parallel with the "New Fire ceremony" of the Maya, for the five days preceding the Heb Sed festival, a fire ceremony called "lighting the flame" served to purify the festival precincts.

The most sacred parts of the rite occurred in a secret chamber – and the question is where this chamber was located. From the reliefs of Niuserre, the 6th ruler of the 5th Dynasty, we know that this chamber contained a bed (a couch?), though other depictions show that in certain cases a sarcophagus was used.

The main purpose of the Heb Sed festival was confirmation that the pharaoh was still "fit to rule", but it is equally clear that his fitness was closely linked with the king's prepardness to make a successful voyage after death – it was a test run for his ascension. The "fit state of mind" that the pharaoh had to be in was known as "akh". Intriguingly, the pharaoh accomplished this state in a place known as the "akhet", as we know often translated as "horizon", but which should be interpreted as a place of spiritual illumination, which Mircea Eliade labelled "an awakening" as well as "ascension", and hence the reason why we used the same terminology. As mentioned earlier in this chapter, Lehner has suggested that this akhet is the Gizeh plateau and hence we need to wonder whether this state of mind or consciousness was indeed attained in Gizeh… which equally means that the secret chamber of the festival in which the "state of akh" was accomplished should be located somewhere on the plateau too.

But before scouring the plateau, let us note that there are scenes on the walls of Nuiserre's chamber in which the glyph "Awake" is shown. At this point of the ritual, the pharaoh is depicted lying on his stomach, "like a sphinx", while "his son" (identified with the god Horus) presents him with the symbols of life. What is this symbol of life? The sun, specifically the first ray of light of the morning. East, of course, is the direction towards which the Sphinx of Egypt directs his gaze, and from which he receives the first ray of light of the morning. The sphinx obviously lies on his stomach "like a sphinx", but I also note that in the New Kingdom, the god Harmakhet ("Horus in the Horizon") became the god of the rising and setting sun and the Sphinx became associated with this deity. Coincidence?

Naydler has titled one of the chapters of his book "The pyramids as the locus of secret rites". He argues that the Heb Sed festivals were performed in pyramids. There is an obvious contradiction in the fact that the construction of a pyramid seemed to be abandoned as soon as a pharaoh died. When he was most in need of a tomb, all work on his tomb was stopped? Let us note that several pharaohs who did not live long enough, had no pyramids whatsoever. Djedefra, Khufu's son, did not live very long and his pyramid was never completed – though he clearly died, the son of a dynasty of pyramid builders extraordinaire who could surely have spared some men to build at least a small or minuscule tomb for this king? This makes little sense. Surely his successor – often his beloved son – on occasion would desire to have his father's and/or predecessor's tomb to be completed, so that his father could be buried inside, before work commenced on his own pyramid? If the successor was in his early twenties when he ascended to the throne, there was more than enough time left before he had to wonder about death, as the life expectancy of an Egyptian pharaoh was not too different from most of us. But each time, work is stopped, as if the pyramid is no longer required now that the pharaoh is dead. In the "pyramid = tomb"-equation, that does not make sense.

From the little evidence available, it is clear that the Heb Sed festival is the key to unlock the true purpose of the pyramid. The Heb Sed festival was normally going to be held for the 30th year of rule of the king. Is it a coincidence therefore that Khufu was said to have taken ten years for the planning of his pyramid, which included the diversion of the river Nile; it then took a further twenty years of work on actually building the pyramids. According to Rainer Stadelman, two of the three pyramids of Sneferu were built between his 14th and 30th year of his reign. Coincidence, or evidence of a link with the Heb Sed festival?

This interpretation also ties in with the conclusions reached by Willem Zitman, who stresses that the image of the "Strong Hand" is expressed in the layout of the pyramids. This stance was the symbol of the king showing his reign over the world – showing that he was "fit to rule" and it should come not as a surprise to find that the pose of the strong hand was central both to the coronation and the Heb Sed ceremonies.

In summary, Naydler has found evidence for the practice of this festival in most pyramids (including the non-violated pyramid of Sekhemkhet), but he – and we – will focus on the Zoser complex, if only because it is perhaps the best remaining evidence – and was after all "Egypt's original pyramid". For one, the walls of the Zoser pyramid complex are not blank as they are at Gizeh. Of all the possible scenes they could display, the texts and depictions show various stages of a Heb Sed festival – if they were tombs, why not show scenes from the Afterlife? To use Naydler's own words: "As these are the only reliefs inside the pyramid, there could be no stronger evidence to demonstrate that the interior of the pyramid was as much associated with the Heb Sed festival as were the buildings and architectural spaces in its vicinity."[45] Let us also add that the causeway of the Great Pyramid also has scenes of Khufu's Heb Sed festival. There is also the famous Heb Sed dance, in which the king circumambulated the courtyard, which represented the country of Egypt. Such large courtyards stand in front of the Pyramid of Zoser, but are also present at the Gizeh pyramids of Khufu and his successor Khafre. We can only wonder whether they are an Egyptian equivalent to the ballcourt of Chichen Itza or other squares, such as the Nunnery of Uxmal.

To describe the entire Heb Sed ceremony: the pharaoh would arrive by boat (!) and moor at the Valley Temple. From there, the ceremony would make its way upwards the causeway, which at the time was actually a covered walkway, with only a slit in the roof to allow daylight to penetrate. The next stop would be at the Pyramid Temple, from which entrance into the pyramid would be the logi-cal – and only available – next step. The chamber inside the pyra-mid would thus be the secret chamber, with the sarcophagus being the site where the secret ceremony of the Heb Sed would occur. What was this ceremony? Details are sketchy, but it was described as the king "unifying" the two dimensions, the "Divine Realm" and Earth. In mythology, this occurred at a "Mound of Creation" and we have noted that the pyramid was indeed considered to be just that: a place where "Heaven" and "Earth" met. During the Heb Sed festival, the king had united the Land of the Gods and our Reality – the old boy could still do it. Egypt rejoiced.

The Zoser complex also incorporated robbing chambers, as well as chapels for the visiting gods of the regions of Egypt, who attended the ceremony. It also fits with Dormion's observation that the gallery leading into the Queen's Chamber originally had niches for statues; other pyramids have similar "niched corridors", all of which have been found to be empty, and which were therefore interrupted as evidence of tomb robbers. But if used for the Heb Sed festival, the niches would only ever have contained a statue during the festival, after which the statues returned to their temples elsewhere in Egypt.

The usage of either a bed, couch or sarcophagus during the ritual may explain why some of the pyramids, like those at Dashur, do not have a sarcophagus. Furthermore, as the ritual was to be performed every thirty years, but many pharaohs performed it more frequently, pharaohs like Sneferu could have held three such ceremonies in their lifetime – or he may have held it twice, making preparations for a third festival, when death intervened. It is commonly accepted that he ruled for 34 years, and thus would have needed – "by law" – to perform at least one festival. Pharaohs that had problems convincing their people of their power and fitness to rule may have performed the ceremonies as frequently as politically expedient. Finally and most importantly, this could explain why some pyramids were never finished: when the king died, the festival was not going to be held. The project was thus abandoned. The king still needed a tomb, but no longer a pyramid...

Where does this leave the "theory" that the pyramids are tombs? Naydler himself has pointed out that the two options are not mutually exclusive: pharaohs could at the end of their life have been buried in their pyramid – if they so desired. But it seems clear that we should not take this as the rule, but more like the exception. What about Dormion's notion about the Great Pyramid and the possibility that the tomb of Khufu is still hidden inside? Dormion observed that the niches in one corridor of the Great Pyramid were afterwards blocked up. Was this following an order by Khufu to transform the pyramid that he had used for his Heb Sed festival into the site of his burial? Perhaps Khufu indeed frequently changed his mind during the construction of the Great Pyramid as to where he wanted to be buried, but it is equally possible that some of these changes may have been done for the simple reason that some of the inner structures (such as the niches) were evidence of its later change in use – to prepare for Khufu's royal funeral. Finally, we need to underline that the coronation ceremony of the new pharaoh required this "secret chamber", but also required the physical proximity of the mortal remains of the predecessor, whom the new king physically had to embrace, showing the succession of the old to the new king, the new king (identified with the god Horus) having "embraced" his father (Osiris). It also suggests a logical conclusion that the secret chamber of the coronation ceremony may have been performed inside the pyramid of the king's predecessor – provided, of course, a pyramid was present. In short, I would argue that we look towards pyramids as temples and occasional tombs. And though they thus fit with the pyramid template found elsewhere, it is equally clear that we should not consider each individual pyramid project to be exactly the same as another pyramid project; they were physically quite often slightly different, and hence ceremony-wise, the festivals in which they would feature, will equally have had minor if not major differences. That is the case now; it was likely the case in Egypt; and elsewhere.

With this interpretation, we have explained the pyramids of Egypt within the emerging framework that is slowly replacing the outdated Egyptological dogma. Remarkably, it appears that the rituals and symbols of the Egyptian pyramids are similar and sometimes identical with their colleagues across the world. So can we list a "universal message" that was encoded into the pyramid template?

CHAPTER 8

BEYOND TIME AND SPACE

HIEROTHESION

We have one more pyramid to go and this pyramid is located in Turkey, in Kurdistan. Nemrud, or Mount Nimrod, is is a 2,150 meters high mountain in eastern Anatolia, the highest peak in the region. In 62 BC, at the top of the mountain, King Antiochus Theos of Commagene built his tomb-sanctuary, along with huge statues (each eight to nine metres tall) of himself and various Greek and Persian gods. The tomb was excavated in 1881 by Karl Sester, a German engineer; his and subsequent excavations have however failed to reveal the tomb of Antiochus.

Antiochus was the son of king Mithradates I Callinicus and the Seleucid princess Laodice, daughter of the Syrian King Antiochus VIII. This marriage had been arranged as part of a settlement by Mithradates' father Samos II to ensure peace between the Kingdom of Commagene and the Seleucid Empire. Antiochus tried to balance the interests of his kingdom with the reality of the power of the Roman Empire and preserve as much as possible Commagene's independence. Despite his efforts, his reign ended with the Commagene submitting to Rome, becoming a client-state under Emperor Augustus.

What is of interest to us, is that this sanctuary is a pyramid, created as an artificial peak for this natural mountain, adding an additional fifty metres to its height. The Turks consider it to be the eight wonder of the world, if only because of the altitude at which the work was accomplished. If pyramids are meant to represent mountains, the builders of this one had gone a step further by placing it on top of a real mountain.

Antiochus was a king who took his religion, a Hellenized form of Zoroastrianism, very seriously. As his religion was of mixed Greek-Persian descent, the gods he worshipped were an amalgamation of both pantheons, some of them personifications of the Sun, Moon and planets. He is also said to have practised a very esoteric type of astrology, and to have laid the basis for a calendrical reform, by linking the Commagene year, which until then had been based on the movements of the Moon, to the Sothic cycle (based on the star Sirius) used by the Egyptians as the basis of their calendar. As such, his "Hierothesion" on top of Mount Nimrod was not merely going to be his tomb; for Antiochus, it was a place where he could gather his people for religious festivities connected with either his birthday or coronation – an ambition which must begin to sound familiar...

The central figure in a series of five seated gods, apparently watching the sunrise in the east, was Zeus, equated by Antiochus with the Persian Ohrmazd. On his right hand side stood Antiochus himself; on his left hand stood what is believed to have been the land of Commagene, represented as a woman. She was flanked by Apollo-Helios (Mithras) and Antiochus by Heracles (Verethragna). These five gods themselves were flanked on each side by paired statues of an eagle and lion, the heraldic animals of the Royal House of Commagene. In front was a Zoroastrian fire altar – dare we speculate for what type of ceremony it would have been used?

The complex was erected at the highest point of his kingdom, where the people and the gods were closest to each other, and where Antiochus had installed a sacred for his nation. We may be able to precisely date the festival of his coronation that occurred here: Commagene possessed the so-called "Lion Horoscope", which van Hoesen and Neugebauer had been able to link with a date of July 7, 62 BC. The sky of that time incorporated precisely the five stellar objects that were depicted as the five gods (Antiochus=Mercury; Commagene=Moon; Zeus=Jupiter; Apollo=Sun; Heracles=Mars). Van Hoesen and Neugebauer have argued that this date corresponded to the date of his coronation, which Antiochus had decreed as a feastday.

The Hierothesion reveals, once again, an intimate connection between the king's coronation (or similar royal festival), his possible tomb, a cyclical calendar system involving rejuvenation and the birth of a new era, and a pyramid as the central feature of a religious complex, which interplays with the landscape and which often involves a sacred mountain, identified as the residence of the gods; it are these items that define the pyramid template. For an archaeologist, it is only the pyramid and the tomb that is tangible; evidence of a coronation will only be uncovered if writings survived the test of time; evidence for a calendar largely depends on texts too, plus sufficient knowledge and data to be able to reconstruct it. In short, in order to arrive at a true understanding of a pyramid complex, the hope that Time has not destroyed too much is an important ingredient.

But many of these elements are present in Egypt and thus the fact that we have no genuine understanding of the pyramid and its importance to the ancient Egyptians is largely due to the fact that

Egyptologists have far too long looked at the tomb and the pyramid and disregarded all other aspects. As such, there was no real genuine drive for understanding. Two of four ingredients were used to explain the entire recipe. It has never worked and it is why Egyptian pyramids have remained enigmas for far longer than all other pyramids elsewhere. Still, we cannot totally blame Egyptologists for this, as they largely stood at the cradle of archaeology and worked with some of the oldest monuments around... in short, their task has been the most difficult, but in recent decades, it is clear that their colleagues elsewhere have been able to accelerate their learning curve, whereas Egyptologists, when it comes to the pyramids, have been largely left behind; only two, Hawass and Lehner, have been able to keep abreast, and though their efforts should be lauded, when compared to the work of their fellow archaeologists outside of Egypt, it is less than what they could have accomplished.

THE MESSAGE OF THE PYRAMID

All Egyptian pyramids were built, without exception, on the west bank of the Nile. The Gizeh plateau sits on the west bank of the Nile. So why should we ask the question why the Great Pyramid was built at Gizeh? It seems a bizarre question, but it are often bizarre questions that lead to intriguing answers.

The Great Pyramid weighs around seven million tons and such a structure requires a solid rock base; elsewhere, it would simply not remain erect, sinking into the sands. The rock surface of the Gizeh plateau therefore made it ideally suited for the construction of this structure. The question is whether this is the sole reason for why it was built there.

In 1912, James Henry Breasted argued that the pyramid represented the benben, the primoridial mound of creation (point of creation). Both the star Sirius and the morning-star Venus (the Mayan Quetzalcoatl) were also associated with the benu bird, the mythical bird that came to rest on the top of the benben, where he was reborn from his own ashes, signalling a new age – in short, a New Fire ceremony. Since Breasted, the shape of Egyptian pyramids is commonly accepted to represent the primordial mound from which the Egyptians believed the Earth was created. The shape is also thought to be representative of the descending rays of the sun, and most pyramids were faced with polished, highly reflective white limestone, in order to give them a brilliant appearance when viewed from a distance; it could thus be seen as a "mirror", reflecting the solar light from on High on Earth. That this was intentional can be seen from how pyramids were often named in ways that made reference to solar luminescence. For example, the formal name of the Bent Pyramid at Dahshur was "The Southern Shining Pyramid" and that of Senwosret at el-Lahun was "Senwosret is Shining".

The identification of the pyramid with the benben stone brings out intriguing parallels: there is the Sacred Stone at El Purgatorio in Peru; there is the Phoenix who rose from its own ashes, in what is clearly a New Fire ceremony, sitting on top of the benben stone. What is the benben stone?

That answer is found in the creation myths, where we learn that in the beginning was the primordial sea. From this watery surface, there was one particular hill, at that time an island, which was considered to have risen first. This was the "primeval hill", the place of creation – and the benben stone was, or represented, this primeval hill.

The primeval hill marked the "point of creation" and it is this point that was localised by building a pyramid on top. We have seen this in Chichen Itza, we can also see it at La Venta, on the Gulf of Mexico, where the Olmecs built their pyramid on an island – likely representing the primeval island of their creation mythology. British author John Michell wrote: "In every traditional society [...] a rock or pillar within the national sanctuary [...] is known to be the generation centre of mankind and the spot where the pole of the universe penetrates the earth."[46] This "central spot" was not only deemed to be the centre from which everything else came into existence, it was also the place where Heaven and Earth – and the Underworld – met. It was an "interdimensional stargate" – and hence a place where the king, like the tribal shamans before him, could "link" all dimensions – and "sail" between them.

Professor Stefan Maul of the University of Heidelberg has provided a Sumerian perspective on this mythology, stating that the "sacred hill, one believed, arose at the beginning of the world from pre-temporal primeval water, in which salt water and fresh water had not yet been separated, and from this hill the nucleus of all things arose. The idea of a primeval hill probably arose from fundamental experiences of Mesopotamian life. At the mouth of the Tigris and Euphrates rivers, where salt water and fresh water still mix today, the new, fertile land of the Mesopotamian alluvial plane arises. In the still unordered world, this primeval hill was thought to be the origin of all ordered existence and thus the nucleus or the navel of the world. In the walled pedestal at the vestibule of the temple, understood as the mythical primeval hill, the pre-world – the primeval beginning of all existence and all time

– pushed itself, so to speak, out into the present of the Babylonians."[47] For the ancient Sumerians, it was at the primeval hill that the separation of order (fresh water) and chaos (salt water) began to occur, through the intervention of the Creator God, residing at the primeval hill, who created a balance – order – between these two waters. In Egypt, the two ingredients that mixed and which had to be separated was not fresh and salt water, but the "normal water" of the Nile and the special waters that arrived at the time of the Deluge, which many compared with the Nile giving birth, the fertile waters seen as the "breaking of the waters" that accompanies human birth – a flood, linked with birth and the birth of a "new age". It is here too that we find the origin of the story of the Deluge in the Bible, with the Ark landing on Mount Ararat... which would be a primeval hill, an island, as the waters recided from the Earth – though in the bible, I would imagine that we are not speaking of a physical flood, but of a symbolic regeneration of the entire Earth. Let us also note that Ararat is not too distant from Mt. Nimrod, the primeval hill for the Commagene.

So, the benben, the primeval hill, was symbolised as a pyramid. The hieroglyph for the primeval mound was indeed a step pyramid. Mark Lehner described the pyramid as "an image of the primeval mound... a place of creation and rebirth in the abyss." RT Rundle-Clark added: "There was no fixed form for the Primeval Hill... the mound was soon formalised into an eminence with sloping or battered sides or a platform surrounded by steps on each side. This became the most usual symbol. It is probably what the step pyramid represents." And it is here that we find confirmation of the variation in how this primeval hill would be built: though there are stepped pyramids and "true" pyramids, to a large extent, we could have equally included a series of conical hills, like Silbury Hill at Avebury, as evidence of such primeval hills.

The symbol of the "primeval hill" was known worldwide, showing that the origins of this idea might be as old as Mankind. Was there a "central" point of creation? A "central centre of creation"? Perhaps. But it is equally clear that every culture had "his" centre of the world; every region had its centre; every town had its own centre. The Sumerian town of Eridu, from which many believe the name "Earth" comes from, was the oldest sanctuary in Sumer and had its own primeval hill. But though Eridu was primary in Sumer, it was not the only primeval hill. The House of Enlil at Nippur, which was built on an artificially raised platform in the centre of the town, had the E.KUR, the Mountain House, because it resembled a mountain…the primeval hill. In the town of Uruk, the Sumerian supreme deity Anu had his temple, the EANNA. The EANNA was a huge man-made mound, with the temple on the top; a ziggurat. It was called "House for Descending from Heaven", underlining once again the connection between Heaven and Earth that was or could be established at that site.

The word ziggurat itself is from the term "zaqaru", "to build high" or "raised up". Michael Rice pointed out that both pyramid and ziggurat were obvious forms of the "sacred mountain" and that this concept went back to the remotest antiquity. The pyramid and the ziggurat were man-made "primeval hills", to identify the sacred location of Creation, where worship to the gods was performed. Equally, the Egyptian word for pyramid is "mer". As Mark Lehner has pointed out, this is possibly derived from "m", meaning "instrument" or "place", and ar meaning "ascension". Therefore, the pyramid is either the "place of ascension" or the "instrument of ascension", or both. It is therefore very close to the Sumerian aspect of creating the bond between Heaven and Earth... and the Mesoamerican concept of a place where "men became gods".

I.E.S. Edwards also identified "mer" or "mr" as "instrument/place of ascension", but added a note of caution, stating that the interpretation was still "open to justifiable doubt". What the word meant, nobody knew for sure, as the m-er conjunction is indeed unusual in Egyptian grammar. But it is equally clear that in Egyptian hieroglyphs, mer *is* written as a pyramid, capturing the essence.

THE PRIMEVAL HILLS OF EGYPT

Though Lehner and Hawass have interpreted the pyramids in innovative ways, what they and their fellow Egyptologists have so far failed to do is interpret the pyramids within the local landscape. For the pyramids of Gizeh, this stretches as far as Heliopolis, now a suburb of Cairo. It was the centre of the Heliopolitan creation myth, focused on the self-begotten Creator God Atum, who created the world from the primeval island through the act of masturbation.

Where is Atum's primeval hill? Though the Greek geographer Strabo mentioned that Heliopolis was situated on top of a noteworthy mound, it seems likely that the primordial hill of their mythology was not located in Heliopolis itself, but at Gizeh. The strong link between both sites was picked up by Robert Bauval, quoting Robin J. Cook: "The Gizeh group probably represents a symbolic expression of the Heliopolitan myth."[48] I.E.S. Edwards described how the Sphinx was said to guard the "Splendid Place of the Beginning of All Time", which is of course the primeval hill – the Mound of Creation. Furthermore, Gizeh and Heliopolis were connected by the "Sacred Roads of the Gods". Anyone travelling from modern central Cairo towards Gizeh can cross one of the southern bridges. They will see the majesty of the pyramids rising in front of them. The two greatest pyramids rise like two mountains, next to each other. It is a magical sight that has lost little of its splendour when the casing stones were removed.

As the primeval hill was a place of descent for the Creator God, was the myth of Atum descending to Earth related to the Gizeh plateau? There is an account of how Khufu mentions that an old sycamore tree that grew near the Sphinx was damaged "when the Lord of Heaven descended upon the Place of Hor-em-Akhet", the latter translated as "the place of the Falcon God (Horus) of the Horizon", identified with the Sphinx as Harmakhet. This tree was linked to Atum and in Heliopolis there was a chapel to "Atum of the Sycamore tree". This suggests, once again, that Gizeh and Heliopolis were two aspects of the cult of the Creator God Atum.

Egyptologist I.E.S. Edward too believed that the primeval hill was the Gizeh plateau. He thus stepped in the footsteps of Diodorus Siculus, who, in ca. 60 BC, wrote that the Great Pyramid took twenty years to build and how "a cut was made from the Nile, so that the water turned the site into an island". The desire to make the plateau into an island was therefore a specific human intervention. Some have seen the reorientation of the Nile towards Gizeh in pure engineering terms: to ease access to the construction site. Though naval access would be highly desirable, there would be no need to make the plateau into an island. In my opinion, this engineering work served at least two purposes: a practical and a

Natural pyramid above Valley of the Kings, Luxor

religious. Within its religious framework, Khufu turned the plateau into an island, to forcefully portray the creation myth of the primeval hill, an event that must have been most profound at the time of the Flooding of the Nile. As the floodwaters receded, the primeval hill of Gizeh would rise from the Waters of Chaos; a new land was born – a new era, a new year had begun.

The primeval mound was therefore the location where the Creation had occurred; it was the site sacred to the Creator God, the god to whom we would return at the ascension. The original word for "mound of creation" is "niwt", which means the numinous centre of the universe, the seat of God. Psychologist Erich Neumann pointed out that this seat was linked with Isis, and that in her role of the mother goddess, a cleft passage or a twin-peaked mountain was her symbol. These "twin peaked mountains" are exactly the image that the two pyramids of Gizeh convey to the traveller arriving at the plateau from Heliopolis; it were the "two hills" in between of which the sun sank – Khufu's horizon, as Lehner pointed out. Let us also note that it was Isis who assisted in the ascension of Osiris and that it was Isis' star, Sirius that controlled the calendar and marked the New Year. It was through her magical operations that her dead husband became Lord of the Underworld.

The Gizeh plateau was not the only location where the ancient Egyptians incorporated this design into the landscape. Primeval hills can be found across the length of the Nile. Hence, we find how nearby Memphis claimed to be the "Divine Emerging Primeval Island", containing Osiris' body, with the same applying to Hermopolis and Thebes (Luxor). We note that Saqqara was the site near Memphis where the first ever Egyptian pyramid was erected; but in Hermopolis or Thebes, no pyramids ever reached for the sky. Still, Thebes was known as the "Island emerging in Nun, which first came into being when all other places were still in obscurity". On the other side of the Nile rises another primeval hill, towering above the Valley of the Kings, where the pharaohs that had ruled from Thebes were buried. This most prominent geological landscape feature, a natural pyramid, can be seen from Thebes itself. The ancient Egyptians regarded this mountain as sacred and referred to it as "The Horn of the West". It may be why the valley below was selected for the royal burials of the kings. In the texts of the Amduat, written on the walls of Thutmoses III's tomb, "The Horn of the West" is referred to as a "gate", a place where souls, gods and spirits reside.

At the beginning of the book of the Amduat, in the first hour, Ra Horakhty descends from the solar boat on the western horizon and orders the dead king to open the doors of the Underworld for him. When standing at an angle mid-point between the temples of Karnak and Luxor, the sun sets directly into this depression. The phenomenon gives the observer the impression that the sun has sunk right into the mountainside and at the same time formed a solar boat. This imagery, of course, is identical to that observed by Lehner from the Sphinx, where the sun sinks between the two "breasts" of Isis: the two largest pyramids of the Gizeh plateau.

During the New Kingdom, the Horn of the West was indeed venerated as a goddess, Meretseger, whose name signified "the beloved of him who makes silence", identifying the beloved with Osiris and hence Meretseger with Isis. Observers have noted that if you look up at the peak from the floor of the Valley of the Kings, you will see that against the horizon it forms the image of a woman's breast facing towards the sky. In short, a twin-peaked mountain, but in this case, no human hands were required to build a pyramid – Nature, the Creator God, had done it himself.

POINTS OF CREATION

Not only have we found that the Egyptian pyramids correspond to the pyramid template, Egypt has actually corroborated the reason why the pyramid template was applied to sacred sites: because these sites were seen as representing the primeval hills, the point of creation.

Once this "awakening" has occurred, it is easy to identify the template and recognise for that it is. The Sumerian town of Nippur, NIBRU.KI, "Earth's Crossing", equally has all the necessary ingredients: in the centre of Nippur stood an artificially raised platform, called KI.UR ("Place of Earth's Root"), which was the place where the connection between Earth and Heaven was maintained. At this centre stood a pillar, which was used by the resident god Enlil to send his word to Heaven; when it was heard in Heaven, abundance would pour down to Earth. On the platform was also a DIR.GA, a dark chamber, "as mysterious as the distant Waters, as the Heavenly Zenith. Among its ... emblems, the emblems of the stars. The ME it carries to perfection. Its words are for utterance... Its words are gracious oracles."

The "dark chamber" was the Holiest of Holies, housing the "me" and the comparison with the "secret chamber" inside the Egyptian pyramids comes rather naturally. In this Holiest of Holies, which in Sumer was a closed area at the back of the temple, stood the statue of the god (in this case Enlil), which was only shown to the people on high days and holidays. These statues were tended to with offerings of food, clothing, incense and ointments. It was these statues that travelled to other assemblies for important rituals, such as the Heb Sed festival of Zoser at his step pyramid of Saqqara.

But probably the most famous sacred centre is Jerusalem and the most famous Holiest of Holies was definitely the Temple of Solomon, sitting on top of a sacred hill – though no pyramid was ever constructed here. The "me" in the Temple of Jerusalem was where the Tables of Destiny and the Ark of the Covenant were housed. The Tables were envisaged as a "bond", a "contract" between God in Heaven and Man on Earth; similarly, the Ark of the Covenant was deemed to be able to communicate with Jahweh – in fact, be his residence.

Jerusalem as a "centre of the world" kept its sacredness well into medieval times – if not into our present era. It was the sacred quest of the Crusades and identified as the centre of the Christian religion – rather than Rome. The biblical texts of Jubilees 8 and Ezekiel specifically identify Jerusalem as the navel of the Earth, where the umbilical cord connects the child with the mother, which in an Egyptian setting would be seen as Horus with Isis, or in a Christian context the child Jesus with the Virgin Mary.

This rock, called in Hebrew "Ebhen Shetiyyah" (the Stone of Foundation), was the first solid thing to be created, and was placed by God amidst the as yet boundless fluid of the primeval waters. Legend has it that just as the body of an embryo is built up in its mother's womb from its navel, so God built up the Earth concentrically around this stone, the Navel of the Earth. And just as the body of the embryo receives its nourishment from the navel, so the whole Earth receives the waters that nourish it from this Navel. To quote John Michell: "the centre of the human body, half way up and half way down its front, is the navel. For this reason, and because it was once attached by the umbilical cord to our maternal source of life and nourishment, the navel provides an image of the notional world-centre, the spot on the earth's surface through which runs the universal pole."[49] And this explains why ancient cultures used the image of human birth, the breaking of the waters and the umbilical cord to respectively symbolise the advent of a new age, the flood and a point of creation, which had in origin been a nurturing link between the body below (Earth; the child) and the mother "above" (Heaven; the Creator God). The navel was a sacred site, on Earth corresponding to the primeval hill, which as the site of this umbilical connection between Earth and Heaven, a bond which the shamans – and the kings – (re-)established at important times in the calendar, such as their coronation and the New Year.

Islam is an example of a modern religion that has largely retained the concept that one culture can have more than one sacred centre. Apart from Jerusalem, another sacred centre is

Mecca, the home of the Ka'aba, another "foundation stone". The sacred stone was said to have been brought to Earth by an angel to record the deeds of the faithful, to be examined hereafter on the Day of Judgement – a concept similar to ascension. The sacred stone was the sole object of the pagan temple that the prophet Muhammad kept when he converted the shrine at Mecca into an Islamic temple. The poet Ikbal Ali Shah stated that the Ka'aba was the heart of the body of the world: "And the stone that you call the Black Stone was itself a ball of dazzling light. In ages past, the Prophet said, it shone like the crescent moon, until at last the shadows, falling from the sinful hearts of those who gazed on it, turned its surface black. And since this amber gem, which came to earth from paradise with the Holy Ghost, has received such impressions upon itself, what should be the impressions which our hearts receive? Indeed, whoever shall touch it, being pure of conscience, is like him who has shaken hands with God." This single quote contains all the basic ingredients of the "pyramid template", though not a pyramid is in sight. There is the "stone that shone", similar to the bright shine of the pyramids; we are told that this stone came from Heaven itself; those who are pure of conscience (which other religions would have labelled "ready for ascension" or "awakening") and touch it, will be reunited with god – ascend.

What were these stones that were able to accomplish such magical features? Some have concluded that they were of meteoric origin, "shining" in the sky, but when fallen on earth, black. The benben stone of Heliopolis has thus been labelled a meteorite, even though the stone itself has disappeared into the mists of time and is hence impossible to study. Author Alan Alford has argued that the sarcophagus inside the King's Chamber was built to hold some of these meteoric stones, which in his opinion were considered to be identical to the gods.

Probably the most unlikely place to chance upon such foundation stones is the medieval story of the Grail. Specifically, it is found within the Grail story of Wolfram von Eschenbach, *Parzival*. He identified Knights of the Grail, who resided in a sacred castle: "By a stone they live, and that stone is both pure and precious. Its name you have never heard? ... But young you will live forever – And this stone all men call the Grail." Here we chance upon the subject of immortality – in fact, in Wolfram's story, the stone offers this immortality. Like the stone of the Ka'aba, the Grail had been brought down from Heaven by angels, who then returned on high because of the sins of Mankind. On Good Friday, a dove flew down with the white Host to lie on the stone. This part of the story is very similar to the Egyptian Phoenix bird. Wolfram's story was taken up in the *Jungerer Titurel*, by Albrecht. He enhanced the vision of Wolfram, and in the Grail Castle, the floating stone became the centre of the world; "In that stone was the secret of life."

Another sacred site without a pyramid but with a foundation stone was Delphi, the most sacred site of ancient Greece. The omphalos stone at Delphi sat in the most important part of the temple of Apollo: the Adyton, the seat of the Pythia. Archaeologists were able to retrieve two of the omphalos stones of Delphi – for the site is believed to have had more than one. Today, the most beautiful omphalos stone sits in the museum, while another omphalos stone sits on the Sacred Way, near the Treasury of Athens, just below the Temple of Apollo. The omphalos stone was connected to Zeus and consists of a single piece of marble. After the confirmation that the ancient accounts were indeed correct and that the Adyton of Delphi more than likely did indeed have a chasm from which vapours rose, geologist Jelle de Boer has proposed that the stone actually sat across this chasm.[50] I find this suggestion compelling, for the "foundation stone" in legend was supposed to sit on top of the Abyss... and a chasm out of which trance-enducing vapours rose that brought the Pythia in contact with the gods in Heaven definitely qualifies as a representation of the Underworld.

THE ACT OF CREATION

A clear insight into the act of creation can be seen when Akhenaten needed to establish a new centre for his new monotheistic cult of the Aten, represented by the sun disc. He wanted to locate his new capital in the exact centre between Heliopolis and Thebes. It was Akhenaten's attempt to balance the power of the old with that of the new, with something of his own... a New Era. A new point of creation, a new anchor both in time and in space... and a new god, the Aten, the visible aspect of the sun god Ra, the chief deity. There are documents that explain how the new capital was created. First, a site was selected, equidistant between Heliopolis and Thebes. Apparently, the site was chosen by Aten himself, according to the inscription on the stela. The new city, Akhetaten, was then laid out and fourteen boundary stelae were erected. These were round-topped stones carved out of solid rock. Each bore a relief and a hieroglyphic inscription that proclaimed the king's commitment to Ra-Harakthy-Aten. After the careful selection of a site, the setting of the town's boundary, only then did the building work begin. These may seem logical if not obvious steps, but what the texts reveal is that each step was seen as a religious act. Though in the case of Akhenaten, it did not involve the construction of a pyramid; his and other examples of sacred centres have provided us with an insight in the extensive rituals that were available for the foundation of a new "centre". In short, the "pyramid template" was an optional part of a larger whole, "the point of creation template". But that is another story…

CONCLUSION

THE OLD AND NEW PYRAMID AGE

Though some pyramids continue to be built to this very day, it is clear that few – perhaps with the exception of the glass pyramid in the Louvre – occupy sacred space, or feature as a monument built to symbolise a place that sits outside of space and time, though the Luxor pyramid in Las Vegas does probably embody that principle best for a 21st century human being.

Leaving aside notions that the Great Pyramid dates from 10,800 BC and that Martian pyramids may exist from several hundred of thousands of years ago, our voyage has made it clear that it was around 3000 BC that Mankind became obsessed with pyramid building. For a long time, it was believed to have been a pure Egyptian-Mesopotamian phenomenon, then spreading out in space and time to other cultures. The Mayans of the New World were believed to have stumbled upon the same concept independently. But with the recent discovery of Caral, it is clear that pyramid building originated on both sides of the ocean largely contemporaneously. Other pyramids, such as those of Bosnia, remain undated, but are likely to come in at 3000-1500 BC. This may seem an extraordinary claim, but we note how (small) pyramids in Greece have already been dated to 2900 BC – the same timeframe.

We may think that Egypt is the cradle of the Pyramid Age, but in truth, it seems that Mankind almost received a "cosmic imperative" to start building pyramid. Or perhaps Mankind was finally able to express the Creation Myth in stone – a pyramid. But if there was indeed a cosmic imperative, then we could look towards an extraterrestrial being telling us what to do. But this is more than unlikely the right answer. Instead, perhaps we should wonder whether there is any connection at all with the start of the Mayan calendar, August 12, 3114 BC, a date which seems to have had no specific significance for the Mayan civilisation, which did not yet exist at the time. It was a date predating their culture, but which was clearly an important date. Why? And what are we to make of the end of this calendrical event, December 21, 2012 AD? Is it a coincidence that it is in the two decades leading up to 2012 AD, in fact since 1994, that Mankind has grown to understand the message of the pyramids? For centuries, they have intrigued us – but they equally puzzled us. Then, since 1994, we are suddenly finding answers, new pyramids, new interpretations, as if a cycle of time is about to end and this type of information is linked with such key calendrical dates. If it is mere coincidence, what an intriguing coincidence it is.

What is also amazing is not that we find pyramids in various areas of the world. What amazes, is that they all conform to a clearly identifiable "pyramid template", which, as any template, was adapted according to local circumstances. Though details of the template may vary across cultures – though often within one culture as well – the core of the message remains the same: if you see a pyramid, you have found "a place of creation", linked with sacred kingship and rule, linked with the Creator God.

At Palenque, the Temple of Inscriptions contains the sarcophagus lid of Lord Shield (in the Mayan language known as

"Pacal"), who ascended the throne at age 12 on July 29, 615 AD, and lived to the age of 80. The tomb on site is currently off-limits, but a   replica of the tomb is on display inside the museum in Mexico City.

Pacal's tomb was opened in 1952 by archaeologist Alberto Ruz Lhuillier. His skeletal remains were still lying in his coffin, wearing a jade mask and bead necklaces, surrounded by sculptures and stucco reliefs depicting the king's transformation (ascension) to divinity and figures from Mayan mythology. It remains one of the most spectacular finds in Mexico's history. Though in some interpretations Pacal was seen as riding some type of "air motor bike", what is actually depicted is how the sun is depicted as sinking into the jaws of the underworld, descending with Lord Pacal. It is identical to how on the Gizeh plateau the sun sinks in the akhet, the "jaw" or "twin peaks" of the horizon, taking the soul of the pharaoh with him into the Otherworld. In both instances, across two continents and three millennia, the same template was applied, in all of its detail.

Though on numerous occasions in the past, such correspondences across continents and space have been seen as evidence of extra-terrestrial interventionalism, in my opinion, it shows that we are face to face with a core myth of Mankind, one that it possessed from its earliest origins as a species, before it began to disperse across the world. Within a biblical setting, we should call it a myth dating from the "Garden of Eden", before the "Tower of Babel" dispersed the people across the face of the Earth. Within a scientific setting, it may mean that this myth dates to 20,000 years old, perhaps even older... This may seem extremely old, but I note that Mankind, in its present form, has been around for at least

30,000 years, and possibly longer. It is about 20,000 years ago that there is clear evidence that we were spreading ourselves about the Earth. We know that more than 20,000 years ago, our ancestors were decorating certain inner chambers of massive cave systems in the south of France and Northern Spain with extra-ordinary paintings. They are evidence of a structured and complex religion, in which paleontologists have noted certain correspondences between cave paintings found in France and Spain and caves in Southern Africa. Indeed, our ancestors seem to have possessed several templates...

Like the pyramids, the paleolithic cave paintings have been subjected to much controversy and speculation. In one incredible instance, one paleoontologist suggested that they should no longer try to interpret these paintings, but instead merely catalogue them: "just archive, don't think."

It is equally clear that whether you believe in the bible or in the theory of evolution, that originally, we were "created" or we "evolved" in one specific location... from which we later dispersed. I suggest that in the period of living together in a relatively small and contained area, which may have taken from anything of one thousand to 20,000 years, it was there that Mankind created the "point of creation template", as well as the "pyramid template". And so, as Mankind went across the globe, wherever and whenever it settled, it applied this "point of creation template", and if circumstances allowed for it, followed it up with the "pyramid template".

Wherever and whenever we established "true" kingship, we have built pyramids. The pyramids scattered about the surface of the Earth are the legacy of this knowledge... The Great Pyramid, the Pyramid of the Sun in Teotihuacan, but equally the small pyramid of Falicon in France, incorporate natural caves, suggesting that the sites on which the pyramids were constructed were deemed to be sacred before the first stone of the pyramid was placed – they had already been mapped according to the "point of creation template".

Though we have made great progress since 1994, certain vital steps need to be made. The pyramids are more than just tombs. For an Egyptologist, it is the threshold he needs to cross, however dangerous it can be for a career. Lehner and Hawass seem somewhat daring to go beyond, though it is with trepadation in their steps. The naturalist Thomas Shaw visited Cairo in 1721. When he entered the Great Pyramid, he felt its interior was not suited to be a tomb and therefore considered it to be a temple. He interpreted the sarcophagus as an implement for the mystical worship of Osiris. Others agreed, including the physician Charles Perry and Cornelius de Pauw. They described them as temples for the worship of "the Being who filled the universe with light", viewing the interior chambers as the tomb of Osiris. At the same time, Abbé Terrasson raised the notion that the pyramids had served as places of initiation, which he outlined in his novel *Séthos*, published in 1731. Terrasson wrote at a time when Freemasonry had just come in vogue; and Freemasonry used Egyptian imagery into the construction of their rituals and initiations.

Almost three centuries later, the fascination with ancient Egypt and the pyramids remain. Rainer Stadelmann described how "before and just after sunrise, the faithful of the pyramid mystery sects, along with members of Masonic lodges with mystical leanings, gather in the tomb chamber and the so-called Queen's Chamber and devote themselves to hours of meditation and soft chanting." Many Egyptologists scoff at the notion that these pyramids are used as such (in fact, some seem incapable of understanding that other people than they may have a right to enter an archaeological site). But even if the pyramids were "just" tombs, it is clear that they thus were a religious building... which incorporated religious services: prayers, meditations and perhaps even hours of soft chanting for the soul of the deceased king.

Pyramids are not just relics of the past, there as mute and dead witnesses of a by-gone age that by all accounts should be left alone. They still exist and though at one point our ancestors stopped the religious obedience their builders desired, any such return would coincide with the intended desire and purpose of the builder. And it are his wishes we should place central, not that of a chorus of people believing they are the sole guardians of these monuments and its builders. That doesn't solely apply to Egypt... it applies to every pyramid, if not any monument.

But it is unlikely that the pyramids were just tombs. The rituals performed in or around them were not purely the quiet prayers by the widows and children of the king. There were rites of coronation, in which a human being took control of his nation and was at that moment in time identified as someone who was still amongst them, but who would, upon death, become a god; someone who would ascend. In Egypt, at the Gizeh plateau, it was symbolised by the akhet, the place of transformation into a spiritual entity and the word akhet itself was known as a mental state. As in Egypt, so in Mexico, where Teotihuacan was known as the place where men also could become gods. On both sides of the

Atlantic Ocean, we find specific references to fire ceremonies. Every 52 years, the Mayans practiced a New Fire ceremony, in which all the fires throughout the Mayan lands were put out for one night, before they were rekindled the next day. In the Inca empire, an identical ceremony was performed every year. In the Mayan world, to underline that this was a true cleansing of the past and a new era, even debts were erased. The ancient Egyptians had a similar "New Fire Ceremony", which occurred at least every thirty years, and which was known as the Heb Sed festival, in which the pharaoh underlined his ability to be able to unite the various dimensions and act as a mediator between these worlds. We thus find "the Vision Serpent" in the New World, where it was known as Quetzalcoatl; this serpent shed its skin, like the phoenix was reborn from his ashes. Quetzalcoatl was a "feathered serpent", thus closely related to the phoenix bird, both able to fly – and both linked with the star Venus.

In the Mayan world, we have descriptions of the ceremonies to this Vision Serpent and in some areas of Mexico, these rituals continue to be performed to this very day. They bring alive – illustrate – the world and the importance of the pyramid. Hence, we know that during these rituals, participants would experience visions in which they communicated with the ancestors and/or the gods. These visions took the form of a giant serpent "which served as a gateway to the spirit realm". The ancestor or god who was being contacted was depicted as emerging from the serpent's mouth. The vision serpent thus came to be the method in which ancestors or Gods manifested themselves to the Maya. Schele and Friedel noted that the Vision Serpent is linked with this "sacred centre": "It is in the center axis atop the World Tree. Essentially the

World Tree and the Vision Serpent, representing the king, created the center axis which communicates between the spiritual and the earthly worlds or planes. It is through ritual that the king could bring the center axis into existence in the temples and create a doorway to the spiritual world, and with it power."[51]

One of the most common rituals associated with the Vision serpent involved invoking ancestral sprits. Especially during coronation rites, the kings would contact the spirits for guidance and blessings. It was the Vision Serpent that provided the medium for contacting these deities. Is it any coincidence that Lord Pakal's sarcophagus lid has been described as "the single most comprehensive image which relates the Vision Serpent to Maya religion"?

In Egypt, we have the story of Kematef, the primordial snake. Kematef was said to have been the self-begotten or the creator of his own egg and can be seen as a variation of the Creator God Atum-Ra. In the Theban creation myth, the serpent personified the

Gebel Ghibli, which resembles a serpent's head, Gizeh

soul of the primeval island. The coils of Kematef were seen as the stepped terraces that wound their way around the primeval hill. Hence, a spiral path was believed to ascend the primeval hill, the path of the serpent.

Another name for the serpent was Nehebkau, which means "Provider of Life Energies" and in the Pyramid texts it is referred to as "I am the Outflow of the Primeval Flood, he who emerges from the waters. I am Nehebkau, the serpent of many coils". The coils were believed to entrap the life energies in a state of unrealised potential, which Mankind was invited to release[52] – a clear parallel with the Mayan Vision Serpent.

Another symbol which involves a serpent is the ouroboros, the serpent in a circle, the animal having its tail in its own mouth – no actual serpent actually does this. The ouroboros is one of the most powerful symbols associated with alchemy. I feel there is one aspect of the Gizeh plateau which, to my knowledge, no-one has ever observed. Everyone knows that pyramids rise from the Gizeh plateau and that below, there are more temples and the Sphinx. But that is not all. From one particular vantage point, there is more to see. This vantage point is the so-called "Southern Hill of Gizeh", known as Gebel Ghibli and is known to the tourists – and Egyptians selling camel rides – as the only place from where you can see all nine pyramids. From this hill, we see the pyramids in front of us; to our right is Cairo, to our left is the desert. But there is more to see, for those with good "vision". From our right, a chain of hills begins to rise, slowly, making its way around the pyramids in front of us; the hills rise towards our left, ending in the place we are standing on. When we descend from this hill and return to the area around the Sphinx and look back upon Gebel

Ghibli, with some imagination (vision?), this hill looks like a serpent's head. So, we have a ring of hills, which rises slowly out of the sand, in front of the pyramids, encircling them, ending in Gebel Ghibli, which looks like a serpent's head. Do we see an ouroboros in this landscape?

Of course, we are all familiar with the story of the serpent in the Garden of Eden...

J.T. Fraser in *Time: The Familiar Stranger* wrote that "the Mayan civilization was based on a 'chronovision', a total absorption of the individual and collective life in the rhythms of nature, mapped into a mathematical system that had several cyclical counts running simultaneously."[53] We should ask the question why they were so obsessed and what these cycles of time really mean. We know that 3114 BC and 2012 AD were somehow important, but why they are so important, has hardly been studied.

Within these cosmic spirals of time, the Mayan kings acted as portals between different planes of reality. Through bloodletting, they conjured "the way" (the path) and the "ch'u", the companion spirits and gods. The Mayan king was considered the chief possessor of "itz", the cosmic sap that could be used to heal or kill. It was the task of the rulers to maintain the balance of the cosmic forces through his magical powers. Likewise, the balance of the universal world order in Egypt was known as Maat, which was, if anything, a state of mind... a state of balance, in which life was good and society was in balance. It was trying to bring Heaven down to Earth and it was the task of the pharaoh to accomplish this.

Since 1994, we may speak of a "New Pyramid Age", or perhaps it is the "End of the Pyramid Age", when we finally begin to understand the legacy of the pyramids. But it is equally clear that so far, we have only been able to uncover part of its message within its context; true understanding remains a distant hope. In Mesoamerica, it will involve archaeologists who will be willing to incorporate the modern knowledge of the surviving Mexican shamans, listen to them and use their knowledge to fully understand the pyramids. The problem and the challenge for Egypt has already been discussed. In short, there is still a way to go.

But there is at least hope. During the writing of this book, a newspaper ran the article that "Aymara Language and Gesture Point to Mirror-Image View of Time." It reported that new analysis of the language and gesture of South America's indigenous Aymara people indicated a reverse concept of time. The study provided a unique insight into "points of creation" and ancient civilisation's obsessions with calendars. The article stated that contrary to what had been thought to be a cognitive universal among humans – a spatial metaphor for chronology, based partly on our bodies' orientation and locomotion, that places the future ahead of oneself and the past behind – the Amerindian group located this imaginary abstraction the other way around: with the past ahead and the future behind. The scientific study noted that "cognition of such everyday abstractions as time is at least partly a cultural phenomenon. With the same bodies – the same neuroanatomy, neurotransmitters and all – here we have a basic concept that is utterly different."

In the 1920s, Arthur Eddington was one of the first physicists to propose that the Relativity Theory suggested that "the stuff of the world is mind stuff" and that this "mind stuff" is not spread out in space and time; "these are part of the cyclic scheme ultimately derived from it". What science found out was the central role of consciousness and how it seems to enter into another dimension – or even a multitude, such as Heaven and Hell – may have been practically known by our ancestors for thousands of years and may have been at the core of the "point of creation template" – and the pyramid.

We look towards chronology and time and try to place the pyramids within this construct. It is the scientific method and it has helped us a long way. But to go the final furlong and truly understand the pyramid in all of its importance that it held for these communities that worked years and sometimes centuries to construct it, our modern approach will fall short. We will need to let go of our own habits, acquire new capabilities, and transform science itself into a method of understanding – true understanding.

For the Aymara, neither time nor space exists as it does for us; we may share a world, but not a reality. And what we see as a long sequence of events, seeing history as linear, our ancestors saw as cycles. The pyramid was seen as a sign of creation – a place outside of time, and a time unaffected by space. Time fears the pyramids, indeed.

BIBLIOGRAPHY

Abdel-Aziz Saleh. *Excavations at Heliopolis. Ancient Egyptian Ounu*. Cairo: Cairo University, 1981/3.

Alford, Alan F. *Pyramid of Secrets: The Architecture of the Great Pyramid Reconsidered in the Light of Creational Mythology*. Walsall: Eridu Books, 2003.

Alford, Alan F. *The Midnight Sun. The Death and Rebirth of God in Ancient Egypt*. Walsall: Eridu Books, 2004.

Alford, Alan. *The Phoenix Solution. Secrets of a Lost Civilisation*. London: Hodder & Stoughton, 1998.

Alford, Alan. *When the Gods came down. The Catastrophic Roots of Religion Revealed*. London: Hodder & Stoughton, 2000.

Allen, Richard Hinckley. *Star-Names and their Meanings*. London: G.E. Stechert, 1899.

Appleby, Nigel. *Hall of the Gods. The Quest to Discovery the Knowledge of the Ancients*. London: William Heinemann, 1998.

Bauval, Robert. *Secret Chamber. The Quest for the Hall of Records*. London: Century Books, 1999.

Bauval, Robert. *The Egypt Code*. London: Century, 2006.

Bauval, Robert & Adrian Gilbert. *The Orion Mystery. Unlocking the Secrets of the Pyramids*. London: William Heinemann, 1994.

Budge, E.A. Wallis. *From Fetish to God in Ancient Egypt*. New York: Dover Publications, 1989.

Budge, E.A. Wallis. *The Egyptian Heaven and Hell*. Chicago: Open Court, 1925.

Budge, E.A. Wallis. *Introduction to the Book of the Dead*. New

York: Dover Books.

Budge, E.A. Wallis. *Osiris and the Egyptian Resurrection*. New York: Dover Books, 1973.

Budge, E.A. Wallis. *The Gods of the Egyptians, or Studies in Egyptian Mythology*. London: Methuen and Co., 1904.

Burl, Aubrey. *Prehistoric Avebury* (Second Edition). New Haven & London: Yale University Press, 2002.

Chatelain, Maurice. *Our Cosmic Ancestors*. Sedona, Arizona: Temple Golden Publications, 1988.

Childress, David Hatcher. *Lost Cities of China, Central Asia & India*. Stelle: Adventures Unlimited Press, 1985.

Childress, David Hatcher. *Extraterrestrial Archaeology. Incredible Proof We Are Not Alone*. Stelle, Illinois: Adventures Unlimited Press, 1994.

Childress, David Hatcher. *Lost Cities of Atlantis, ancient Europe and the Mediterranean*. Kempton: Adventures Unlimited Press, 1996.

Childress, David Hatcher. *Ancient Tonga & The Lost City of Mu'a*. Kempton: Adventures Unlimited Press, 1996.

Clark, R.T. Rundle. *Myth and Symbol in Ancient Egypt*. London: Thames & Hudson, 1959.

Collins, Andrew. *Gods of Eden. Egypt's Lost Legacy and the Genesis of Civilisation*. London: Headline, 1998.

Crowley, Brian and James J. Hurtak. *The Face on Mars. The Evidence of a Lost Martian Civilization*. South Melbourne: Sun Books, 1986.

Davidovits, Joseph. *La nouvelle histoire des Pyramides*. Paris :

Jean-Cyrille Godefroy, 2004.

Davidovits, Joseph. *Ils ont bâti les pyramides*. Paris: Jean-Cyrille Godefroy, 2002.

Devereux, Paul. *Symbolic Landscapes. The Dreamtime Earth and Avebury's Open Secrets*. Glastonbury: Gothic Image, 1992.

Devereux, Paul. *Re-Visioning the Earth*. New York: Simon & Schuster, 1996.

Devereux, Paul. *Mysterious Ancient America. An Investigation into the Enigmas of America's Pre-history*. London: Vega, 2002.

Dormion, Gilles. *La chambre de Chéops. Analyse architecturale*. Paris: Fayard, 2004.

Dunn, Christopher. *The Giza Power Plant. Technologies of Ancient Egypt*. Santa Fe, New Mexico: Bear & Co, 1998.

Edwards, I.E.S. *The Pyramids of Egypt* (revised edition). London: Penguin Books, 1980.

El Mahdy, Christine. *The Pyramid Builder. Cheops, The Man Behind The Great Pyramid*. London: Headline, 2003.

Frankfort, Henri. *The Birth of Civilisation in the Near East*. Ernest Benn.

Fraser, P.M. Ptolemaic Alexandria: Text, Notes, Indexes. 1972. Clarendon Press, Reissue edition, 1985.

Gilbert, Adrian. *Magi. The Quest for a Secret Tradition*. London: Bloomsbury, 1996.

Goswami, Amit. *The Self-aware Universe: How Consciousness Creates the Material World*. New York: Jeremy P Tarcher, 1995.

Goswami, Amit. *Physics of the Soul: The Quantum Book of Living,*

Dying, Reincarnation and Immortality. New York: Hampton Roads Publishing Company, 2001.

Hancock, Graham. *Fingerprints of the Gods. A Quest for the beginning and the end.* London: Heinemann, 1995.

Hancock, Graham & Robert Bauval. Talisman. *Sacred Cities, Secret Faith.* London: Michael Joseph, 2004.

Hancock, Graham & Robert Bauval. *Keepers of Genesis. A Quest for the hidden legacy of Mankind.* London: Heinemann, 1996.

Hancock, Graham.*Underworld. Flooded Kingdoms of the Ice Age.* London: Michael Joseph, 2002.

Hausdorf, Hartwig. *Die Weisse Pyramide. Ausserirdische Spuren in Ostasien.* Munich: Langen Müller, 1994.

Hoagland, Richard. *The Monuments of Mars. A City on the Edge of Forever.* Berkeley, California: Frog Ltd, 1996.

Hope, Murry. The *Sirius Connection. Unlocking the secrets of ancient Egypt. Shaftesbury: Element Books, 1996.*

Hornung, Erik. *The Secret Lore of Egypt. Its Impact on the West.* Ithaca & London: Cornell University Press, 2001.

James, Peter and Nick Thorpe. *Ancient Mysteries.* New York: Ballantine Books, 1999.

Jenkins, John Major and Martin Matz. *Pyramid of Fire. The Lost Aztec Codex.* Rochester, Vermont: Bear & Company, 2004.

Jenkins, John Major. *Galactic Alignment. The Transformation of Consciousness according to Mayan, Egyptian and Vedic Traditions.* Rochester, Vermont: Bear & Company, 2002.

Jenkins, John Major. *Maya Cosmogenesis 2012. The true meaning of the Maya calendar end-date.* Rochester, Vermont: Bear & Company, 1998.

Joseph, Frank. *The Lost Pyramids of Rock Lake. Wisconsin's Sunken Civilization.* St Paul, Minnesota: Galde Press, 1992.

Joseph, Frank. *Atlantis in Wisconsin. New Revelations About Lost Sunken City.* St Paul, Minnesota: Galde Press, 1995.

Krupp, E.C. *Skywatchers, Shamans & Kings. Astronomy and the archaeology of power.* New York: John Wiley & Sons, 1997.

Lawton, Ian & Chris Ogilvie-Herald. *Gizeh: The Truth. The People, Politics & history behind the world's most famous archaeological site.* London: Virgin books, 1999.

Lehner, Mark. *The Complete Pyramids.* London: Thames & Hudson, 1997.

Lutz, Henry L.F. Canopus, The City of "the chest of heaven".

McCulloch, Kenneth C. *Mankind: Citizen of the Galaxy*: The Pas, Manitoba: The Rings of Saturn Publishing, 1985.

McDaniel, Stanley V. The McDaniel Report. On the Failure of Executive, Congressional and Scientific Responsibility in Investigating Possible Evidence of Artificial Structures on the Surface of Mars and in setting Mission Priorities for NASA's Mars Exploration Program. Berkeley: North Atlantic Books, 1993.

Mehler, Stephen S. The Land of Osiris. An Introduction to Khemitology. Kempton: Adventures Unlimited Press, 2001

Michell, John. *The Dimensions of Paradise. The Proportions and Symbolic Numbers of Ancient Cosmology.* San Francisco: Harper & Row, 1988.

Michell, John. *At the Centre of the World. Polar Symbolism discovered in Celtic, Norse and Other Ritualized Landscapes.* London:

Thames & Hudson, 1994.

Morrison, Tony. *Pathways to the Gods. The Mystery of the Andes Lines.* Chicago: Academy Chicago Publishers, 1988.

Musaios (Charles Muses). *The Lion Path: You Can Take it With You.* Sardis, British Columbia: House of Horus, 1990.

Naydler, Jeremy. *Temple of the Cosmos. The Ancient Egyptian Experience of the Sacred.* Rochester, Vermont: Inner Traditions, 1996.

Naydler, Jeremy. *Shamanic Wisdom in the Pyramid Texts. The Mystical Tradition of Ancient Egypt.* Rochester, Vermont: Inner Traditions, 2005.

Neugebauer, Otto & Richard A. Parker. Egyptian *Astronomical Texts I: The Early Decans.* Brown University Press, 1960.

Parker, Richard A.. The Calendars of Ancient Egypt. 1950

Percy, David S, & David Myers and Mary Bennett. *Two-Thirds. A History of our Galaxy.* London: Aulis Publishers, 1993.

Picknett, Lynn & Clive Prince. *The Stargate Conspiracy. Revealing the truth behind extraterrestrial contact, military intelligence and the mysteries of ancient Egypt.* London: Little, Brown & Co, 1999.

Pinchbeck, Daniel. 2012: *The Return of Quetzalcoatl.* New York: Jeremy Tarcher, 2006.

Poe, Richard. *Black Spark, White Fire. Did African Explorers Civilize Ancient Europe?* Rocklin, CA: Prima Publishing, 1997.

Plutarch, *The History of Isis and Osiris.*

Rice, Michael. *Egypt's Making. The Origins of Ancient Egypt 5000-2000 BC.* London: Routledge, 1990.

Salazar, Fernando & Edgar. Cuzco and the Sacred Valley of the Incas. Cuzco, Tanpu, 2003.

Schele, Linda; and David Friedel. A Forest of Kings: The Untold Story of the Ancient Maya. New York: William Morrow, 1990.

Schele, Linda & Peter Mathews. The Code of Kings. The Language of Seven Sacred Maya Temples and Tombs. New York: Scribner, 1998.

Sellers, Jane. The Death of the Gods in Ancient Egypt. An Essay on Egyptian Religion and the Frame of Time. London: Penguin, 1992.

Sitchin, Zecharia. *The 12th Planet*. New York: Avon Books, 1976.

Stricker, Bruno. Het Corpus Hermeticum: Index op gecommentarieerde passages. Leiden: 1993.

Stricker, Bruno. De Brief van Aristas. Leiden: Leiden University, 1956.

Sullivan, William. *The Secret of the Incas. Myth, Astronomy, and the War Against Time*. New York: Crown Publishers, 1996.

Temple, Robert. *The Sirius Mystery*. London: Sidgwick & Jackson, 1976.

Temple, Robert. *The Crystal Sun. Rediscovering a lost technology of the ancient world*. London: Century, 2000.

von Dechend, Hertha & Giorgio de Santillana. Hamlet's Mill. An Essay investigating the origins of human knowledge and its transmission through myth. Boston: Nonpareil, 1969.

Wilkinson, Toby. *Genesis of the Pharaohs. Dramatic new discoveries that rewrite the origins of the Ancient Egypt*. London:

Thames & Hudson, 2003.

Zitman, Wim. Kosmische Slinger der Tijden. Hollandscheveld: De Ring, 1993.

Zitman, Wim. Sterrenbeeld van Horus. Uniek kleitablet brengt bakermat van voorouders van de Egyptische beschaving in kaart. Baarn: Tirion, 2000.

NOTES

1 Michael Rice, *Egypt's Making*, p. 281.

2 Colin Wilson, *From Atlantis to the Sphinx*, p. 55-6.

3 The water fuel cell theory was proposed by Alan Alford, who later abandoned this idea. The Tesla harmonics device was proposed by Christopher Dunn in *The Giza Power Plant*.

4 X-Ray Analysis and X-Ray Diffraction of Casing Stones from the Pyramids of Egypt, and the Limestone of the Associated Quarries (1984) by Joseph Davidovits, published in *Science in Egyptology*, Proceedings of the Science in Egyptology Symposia, Manchester (UK), pp. 511-520, 1984.

5 Otto Neugebauer, The Exact Sciences in Antiquity, quoted in Jeremy Naydler, *The Shamanic Wisdom in the Pyramid Texts*, p. 26.

6 Kurt Mendelssohn, *The Riddle of the Pyramids*, p. 74.

7 SRI: Stanford Research Institute, now known as SRI International. Independent from Stanford since 1970, SRI International is an independent, nonprofit research institute conducting client-sponsored research and development for government agencies, commercial businesses, foundations, and other organisations.

8 David Pratt, The Great Pyramid, http://ourworld.compuserve.com/homepages/DP5/pyramid.htm.

9 Lawton, Ian & Chris Ogilvie-Herald. *Gizeh: The Truth*, p. 148-9.

10 James Norman, Ancestral Voices: Decoding Ancient Languages (New York: Barnes & Noble, 1975), p. 137, quoted in

Richard Poe, *Black Spark, White Fire.*

11   Pluto is a very small "planet" and in August 2006 was actually downgraded, as astronomers argued that several other objects in orbit around the sun are equally large as Pluto, yet are not called planet.

12   Graham Hancock, *Fingerprints of the Gods*, p. 171.

13   John Major Jenkins, *Maya Cosmogenesis 2012.* p. 76.

14   Aubrey Burl, *Prehistoric Avebury*, p. 172.

15   Maurice Chatelain, *Our Cosmic Ancestors*, p. 85.

16   Graham Hancock, Robert Bauval & John Grigsby, *The Mars Mystery*, p. 75.

17   Kenneth McCulloch, *Mankind: Citizen of the Galaxy*, p. 186.

18   Diodorus Siculus, I. 89. 3.

19   Pausanias, 9.25.7.

20   Richard Poe, *Black Fire, White Spark*, p. 325.

21   P. 45 of the reported book.

22   The pyramid at Cholula, Mexico, and the two largest pyramids at the Gizeh plateau precede it.

23   Some estimates range from 50 to 140 million bricks.

24   A map of the soul, the landscape encountered by the soul after death.

25   Fernando & Edgar Salazar, *Cuzco and the Sacred Valley of the Incas*, p. 97-101.

26   Fernando & Edgar Salazar, *Cuzco and the Sacred Valley of the Incas*, p. 97-101. The other quotes from the Salazar book also come from these pages.

27   William Sullivan, *The Secret of the Incas*, p. 351.

28   William Sullivan, *The Secret of the Incas*, p. 351.

29   See www.realitytest.com/gcpe/2004.htm for the report.

30   Apollodorus, *Bibliotheca*, III, 5.

31   Christine El Mahdy, The Pyramid Builder, p. 59.

32   Robert Temple, The Crystal Sun, p. 370.

33   Maurice Chatelain, Our Cosmic Ancestors, p. 67. Chatelain uses 984 feet for the base, the height 164 yards and the apothem 205 yards.

34   Kenneth McCulloch. Mankind: Citizen of the Galaxy, p. 182.

35   Kenneth McCulloch. Mankind: Citizen of the Galaxy, p. 183.

36   E.C. Krupp, Skywatchers, Shamans, and Kings, p. 292

37   Gaston Maspero, *Etudes de Mythologie et d'Archéologie Egyptiennes*, vol. 2, p. 236.

38   Erman in Zeitschrift der Deutschen Morgenländischen Gesellschaft, vol. 46, p. 94, Wallis Budge in various prefaces to the Book of the Dead, including 1913 and 1895 editions.

39   Wallis Budge in various prefaces to the Book of the Dead, 1913 (p. xiv) and 1895 (p. vi) editions.

40   British Museum No. 10477, Utterance 64.

41   The Coffin Texts were a later version of the Pyramid Texts, this time written on the coffin of the deceased itself, rather than inside the pyramid.

42   Musaios, *The Lion Path*, 1990 Edition, p. 87.

43   Jeremy Naydler, Shamanic Wisdom in the Pyramid Texts, p. 49.

44   Jeremy Naydler, Shamanic Wisdom in the Pyramid Texts, p. 24.

45   Jeremy Naydler, Shamanic Wisdom in the Pyramid Texts, p. 94.

46   John Michell, *The Dimensions of Paradise*.

47   Stanford Presidential Lectures and Symposia in the Humanities and Arts, http://prelectur.stanford.edu/lecturers/maul/ancientcapitals.html.

48   Robert Bauval, *The Orion Mystery*, p. 216.

49 John Michell, *The Dimensions of Paradise.*

50 William J. Broad, *The Oracle*, throughout, but page 224 specifically.

51 Schele, Linda; and David Friedel. *A Forest of Kings: The Untold Story of the Ancient Maya*, p. 68.

52 Naydler, Jeremy. Temple of the Cosmos, p. 36.

53 Quoted in Daniel Pinchbeck, 2012: The Return of Quetzalcoatl, p. 190.

O

is a symbol of the world,
of oneness and unity. O Books
explores the many paths of wholeness
and spiritual understanding which
different traditions have developed down
the ages. It aims to bring this knowledge
in accessible form, to a general readership,
providing practical spirituality to today's seekers.

For the full list of over 200 titles covering:

- CHILDREN'S PRAYER, NOVELTY AND GIFT BOOKS
- CHILDREN'S CHRISTIAN AND SPIRITUALITY
- CHRISTMAS AND EASTER
- RELIGION/PHILOSOPHY
- SCHOOL TITLES
- ANGELS/CHANNELLING
- HEALING/MEDITATION
- SELF-HELP/RELATIONSHIPS
- ASTROLOGY/NUMEROLOGY
- SPIRITUAL ENQUIRY
- CHRISTIANITY, EVANGELICAL
  AND LIBERAL/RADICAL
- CURRENT AFFAIRS
- HISTORY/BIOGRAPHY
- INSPIRATIONAL/DEVOTIONAL
- WORLD RELIGIONS/INTERFAITH
- BIOGRAPHY AND FICTION
- BIBLE AND REFERENCE
- SCIENCE/PSYCHOLOGY

Please visit our website,
www.O-books.net

SOME RECENT O BOOKS

The Fall
The evidence for a Golden Age, 6,000 years of insanity, and the dawning of a new era

Steve Taylor

Taylor provides us with the most overwhelming evidence of the existence of an Age of Perfection at the onset of human evolution, and of the fact that human spiritual, social and cultural evolution and history have been a process of degeneration. The Fall is one of the most notable works of the first years of our century, and I am convinced it will be one of the most important books of the whole century.

Elias Capriles International Journal of Transpersonal Studies
1905047207 352pp **£12.99 $24.95**

The Light of Civilisation
How the vision of God has inspired all the great civilizations

Nicholas Hagger

In the most monumental study of the history of civilizations for several generations, Nicholas Hagger describes the grand sweep of history in the style of Gibbon, Toynbee and Spengler. An extraordinary book.

David Gascoyne
1905047630 656pp 230/153mm **£24.99 $49.95**

Mayflower: The Voyage that Changed the World
Anthea and Julia Ballam

This new account of the famous voyage of the Mayflower and the establishment of the Pilgrims in America is the clearest the most vivid I have ever read. This is a timeless, inspirational story that will be enjoyed by people of all ages: exciting, informative and beautifully retold.

Nigel Hamilton, biographer.

1903816386 160pp 216/140 b/w and colour illustrations throughout
£11.99 $17.95 cl

Nostradamus: The Illustrated Prophecies
Peter Lemesurier

2nd printing

A revelation. I am amazed by the translations' objectivity and Lemesurier's refusal to interpret the prophecies beyond what the text itself suggests. The handsomely produced book is a supremely important volume to stock in your store.

New Age Retailer

1903816483 512pp 230/153mm b/w + colour illustrations **£19.99 $29.95** cl

Renewed by the Word
The Bible and Christian revival since the Reformation
Jeremy Morris

Renewed by the Word captures the restless, endlessly self-regenerating character of Christianity, rooted as it is in a particular body of texts witnessing to Jesus Christ but lived out in real human communities, or churches.

1842981471 160pp 230/153mm **£14.99** cl

Rosslyn Revealed
A secret library in stone
Alan Butler and John Ritchie

Rosslyn Revealed gets to the bottom of the mystery of the chapel featured in the Da Vinci Code. The results of a lifetime of careful research and study demonstrate that truth really is stranger than fiction; a library of philosophical ideas and mystery rites, that were heresy in their time, have been disguised in the extraordinarily elaborate stone carvings.

1905047924 260pp b/w + colour illustrations **£19.95 $29.95** cl

The Secret History of the West
The influence of secret organisations from the Renaissance to the 20th century
Nicholas Hagger

If you think that the history of Western civilization is all about progressive leaps and bounds, with Utopian visions often ending in wars, then think again. Nicholas Hagger has produced an enticing narrative analysing the roots and histories of large and small revolutions since the Renaissance. He courageously covers a broad territory with a stunning array of "heretical" sects that have shaped and continue to shape our world behind the scenes.

Nexus

1905047045 592pp 230/153mm **£16.99 $29.95**

Sheep
The remarkable story of the humble animal that built the modern world

Alan Butler

The story of the sheep 'is' the story of humanity, a surprisingly exciting and gripping tale that deserves to be told. Spanning a vast period of time, it includes some of the most famous names that have been left to us by history, and many that deserve to better recognised.
1905047681 224pp **£9.95 $19.95** cl

The Syndicate
The story of the coming world government

Nicholas Hagger

2nd printing

Finally, a solid book about this pressing matter, and refreshingly without the usual hysteria or excessive speculation. Hagger has done his homework and is initially just concerned with supplying extensive data. Upon this he builds his case: contrary to popular belief, the desire for world domination has never died down. There is a clandestine group, let's call them 'the Syndicate', which desires to achieve this aim. Most of the defining events of the 20th century have been orchestrated by this club, and now the machinery is in place. The world is on the eve of global government, and nothing can prevent it.

Amazon Review

1903816858 456pp 230/153mm **£11.99 $17.95**